# PHILOSOPHY
# OF ECONOMICS

## C. Dyke

TEMPLE UNIVERSITY

*PRENTICE-HALL, INC.*
*Englewood Cliffs, New Jersey 07632*

*Library of Congress Cataloging in Publication Data*

Dyke, Charles E. (date)
    Philosophy of economics.

    (Prentice-Hall foundations of philosophy series)
    Bibliography: p.
    Includes index.
    1. Economics—Philosophy. I. Title.
HB72.D9      330.1      80-23635
ISBN 0-13-66336-6

Editorial/production supervision
    by Barbara Alexander
Manufacturing buyer: Harry P. Baisley

Printed in the United States of America

10  9  8  7  6  5  4  3  2  1

PRENTICE-HALL INTERNATIONAL, INC., *London*
PRENTICE-HALL OF AUSTRALIA PTY. LIMITED, *Sydney*
PRENTICE-HALL OF CANADA, LTD., *Toronto*
PRENTICE-HALL OF INDIA PRIVATE LIMITED, *New Delhi*
PRENTICE-HALL OF JAPAN, INC., *Tokyo*
PRENTICE-HALL OF SOUTHEAST ASIA PTE. LTD., *Singapore*
WHITEHALL BOOKS LIMITED, *Wellington, New Zealand*

PRENTICE-HALL FOUNDATIONS OF PHILOSOPHY SERIES

| | |
|---|---|
| *Virgil Aldrich* | Philosophy of Art |
| *William Alston* | Philosophy of Language |
| *Roderick M. Chisholm* | Theory of Knowledge |
| *Lawrence H. Davis* | Theory of Action |
| *William Dray* | Philosophy of History |
| *C. Dyke* | Philosophy of Economics |
| *Joel Feinberg* | Social Philosophy |
| *William K. Frankena* | Ethics |
| *Martin P. Golding* | Philosophy of Law |
| *Carl Hempel* | Philosophy of Natural Science |
| *John H. Hick* | Philosophy of Religion |
| *David L. Hull* | Philosophy of Biological Science |
| *James E. McClellan* | Philosophy of Education |
| *Willard Van Orman Quine* | Philosophy of Logic |
| *Richard Rudner* | Philosophy of Social Science |
| *Wesley C. Salmon* | Logic |
| *Jerome Shaffer* | Philosophy of Mind |
| *Richard Taylor* | Metaphysics |

*Elizabeth and Monroe Beardsley, editors*

# FOUNDATIONS OF PHILOSOPHY

Many of the problems of philosophy are of such broad relevance to human concerns, and so complex in their ramifications, that they are, in one form or another, perennially present. Though in the course of time they yield in part to philosophical inquiry, they may need to be rethought by each age in the light of its broader scientific knowledge and deepened ethical and religious experience. Better solutions are found by more refined and rigorous methods. Thus, one who approaches the study of philosophy in the hope of understanding the best of what it affords will look for both fundamental issues and contemporary achievements.

Written by a group of distinguished philosophers, the Foundations of Philosophy Series aims to exhibit some of the main problems in the various fields of philosophy as they stand at the present stage of philosophical history.

While certain fields are likely to be represented in most introductory courses in philosophy, college classes differ widely in emphasis, in method of instruction, and in rate of progress. Every instructor needs freedom to change his course as his own philosophical interests, the size and makeup of his classes, and the needs of his students vary from year to year. The seventeen volumes in the Foundations of Philosophy Series —each complete in itself, but complementing the others—offer a new flexibility to the instructor, who can create his own textbook by combining several volumes as he wishes, and can choose different combinations at different times. Those volumes that are not used in an introductory course will be found valuable, along with other texts or collections of readings, for the more specialized upper-level courses.

*Elizabeth Beardsley*  /  *Monroe Beardsley*

# CONTENTS

# 7

# 8

# 9

# PREFACE

If I've done my job right, there isn't a single original thought in this book. The philosophy of economics is an area of study that cuts right across the interests and expertise of philosophers and economists. Communication between the two hasn't been all that satisfactory for a number of years—though it seems to be getting better lately. The trick is to combine the important insights of the two for general use. This is especially important since everyday life doesn't separate into a philosophical part and an economic part. We simply have to make intelligent decisions based on our values, purposes, and best guesses about how any particular decision is likely to turn out. Philosophy and economics are thoroughly mixed in those decisions. So, I hope that I've put the philosophical thinking and economic thinking together in a useful way, a way that stimulates new thinking about economic life and makes that life more understandable.

Scholarship is best defined as piracy redeemed by footnotes. I certainly hope that I've redeemed all my piracy. In addition, the notes and suggested readings are important for those who want to pursue matters beyond the confines of this book. That ought to be everybody, since I don't pretend to anything but the laying of some foundations here.

I have a number of friends to thank for their help: Monroe and Elizabeth Beardsley, Linda Dyke, George Johnson, Richard Schuldenfrei, Robert Simon, Neal Steinman, and Grace Stuart. That's the short list. The long list includes all the Temple students who've found their way into my classroom.

*C. Dyke*

## CHAPTER ONE

# The Outlines of Rationality and Value

It's only fair that you know right from the outset where you're headed. First I assume that for you, as for me, the economic part of your life is important. It takes up a good deal of your time. It's probably the source of some concern and annoyance. The only sensible response to something with the everyday importance of economics is to understand it as well as you can. Otherwise you become a passive victim of those who *do* understand. Furthermore, the sort of understanding you want to develop is a critical understanding. That is, eventually you want to be able to make intelligent decisions about your economic life. To do this you'll have to be able to sort through policy alternatives in order to decide which ones look right, and which ones look wrong. In a nutshell the aim of this book is to help you make intelligent decisions about your economic life.[1]

[1]Those who haven't yet studied any economics might like to find some handy introduction to the subject. There are many books that could do the job. I like John Kenneth Galbraith and Nicole Salinger, *Almost Everyone's Guide to Economics* (Boston: Houghton Mifflin, 1978). Like any such book, it has to be read in a questioning frame of mind, and you may well come to disagree with parts of it. But at least Galbraith is honest and open about his point of view.

**RATIONALITY AS**              Economic activity, like any human activity, eventu-
**"MAKING SENSE"**              ally has to make sense in human terms. This means
that it has to make sense in *your* terms. We'll be asking questions about
explanation, justification, and rationality. What is it that ties all these
questions together and makes them worth discussing? It is the fact that
the questions are applicable to the day-to-day lives of everyone. As we
focus in on economics, this will become even clearer.

But if economic theories or systems are going to *make sense* to you in
your own terms, then you're going to have to *understand* them in your own
terms. This is, you're going to have to take a step back and look at what
you think your day-to-day life is all about. As we go on to talk about value,
welfare, and freedom, for example, you're going to have to match what
I say and what economists say with what you yourself think. If you fail to
do that, the study of the foundations of economics won't do you any real
good.

In a way you have a choice. The first alternative would be to accept all
the conditions of your economic life without question and refuse to
examine them closely. Then this book would become—for you—an elaborate intellectual exercise—to be treated as a game and forgotten when
the game is over. The second alternative is to decide that this book is
about you: your values, your welfare, your freedom. Then you'll have to
lock horns with the arguments put forward here and think your way
through to your own judgment on the issues raised. There's no way you'll
be able to do this if you're not willing to take that one step back. You will
have to examine your own life and beliefs at the same time you're examining the theoretical views that others provide you.

Reduced to its most fundamental terms, philosophy is nothing more
than taking that one step back and engaging in a critical examination of
basic issues. One of the first known philosophical slogans is "The unex-
amined life is not worth living." That's simply an invitation to step back
and think critically. Furthermore, since everyone has a life to live, the
invitation is wide open to everyone. Philosophical thinking doesn't require you to be some special sort of creature.

If you think about it, you'll realize that nearly everyone has the urge
to engage in philosophical thinking. This urge may not express itself in
a specialized philosophical idiom. Instead of talking about conforming to
particular models of rationality, we're more inclined to talk about people
having their act together or not. But the vocabulary isn't nearly so important as the activity of thinking deeply and critically. We just have to be
careful that the vocabulary we use is clear enough to give us a chance to
get some sensible answers to the questions that come up. Obviously, part
of the job of this book is to give you a vocabulary adequate to the
questions you're going to have to face.

You might think that this would be a good time to define our area of inquiry—to decide what the philosophy of economics is all about. It turns out, though, that definitions of areas of inquiry are dangerous. For instance, it's well known that definitions of economics as an area of inquiry always favor one particular economic theory over another, before any of them is put to a fair test. That is, definitions of subject areas are always tied to attitudes about what economic life should be, in addition to what it is. Later on we'll see more clearly why this is so.

Still, we have to get started, and I think that the way to do it is to take advantage of something that everyone agrees about. Whatever economics may be when defined precisely, it surely involves rationality and value. In our economic activity we try to act as intelligently as we can in the light of the values we have. On this basis it's easy to see what the philosophy of economics is: the process of stepping back and examining our rational pursuit of our values.

We can begin by looking at a situation which may be familiar to you. I think you'll agree that the situation has something to do with economics. It surely plunges us right into the middle of a discussion of rationality and value.

**THE LOTTERY**     Imagine that we're walking down the street together. We pass a newsstand selling lottery tickets. You have a spare dollar in your pocket, and you're tempted to buy a ticket. But you wonder whether a lottery ticket is worth buying; and, since you have me along, you ask my advice. I'm more than willing to oblige and begin as follows.

First, we have to make some assumptions about you. We have to assume that money is the reason why you would enter the lottery. We assume that, for you, $1001 is as much better than $1000 as one dollar is better than nothing—and so on for any dollar added to any amount. We assume that you get no particular kicks from gambling, nor do you feel at all guilty about it. Later on you will learn to wince at some of these assumptions, but for now we'll assume that they're okay.

Second, we set up the facts of the lottery. There are 10,000 tickets in all, each to be sold for a dollar. All the tickets will be sold. The operator will reserve $1000 as his payment for running the lottery. Five tickets will be drawn at random. The first ticket drawn will pay $5000; each of the other four tickets drawn will pay $1000.

Should you buy one lottery ticket, several, or none? In order to decide this we have to see how you could expect to make out. Anyone could guess; you don't need me for that. We presumably want some rational way of working out what you could expect to gain. Let's try this one: First we notice that to be certain of winning as much as possible, you have to buy all the tickets, paying $10,000. In return, you receive $9000 for a net loss of $1000. So it doesn't appear to be rational to buy all the tickets. This means that if you enter the lottery you'll have to take your chances. You'll have some chance of winning and some chance of losing. If you want to make a rational decision about playing or not playing, then you have to determine exactly what your chances are.

Suppose you were to buy one ticket. Then the possible results (or payoffs) would be: win $4999 ($5000 minus the price of the ticket); win $999; lose $1. There would be one chance out of 10,000 to win the $4999, four chances out of 10,000 to win the $999, and 9995 chances out of 10,000 that you would lose the dollar you paid for the ticket. (Remember that we said there would be a random drawing. This means that no given ticket has a better chance of being drawn than any other given ticket.) Now we can express the chances of winning and losing as probabilities. Since certainty is surely 10,000 chances out of 10,000 and

$$\frac{10,000}{10,000} = 1,$$

the reasonable thing to do is to express the probabilities as fractions (or equivalently as decimals) and notice that when the probabilities of all the possible results are added together they must total one. So, the probability of winning $4999 is 1/10,000; the probability of winning $999 is 4/10,000; the probability of losing a dollar is 9995/10,000; and these are all the possibilities.

We can now define a "rational expectation": it's by multiplying each possible payoff by the probability of its occurrence and then adding all the products together. So:

$4000 \times 1/10,000$ plus $999 \times 4/10,000$ plus $-$1 \times 9995/10,000 =$

$$\frac{4999}{10000} + \frac{3996}{10000} - \frac{9995}{10000} = \frac{1000}{10000} = -\$.10$$

Thus –$.10. is the rational expectation associated with buying one lottery ticket.

Now let us notice three things: First, your rational expectation when you don't buy any tickets is 0: that is, you neither win nor lose anything. Second, if you bought all the tickets you'd lose at the rate of $.10 a ticket. And third, if all the tickets are sold—no matter to whom—the average loss per ticket is $.10. All this is no surprise, since we know that the operator skimmed that $.10 a ticket off the top as his payment for running the lottery.

With a final flourish of the pencil I say to you that since your rational expectation is 0 if you don't buy any tickets, and –$.10 if you do buy a ticket, you shouldn't buy a ticket. You look at me and say: "That's stupid. There's no way that I can lose exactly a dime. I'll either lose a dollar or I'll get rich." Of course, you're right; what can I say? Well, try this: "The dollar amount that you get when you calculate the rational expectation is an indication of what you would win or lose in the long run." You point out to me that for the one-time purchase of a lottery ticket there *is* no long run. "Right again," say I, "but if the lottery were run day after day for a long time, and if you bought one ticket each time, then after a long time you could expect to have lost $.10 a ticket." In disgust you reply that until you hit a lucky ticket you'd be losing at the rate of a dollar a ticket, not a dime, and when you hit a lucky ticket you'd quit—stopping the long run. I reply that you can rationally expect that when you quit you'll have played so long that your net result is a loss of $.10 a ticket.

Furthermore, look at it this way. You asked me to give you some way of making a rational decision about buying a lottery ticket. Let's suppose that it's going to be a one-time purchase, so that there's no long run. We know that you'll either win $999 or $4999 or lose $1 so that a loss of $.10 has no literal meaning. Still, you were asking me whether it was worth the risk of a dollar to try to win in the lottery. I've come up with a number which is an indicator of the risk. While it doesn't literally specify any one of the actual outcomes, its relationship to the outcome of not playing at all is clear. I'm simply specifying a concept of rationality in this case. And you had none to begin with. My concept of rationality says: Calculate the rational expectation of a course of action, compare it with the rational expectations of the alternatives, and choose the alternative with the highest number. The numbers rank the alternatives in a rational way (say I) and in some cases the relative sizes of the numbers, and whether they're positive or negative might even give an indication of how risky the various choices might be. All the talk about "in the long run" is simply to give you a sense of why you might want to accept this concept of rationality. It tells you that if you use it over and over in similar situations, then in the long run you have the right to be confident that you have made out better than if you hadn't used it.[2]

The lottery obviously gives us a particular conception of rationality. In fact, as we worked out the buying of a lottery ticket, we specified a precise *rule* of rationality. Similarly, the lottery requires a conception of value:

[2]This method for calculating payoffs in terms of expected gains is called, in general, "Bayesian decision theory." There are many sources: For example, Robert D. Luce and H. Raiffa, *Games and Decision* (New York: Wiley, 1957) chapter 2; R. C. Jeffrey, *The Logic of Decision* (Boston: Houghton Mifflin, 1978); Ben M. Enis and C. L. Broome, *Marketing Decisions: A Bayesian Approach,* (Scranton, Pa.: Intext 1971).

payoffs expressed in terms of dollars. These conceptions of rationality and value seem to suit the situation perfectly well. You might even consider extending their use, situation by situation, until they become your overall conception of rationality and value. But before you adopt them as the way in which you organize your day-to-day activity, you ought to know more about them. This means taking a good look at some alternative conceptions of rationality and value, and a broader view of the whole area.

**WHAT IS IT TO BE RATIONAL?** When you go back and see how the word "rational" was used in ancient times, you find that something was thought of as rational if it was in the right proportion, given other facets of the situation within which it occurred. This isn't surprising since "ratio" means "proportion"—as we know from studying fractions. We even talk of rational numbers: those that can be expressed as a proper fraction. The notion of rationality as proportionality might be a good one to begin with.

Applied to human beings, this conception of rationality would mean that a person is being rational when there is some correct proportion between him and some facet of the surrounding world. Now, how in the world could your relation between yourself and your surroundings be expressed literally in terms of a proportion? Three examples might help: First, you probably know what it is to overeat. To talk about overeating is to think of food intake in proportion to requirements for food. Second, we're sometimes told that we're over-reacting to a situation that doesn't merit such an extreme response. Our reaction is said to be all out of proportion to the importance of the situation. Third, in our attempt to approach the lottery rationally, we were trying to establish a right proportion between the money expended and the payoff expected. In this case the ratio could be stated literally in terms of numbers.

How far can we go in thinking of rationality in terms of proportions and ratios? Well, the ancient Greeks seem to have thought that we could go very far in this direction. That's because they tended to think of the world as a mathematically harmonious whole, with everything (at its best) in harmonious proportion to everything else. We generally don't think of the world in this way any more. (But don't underestimate the attraction of looking at the world in terms of mathematics. As we go along we'll see some of the places where this attraction leads.) If we don't literally think of the world as a harmonious whole, then the notion of proportion as rationality will probably be more metaphorical than literal. It seems to be metaphorical in the second example: over-reacting. It's easy enough to say that someone's reaction was all out of proportion to the demands of a situation. It's a lot harder to write down the fraction that would express the proportion in mathematical terms. In fact, it would be silly to try.

What then can we salvage from the notion of rationality as harmonious proportion? Well, it gives us the basic conception of a whole into which a number of parts have to fit—taking their appropriate place. Then, if you could think of your world or your life as such a whole, you could begin to think of how the parts fit together. You could ask if your day-to-day activities, your attitudes, or the ways you spend your time fit together to add up to some satisfactory whole. I think that this could give us our basic sense of rationality even though it doesn't give us many mathematical ratios. Of course, if the whole you were considering were the family budget, then this conception would fit nicely; and in this case you *would* get explicit ratios.

Since our overall task is an examination of one of the social sciences, let's see how this conception of rationality fits into a social scientific context.[3]

**UNDERSTANDING AND EXPLAINING**       Imagine you're an anthropologist. You've fallen into an anthropologist's dream: You've found a lost tribe. It's never before been investigated by a representative of Western culture. You carefully inch your way into the tribal milieu and try to understand these people whose way of life is so very different from yours. Some of the things they do make perfectly good sense to you. They eat, sleep, have sex, etc. These are normal parts of your own life, and since they have a clear sense within your own life, you make the safe assumption that they have the same clear sense in the lives of the people of the lost tribe. But there are things they do that don't make immediate sense to you. Their ways are different from yours. In fact, it may be that *what* they eat, *how* they eat it, or *when* they eat differs from what you're used to. You might even learn something new about sex from them. It may occur to you that the overall whole into which their activities fit is different from the whole that makes up your life.

Given these differences, could you ever figure out the rationality of the activities of the lost tribe? Maybe so, but you'd have to do it very carefully. Most important, you'd have to avoid falling into the trap of thinking that

[3]The line of thought pursued in this section and the next has its roots in Aristotle, "Nichomachaean Ethics," in Richard McKeon, ed., *Introduction to Aristotle* (New York: The Modern Library, 1947) especially Books 3, 7, and 10; J. L. Austin, "A Plea for Excuses," *Philosophical Papers* (Oxford: Oxford University Press 1961); H. L. A. Hart, "The Ascription of Responsibility and Rights," in A.G.N. Flew, ed., *Essays on Logic and Language* (first series) (Oxford: Basil Blackwell, 1855); A. R. Louch, *Explanation and Human Action* (Berkeley: University of California Press, 1966); Peter Winch, *The Idea of a Social Science* (New York: Humanities Press, 1958); and essays discussing Winch's views in Bryan K. Wilson, ed., *Rationality* (Oxford: Basil Blackwell, 1970).

any overall way of life that made sense had to be very like your own way of life. Why must everything make sense in *your* terms? What's wrong with an activity making sense in *their* terms?

Modern-day anthropologists are very sensitive to the problem of understanding another culture in its own terms. After all, failing to be careful about this leads to what we might call "explanatory imperialism." An explanatory imperialist would claim that the only rational way of life was the one he himself participated in. On the basis of this claim any activity that wouldn't make sense as a part of the explainer's way of life would be dismissed as irrational, "primitive," or "savage." The explainer would disapprove of it and even feel the duty to change it.

Contemporary anthropologists don't want to adopt this attitude toward other cultures. They want to try to appreciate the ways of life of others in their own terms. They want to stop short of approval and disapproval and leave these to the missionaries. They want to be able to use concepts of rationality, understanding, explaining, and making sense which don't prejudge the rightness or wrongness of what they're trying to understand and explain. Unfortunately, our ordinary use of the words "rational" and "irrational" won't cooperate fully with their effort.

When we say that someone or something is irrational, for example, we generally imply that there's something wrong: some thing or person isn't up to scratch. It's hard to imagine agreeing that something you're doing is irrational without considering a change in your ways. Further, you can easily imagine being called irrational and indignantly replying that what you're doing is perfectly rational—if understood properly. Your indignation would be a good indication of your feeling that the "charge" of irrationality was a criticism, a negative judgment of what you were up to.

It's very hard to free the words "rational" and "irrational" (especially the latter) from the context of criticism and defense. For instance, if my eventual advice to you about the lottery ticket was not to buy one, and you went ahead and bought one anyway, I might call you irrational. Now, remember, you'd be irrational in a very precise sense, defined in terms of the maximization of expected gain. Nonetheless, my judgment that you were irrational might sting a bit and lead you to defend yourself. This give and take of criticism and defense is a normal context for the words "rational" and "irrational." It's a natural result of our living a life together. I have to be able to have reasonable expectations about your behavior, and you have to have the same sort of expectations about me. Otherwise we're often going to be at odds, be in each other's way, and in general have a hard time sharing the same living space. So we routinely do two things: First, keep trying to figure each other out; and, second, try to guide and influence each other's behavior. The first of these isn't very different from what the anthropologist does when he tries to understand the lost tribe. Of course, you and I have an easier time understanding each other than the anthropologist does understanding a member of a lost tribe. We share a way of life, which means we share an understanding of the typical wholes that govern the rationality of what we do. We don't understand each other perfectly all the time, but, on the other hand, we're seldom at a total loss. This sharing of a way of life is very important to us. We spend a long time, especially as children, working hard at being sharers. One of the ways a child works at being a sharer is by asking "why" all the time.

The second stage—the guiding and influencing of behavior—is the stage the anthropologist wants to avoid. He doesn't want to participate in a give and take of criticism and defense, for his object is to understand, not to be a co-participant. When he, for example, finds that his lost tribe is a tribe of cannibals, he wants to make sense of the cannibalism in their terms. If they believe that eating human flesh endows them with the virtues and strength of the person eaten, then this fits the cannibalism into a context—a whole—which can be understood. Whether the lost tribe is right or wrong is entirely another matter. Of course, there's an obvious limit to the anthropologist's ability to say "Ah, they're cannibals. How interesting." If he finds himself in the cooking pot, then the lost tribe has involved him as a co-participant, and he'd better try to get involved in a give and take of criticism and defense designed to show them the folly of cannibalism. Otherwise he's cooked.

Well, anthropology is one branch of the social sciences, and economics is another. As we examine what the economist does, we'll have to try to see whether his object is to understand or whether it's to guide and influence action. In his case he's not (in general) dealing with a lost tribe. He's dealing with us. He's one of the sharers, and a co-participant with us in an economic system. When he provides us with a conception of rationality such as the one used to analyze the lottery, is he trying to influence behavior? Is he making judgments about better and worse ways of being? It's easy to see that if he's doing these things, then his conceptions of rationality and value are closely tied to one another. A large part of our task in the course of this book will be to examine the ways in which economic rationality and economic value are tied. Such ties can be found, for example, in explanations in terms of means and ends.

**MEANS AND ENDS**　　Presumably you have some reason for reading this book. Maybe you want to know a bit more about the foundations of economic theory. Maybe you've happened to take a course for which this book is assigned, and you want to get a good grade in the course. Maybe you have both purposes in mind or perhaps some others. In any case reading this book is something you do as a means of achieving some further end you have in mind. Doing something as a means to some further end is one of the most common patterns in our behavior. Some would say that *all* our behavior falls into this pattern.

We might wonder if everything we do fits the means-ends pattern. It seems easy enough to identify cases that *do* fit. Whenever we give reasons for what we do in terms of "in order to . . ." or "for the sake of . . .," we seem to be talking of means and ends. The picture is that of a series of activities in which the rationality of the ones early in the series is established because of their relationship to the ones at the end. Whenever it's difficult to set out such a series, then the appropriateness of the means-ends pattern is subject to doubt. For instance, if someone says she's doing something in order to fulfill a promise, then the words seem to imply that what's being done is an early activity in a series, and that a later activity in the series is "fulfilling a promise." But of course this needn't be so. If she is doing an errand in order to fulfill a promise, then the doing of the errand and the fulfilling of the promise are the same thing. In general there are many times when we use "in order to . . ." in which the activities involved are *not* in a temporal series. This is true in all those cases in which we talk about doing something to fulfill duties or requirements. For example, you might answer some questions right in order to pass a test, but passing the test isn't something you do after answering the questions. "Passing the test" is another way of describing what you're doing when you're answering the questions, a way of describing it which relates your activity to a broader whole that has to be understood if your activity is to be understood. Whether or not cases of this sort can ultimately be looked at as instances of means and ends is the subject of debate among philosophers, but whatever the outcome of the debate it's clear that the obviousness of the means-ends pattern is spoiled by the complications introduced here.

The questionable means-ends cases important for our purposes are slightly different. If you're riding a train, then chances are that you're doing so in order to get to some destination. Your being at that destination is the end, down the line, so to speak, that accounts for the rationality of your being on the train. But what if you're a train buff riding the train for the sheer enjoyment of it. The train's destination may be absolutely irrelevant as a reason for taking the train ride. What would your true end be then? Well, there are two ways of trying to show that the train buff really does conform to the means-ends pattern. Both are relevant to our future investigations.

First, we could take a cue from the phrase "for the sheer enjoyment" and suppose that the train buff was riding the train as a means to the end "enjoyment." In place of "enjoyment" we might write "happiness" or "pleasure." There is a strong tendency, under the influence of the means-ends pattern, to try to find some end, such as happiness, which can be popped in at the end of the phrase "for the sake of . . ." when nothing else seems to fit. This tendency persists even in the face of the many difficulties of saying what happiness, pleasure, or enjoyment is. Later we'll see some of these difficulties. The serious discussion of these matters, as they affect economic theory, will concern us in later chapters, so I'll drop them here for the moment.

The second way we could try to show conformation to the means-ends pattern is by saying that the train buff was not riding the train for the sake of anything else, but for its own sake. For the train buff, riding the train is an "end in itself." This seems all right. Some things have to be ends, else all activities would be left meaningless in a means-ends pattern. Of course we still might not know what makes something an end in itself. Presumably we'd need some further theory to tell us that.

Given the possibility of ends in themselves, though, we can see that in terms of the means-ends pattern we have two possible sorts of reasons we might offer in explanation of something we do. Either we're doing it as a means to some further end, or we're doing it for its own sake. Following the lead of psychologists concerned with motivation, we can call something done for the sake of something else *extrinsically rewarding,* since it depends for its rationale on something beyond itself; and we can call something done for its own sake *intrinsically rewarding,* since it *doesn't* depend on anything beyond itself for its rationale. The train buff thus finds riding the train intrinsically rewarding, while most of us find it extrinsically rewarding as a means of getting where we want to go.

The distinction between intrinsic and extrinsic reward will turn out to have interesting consequences for economic theory. For now, just think of the following two situations: First, a person goes to work every day, works eight hours, and goes home. At the end of the week she gets paid. Is work intrinsically or extrinsically rewarding for her? It could be either, both, or neither, and which it is will have a lot to do with the way we understand her work activity. Second, a person goes to a Moroccan bazaar to buy a rug. Before the bargain is struck an hour of haggling and bargaining takes place. Is the bargaining intrinsically rewarding, extrinsically rewarding, or both? Again, which of these is true is crucial to our understanding of the activity.

There are additional questions to be asked about activities that are extrinsically rewarding. We can ask whether the activity really is rational as a means, and we can ask whether its end is really a rational end. As an example of the first question, think of someone eating lunch as a means to relieve hunger. This seems a rational thing to do, but (following our old example) only if what is eaten and how much is eaten are appropriate to the purpose. As long as overeating is a possibility, we'll have questions about proportioning means to ends. Eating three apple pies may satisfy hunger, it's not a very rational way to satisfy it.

There are other, simpler ways in which means can be irrational with respect to ends. Someone might be in Chicago and take the San Francisco plane in order to get to New York. The wrong means have evidently been adopted. The rationality of means obviously depends above all on their genuinely being ways to bring about the end they're aimed at.

Even if something is rational with respect to some end, we can still question the rationality of the end. The person who took the San Francisco plane to get to New York might after all be better off in San Francisco. Had he thought things out, while in Chicago, he might have come to that decision himself. Or, a little kid might set off to make a bomb in the cellar. Every means he adopts might be just right, so that he ends up with the bomb. But his end—making the bomb—may itself be irrational. Now ask yourself this: When we question ends, are we questioning their rationality or their value? The answer to this question depends on how we find rationality and value intertwined. If we continue to think of rationality as having to do with how parts of a life relate to a whole, then we can question particular ends in terms of how they relate to a broader whole. This would seem to question the rationality of the end, but it might just as well be thought of as questioning the values that a person was pursuing.

It would be convenient if we could confine questions of rationality to means, and questions of value to ends, but this doesn't seem possible. Imagine someone who wants to be President: a noble end and one well worth achieving for those suited to it. Imagine further that the person determines that the only way to become President is by eliminating all the other candidates and the only way to eliminate them is by means of assassination. Now the end is perfectly fine, but there seem to be questions of value that we could ask about the means. It has sometimes been argued that "the end justifies the means," but I'm not willing to accept that in the face of examples like the one presented. Questions of value and rationality seem to be mixed up both in reference to ends and in reference to means.

In summary, the means-ends pattern is one of the most common ways in which we make sense out of what we do. The pattern, however common, is far from simple, since it raises complicated questions about the relation of rationality and value.


**PREFERENCE**                              We now move to the concept of preference. Not only will this concept appear with alarming frequency later on, but we can also deepen our understanding of the connection between rationality and value by considering what it is to prefer one thing to another.

Talk of preference lands us immediately in situations where two or more alternatives are being compared. The simplest sort of case might be the one you face in the morning as you groggily confront your breakfast: Which of two cereals are you going to pour into your bowl? If you cast an eye on each and end up choosing Exxies, we should be able to conclude that of the two cereals you prefer the Exxies—at least this morning. This points out an interesting feature of the way we normally understand preference. Preference is closely tied to the choices we actually make. In normal circumstances we take choice to be a mark of preference and behavior to be a mark of our real likes and dislikes. Someone may swear up and down that she likes chocolate better than vanilla, but if every time she's given a choice between the two she chooses vanilla we feel justified in writing off what she *says* and basing our judgment on what she *does*. "Put your money where your mouth is," we say, insisting that preference and action match up. "Action speaks louder than words." If life were really simple, preference and action *would* match up. But life isn't so simple. Choosing according to your preferences is a luxury. Picking up the box of Exxies rather than the box of Captain X is a choice you can easily base on preference. There's apparently no broad context in which your choice of Exxies means anything. But if there were important things to worry about—questions of nutrition or questions of whether you'd already eaten your fair share and ought to leave some for your brother, for example, then you might, reluctantly, reach for the Captain X despite your preference for Exxies. In general, behavior fits preference only when there are no significant reasons to act otherwise.

Things have gotten complicated enough so that we ought to separate out three things: pure preference, reasoned preference, and preference-all-things-considered. Pure preferences are ones that have no reasons behind them. When asked "Why do you prefer this to that?" and you answer "No reason. I just do," your preference is a *pure preference*. A *reasoned preference,* obviously, is one that you can provide reasons for. Two things may differ with respect to certain features, and by pointing to these features you can explain why you prefer one to the other. You might even be able to sketch out the broader whole in which one of the alternatives fits better than the other. *Preferences-all-things-considered* are a bit more complicated. Given a choice between two alternatives, you might find that you have a pure preference for the first over the second but a reasoned preference for the second over the first. In fact, there may be all sorts of reasons weighing in favor of each of the alternatives. You find that you have to balance out all the reasons (and your pure preference) in order to get to a final judgment. The final result of all the weighing and balancing is a preference-all-things-considered. Now, we have to note two things here. First, the weighing and balancing we talk about in these situations is not a literal weighing and balancing, so if you claim that some choice of yours reflects a preference-all-things-considered you may be challenged to explain how you arrived at your result. Second, the word "all" can't be taken too literally either. No one is omniscient, so no one ever sees the full import of the choices made. The force of the word "all" is to insist on a decent level of conscientiousness in thinking about the ramifications of choices. In real life we alter the level of conscientiousness we insist on depending on the nature and importance of the choice.

Given the three sorts of preferences we've distinguished, it's clear that your choice of Exxies might reflect a preference of any of the three kinds —depending on how we fill in the circumstances of your breakfasting. An observer of your behavior won't, in general, be able to tell which sort of preference is involved just by looking at what you do.

Another thing to notice about *pure* preferences is that we usually get down to them only after a series of choices made on a more reasoned basis. For instance, it would be very strange for a person to say that she had a pure preference for democracy over tyranny—no reason, just preference. I suppose that at a certain level of ignorance someone might not be able to provide any solid reasons for choosing one over the other and so couldn't have a reasoned preference. But if she still expressed a preference, we'd probably be right in saying that given her ignorance her preference was meaningless; she didn't know what she was choosing between.

Imagine, though, that the person has worked out the reasons for preferring democracy to tyranny, knows what they mean, and has the information she needs in order to make an intelligent choice. Imagine that preferring democracy, she finds herself in a two party system and has to choose one of the two parties. Again it would be strange for her to say that she had a pure preference between the parties—if there really were two distinguishable parties with different views on important matters— so we'll imagine that she has a reasoned preference for one of the two parties and goes to vote in their primary election. Now suppose that of two candidates she prefers Leverone over Levertwo for no particular reason at all. She says it's a pure preference. Well, we might accept this; even accept it as perfectly reasonable. It may just be that there's nothing to choose between Leverone and Levertwo. She might just as well vote for the one she likes best.

We've gotten down to a place where pure preference seems reasonable —just as it did in the choice between Exxies and Captain X. But to say that voting for Leverone was a matter of pure preference would be tremendously misleading. We'd be hiding all the thinking, reasoning, and judgment that got her down to the point of voting. The choice between

Leverone and Levertwo may be a matter of pure preference, but the act of voting for Leverone is much more. The vote for Leverone is a consequence of the assessment of political systems, judgments about which of two parties is better, and comparisons between Leverone and Levertwo that result in the judgment that there is nothing to choose between them. In short, behind the apparent pure preference is an enormously complex view of politics.

Imagine the anthropologist we met earlier on leaving his lost tribe and coming around to investigate our voter. He observes her behavior—the vote for Leverone. How is he to understand this behavior? As a pure preference? No, certainly not. If he's worth his salt he's not going to be satisfied until he understands the complex of beliefs, judgments, and institutions which give meaning to the voting behavior.

As we move on to consider economic behavior, we're going to have to keep this example in mind. It may be that there are pure preferences simply to be taken as such. On the other hand, we're going to have to be sure that when we call something a pure preference we're not suppressing all the background that gives meaning to the choice and that, in fact, got the chooser to the point of a pure preference in the first place.[4]

**VALUE**                           Even though we've been sticking pretty close to the concept of rationality so far, we really haven't been able to keep the concept of value out of discussion. It came into the discussion of the lottery as "payoff." It appeared in the discussion of means and ends—especially with respect to ends. And when we talk of preferences we're obviously very close to talking about what we value more or value less. It's time to get a basic overview of value.

Two people thinking about choosing a life partner wonder if they share enough values to make it work. Adolescents struggle with the problem of accepting or rejecting their parents' values. The value of Guy Lafleur to the Montreal Canadiens is immense. The chemicals which comprise Guy Lafleur have a value of about two dollars. The value of the dollar against the lira is fluctuating between 850 and 875. Friendship is valuable, and so are diamonds. Go to a dictionary and look up "value" and its related verbs and adjectives. You'll see why everyone who wants to talk about value carefully tries to provide his own definition of the word. English usage is so broad and varied that we end up at sea when we try to ask "What does the word 'value' mean in English?" There is no simple answer.

[4]A critique of pure preference can be found throughout the writings of Jürgen Habermas. For example, see Jügen Habermas *Theory and Practice* (Boston, Beacon Press, 1973) Chapter 7.

There are many reasons why the concept of value is so complicated. One of these reasons relates to what we glimpsed earlier in this chapter. Concepts of value are related to ways of life. That is, when we talk about a person's values, we make implicit reference to his hopes, aspirations, plans, and self-conception. All these latter things are complicated, and, of course, can vary from person to person. One man's waste is another man's fertilizer.

At the beginning, we can think of values as those things worth having, worth doing, or worth being. This leaves open most of the interesting questions about value: Exactly what *is* worth having, doing, or being? How do we find out what is worth having, doing, or being? If it's up to a person to choose his values, is the choice a considered one? If so, on what considerations should we choose values?

Questions of value always have two dimensions: we ask *what* is valued, and also *why* it's valued. Some theories use the term "human values" to refer to *what* is valued or ought to be valued; other theories use the term to refer to the *reasons* for valuing certain things or kinds of things. We'll have to make sure that we're clear about what we mean as we go along.[5]

**WANTS AND NEEDS**        We surely wouldn't think a person rational when pursuing frivolities at the expense of the necessities of life. Economic life constantly requires decisions about which of our wants and needs ought to be given priority.

So the next thing we have to examine is the distinction between wants and needs. We'll find this distinction creeping into our future discussions in several different ways. We make use of the distinction in everyday life when we call some things necessities and some things luxuries. In addition, if we live in a society which believes that everyone ought to be assured the basic necessities of life, we have to decide, as a society, what these basic necessities are. The notion of basic needs is tangled up with

[5]An interesting conception of value is that of Monroe Beardsley:

Toward anything whatever, we may act in a variety of favoring ways, or adopt a variety of positive stances: helping to bring it into existence or to preserve and protect it, seeking it out, choosing or selecting it, making it more accessible to ourselves or others, borrowing or buying, taking advantage of its availability, etc. To act in any of these ways is to *elect* that thing, and anything that is or could be elected by someone is eligible. An act of electing something at some time may be one for which a justification can be given—i.e., there is an adequate reason for that act. Then we can say that the thing in question has *warranted eligibility*. A plausible view of value in general is that it is warranted eligibility.

From "In Defense of Aesthetic Value," Presidential Address delivered before the Seventy-Fifth Annual Eastern Meeting of the American Philosophical Association in Washington, D.C., December 28, 1978.

the concept of economic value in ways that make it wise for us to get straight about the concept of needs before we go any further.

Let's start with an easy case: food. We then ask the questions I have suggested: "Is food worth having?"; "Is eating worth doing?"; "Is it worth being someone who eats?" If we leave aside the religious mystic trying to starve himself into union with the divine, then the answer to all three questions is obviously "Yes." The questions are even pretty trivial, we say, *given our biological needs.* Eating isn't just something worth doing; it's something we have to do. We don't have any choice about being someone who eats. *What* we eat and *how much* we eat are up to us, of course—within limits, but *that* we eat is not. Similarly, we are beings who sleep, beings who move, and so forth. In short, we have a fair idea what our biological needs are. They are needs in a plain sense: We can't get along without them.

From time to time we find people proposing that human beings have non-biological needs: for example, psychological needs (for mother love or acceptance by others) or spiritual needs (whatever they might be). It seems reasonable to question these needs. What are they needs for? If you don't eat for a while you start to get sick and then die. It's not hard to see what food is needed for: health and life. But when the range of needs is extended, it gets harder to say why the needs are really necessary. "If's" start to pop up in embarrassing places. For instance we are told "Every child needs the presence of a strong male figure within a stable environment." We look at this, and, if we're able to make sense of it, we are bound to ask: "Needed for what?" Presumably the person claiming that we have such a need can fill us in. The explanation of the need will probably run along the lines: "If you want the child to grow up in a world of male-female relationships . . ." Whatever the specific explanation might be, we have to evaluate it. There are two obvious ways to start: by questioning the means—ends connection that's being put forward or by questioning the end.

The way to question the means-ends connection is by trotting out examples of people who are well adjusted but who had no strong male figure in their childhood environments. If we could find such examples, we would defeat the claim that the male figure is necessary for the end specified. But in reply to our example, the advocate of the necessity for a male figure could move to a slighly different claim. He could say that *under normal circumstances* the male figure is necessary. This would mean that he thought that the counter-examples we had offered were the products of atypical circumstances which, by accident or luck, produced results like the normal ones. So he would still insist upon the need for a male figure in normal circumstances.

The debate over whether something is a need or not has to be interrupted for a moment while we talk about "normal circumstances." It turns out that we'll probably find that part of the "normal circumstances" are human institutions—arrangements that have been set up over the course of a long period of human history. If this is so, then we might want to take a good look at the human institutions in question and think about changing them in order to eliminate the "need" that appeared when they were part of the "normal circumstance." Let's look at a parallel case. Suppose someone says that vitamin pills are necessary for health. He proves it by showing us many people who take vitamin pills and are healthy and many sickly people who don't take vitamins. We counter by showing him a lot of healthy people who never take vitamin pills. We argue from this that vitamin pills are really not a human need. He replies that there is something atypical—even odd—about the healthy people who don't take vitamin pills. They eat a healthful diet instead of hamburgers, french fries, pizza, cola, and TV dinners. Anyone eating the typical junk food diet needs vitamin pills. So apart from aberrant cases, vitamin pills are a human need. It seems reasonable for us to reply that it would be better for everyone to have a healthful diet thus eliminating the need for vitamin pills. But in any case many things that look like basic human needs are needs only against a background of circumstances that might well be changed to eliminate the "need."

Now for a second line of attack on certain alleged needs proposed for us. Since all needs are needs with respect to some end, it's always possible to question the end. To take an extreme example, let's suppose that a mugger decides that to succeed in his craft he needs a gun. We talk it over with him and end up by conceding that he is right. Without a gun he isn't going to be able to make ends meet. But at that point we'd still try to keep him from having a gun. The end for which he needs the gun is unacceptable.

In contrast, we can think of the sculptor who tells us that she needs chisels and a mallet to do her work. She's right about this, and in this case we probably won't try to prevent her from getting the tools she needs. Of course, in contrasting these two cases I'm assuming that our values are alike in that we'd want to discourage mugging but not discourage sculpting. But that's the whole point. Without reference to the value of the end we aren't ready to accept something as a need we should fulfill. So, a society concerned with the needs of its citizens might refuse to give its muggers guns.

To sum up this discussion of needs, we can say this: Anything which is necessary is necessary for some further end or purpose. Sometimes the end or purpose has a value that is, for all intents and purposes, beyond dispute—for example, life and health. But many of the things which are proposed as basic human needs are problematical. Either they're needs only in a particular set of circumstances, and these circumstances might be changed to eliminate the need; or the purposes which the needs serve are themselves of questionable value. As we continue through our study of economics, we're going to have to stay alert to these issues. Many of the really difficult questions at the roots of economic disputes concern differing conceptions of human needs.[6]

**PROGRAM GUIDE**     Now that we have a basic understanding of the concepts of rationality and value, we have to push on to our goal. So that you can keep track of the progress of your understanding, here's a plan of the remainder of the book. We have to see how the search for value that can be calculated and measured has led economists to their present-day concept of value. Then we have to see how their concept fits with our own. As we trace the development of the concept of economic value, we'll encounter some devices which allow more precise accounting of values than you may be used to. Learning how to work with these devices is a must for an appreciation of what the economist is up to and indispensable for a precise understanding of the economic market.

Every economic system embodies a conception of what it is for something to *belong* to somebody. Any economy is incomprehensible until you understand what theory of property underlies it. So, before we can make the transition from value to the market, we have to pause to get a basic understanding of various theories of property.

Next comes an examination of the theory of the market economy. Market systems aren't the only possible sorts of economic systems. But for an American, they're the most important systems to understand. Furthermore, since full understanding involves critical understanding, we have to try to make the theory of the market stand up to the most serious criticisms we can find. The most important questions to be asked

[6]There are as many accounts of human needs as there are accounts of human nature. It is impossible to canvas them. One writer for whom the concept of needs (and *real* needs) is central is Herbert Marcuse. See *Eros and Civilization* (Boston: Beacon Press, 1955); *One Dimensional Man* (Boston: Beacon Press, 1964); *Essay on Liberation* (Boston: Beacon Press, 1969). A very much related issue in political science is the distinction between real and apparent interests. A representative selection of works debating this issue might be Robert Dahl, *Who Governs?* (New Haven: Yale, 1961); Robert Dahl and Charles Lindblom, *Politics, Economics, and Welfare* (New York: Harper and Row, 1953); Peter Bachrach and Morton Baratz, *The Theory of Democratic Elitism: A Critique* (Boston: Little Brown, 1967); William Connolly, *Political Science and Ideology* (New York: Atherton Press, 1967); E. E. Schattschneider, *The Semisovereign People* (New York: Holt, Rinehart & Winston, 1960); Gunnar Myrdal, *Beyond the Welfare State* (New Haven: Yale, University Press, 1960); W. G. Runciman, *Relative Deprivation and Social Justice,* Berkeley (University of California Press, 1966).

about market theory concern the claim that the market is the most efficient possible economic system and the claim that it promotes our freedom better than any other system.

Finally, we have to get a sense of the options open to us. How different could the world be, for example, from the world the market theorist describes for us? This question forces us to take a good look at the nature of economic theories and economic laws.

## CHAPTER TWO

# First Steps
# Toward a Theory
# of Economic Value

It will be easiest to follow the development of the concept of value within economics if we start with the work of Adam Smith, whose *Wealth of Nations* was published in 1776.[1] Smith wrote at a crucial time for economics. A world economy in the full sense had been developing as the era of colonization of America, Asia, and Africa progressed. Furthermore, scientific and technological advances led the way to what we know as the Industrial Revolution. Convenient sources of power, such as the steam engine, made large scale industry possible for the first time. Invention after invention appeared on the scene, making the manufacturing of all sorts of things a factory operation rather than a matter for small household industry.

In a previous age the people of wealth and power had been those who held large amounts of land. More and more, the landowners were being replaced in power by people whose wealth came from manufacturing, commerce, and trade. As all these developments created a world very

---

[1]For everyone's convenience, I will refer to the most easily accessible (abridged) edition of Adam Smith, *The Wealth of Nations,* that edited by Bruce Mazlish (Indianapolis: The Bobbs Merrill Company, 1961).

different from the old one, the need for sophisticated economic theory became more and more pressing. Smith's theory was one of the first attempts to deal with the economics of this new world. In retrospect it is surely the most important of the early theories.[2]

**USE VALUE AND EXCHANGE VALUE**    With few exceptions economic theorists prior to Adam Smith had insisted that the basic source of wealth was land. This certainly seemed reasonable when the wealthiest people were large landowners. But now manufacturers and men of commerce were becoming very rich without a large landowning base. In addition it was noticed that land by itself was not a guarantee of wealth. After all, the *use* of land for various purposes is what makes it valuable, not its mere existence. So there must be other sources of wealth to go along with land. Smith tried to tell us what these other sources of wealth were.

Here we have to pause for a second to try to figure out what wealth is. It seems easy enough. We talk about wealth all the time. But by the time the concept of wealth becomes precise enough to be used by economists it's far from easy. We think that if you've got a lot of money you're wealthy. But we know that there must be more to it than that, because there are many wealthy people who don't have much cash on hand or much money in the bank. They do have possession or control of land, investments, corporations, etc. It seems that money may not so much be wealth but, rather, a yardstick by which we measure wealth. Wealth would then consist of things of value, things which money measures (or can buy). If we think that money can buy anything—either directly or indirectly—then wealth, measured in terms of money, would consist of everything of value. This line of thought will do to get us started, but it has to be made much more precise before we're through.

The next step is to go back to Adam Smith to work out his theory of value. He distinguishes two kinds of value: "value in use"; "value in exchange."[3] Each of these fits some of our basic feelings about economic value. The value in use (or "use value") of something is the value that it has insofar as it is useful. "Useful for what?" Useful for whatever. Just as things are never simply necessary but are necessary *for* something, so things are never simply useful. To specify the usefulness of something you have to spell out what purpose it serves. At this point we can let our imagination and common sense understanding of usefulness and useless-

[2]A good historical account of the development of the theory of utility is George Stigler, "The Development of Utility Theory," in Earl J. Hamilton and others, eds., *Landmarks in Political Economy* (Chicago: University of Chicago Press, 1962).

[3]See Smith, op. cit., p. 29.

ness tell us what sorts of purposes we're talking about. Smith himself spells out the concept of use value in a common sense way. He assumes that ordinary people, leading ordinary lives, won't have any trouble with the concept of usefulness. In general, we can go along with that, but as the concept of usefulness (or "utility," as it comes to be called) is extended, we may begin to have doubts about it.

This concept of use value ("usefulness," "utility") reflects some of our common sense understanding of value. After all, to say that something is valueless and to say that it's useless are, often, the same thing. The concept relates the objects that are manufactured, bought, sold, and traded to the lives in which they are used. Usually we don't try to get something that's going to be useless to us.

Smith's concept of exchange value captures another part of our common sense understanding of value. Many times when we ask about the value of something we want to know what it costs. That means we want to know how much money we'd have to exchange for it. We'd better stop talking loosely about money, though. The *basic* picture Smith wants us to have is that of an economy of barter and trade in which money has not yet been introduced. We're supposed to think of the exchange value of something such as wheat in terms of something such as milk that can be traded for it. This must be extended through all the things that can be traded for one another: shoes for meat; clothes for carrots; cars for stereos; stereos for milk; and on and on. Everyone will inevitably become involved in trade, according to Smith, because it will become clear that people cannot provide themselves with all the things they need and want. A person's own efforts will be best spent producing the things that person produces best. If others do the same, then they'll be able to trade so that they all end up with what they want and need, even though most of it they didn't produce for themselves. The division of labor, says Smith, is a much more efficient way of providing for wants and needs than total independence. Trading will come about as a natural consequence of this.

Well, it's one thing to say that wheat will be traded for milk; it's another to say *how much* wheat will be traded for *how much* milk. If we can't decide between us how much of one thing is to be traded for how much of the other, we're never going to be able to complete the trade. When we *do* decide how much of one thing is to be traded for how much of the other, then we've established between us the *price* of the one thing in terms of the other. Without the establishment of price our trading activity could never take place.

It's clear, then, that if we're going to establish prices we're going to have to establish the *quantities* of the various items traded. These quantities must be measurable. ("How much is that bushel of wheat?" "Five gallons of milk." "Oh, and how much does that come to in lamb chops?"

"Let's see, that would be three pounds of lamb chops.") There is no real problem in measuring such quantities as these (as long as we aren't concerned with the *quality* of the chops), so if prices are expressed in terms of them we have a genuinely quantitative measurement system for exchange value. Unfortunately, this is only the first step, and the later steps are not so easy.

A theory of exchange value ought to be of some use to the people who are doing the exchanging. For instance, if I know that I'll need a bushel of wheat tomorrow, then I'd like to know how much milk I'll have to bring along to trade for the wheat. Today a bushel of wheat is going for five gallons of milk. Suppose I notice this and bring the five gallons of milk the next day. Then the wheat merchant tells me that wheat now costs seven gallons of milk. The price of wheat in terms of milk has changed. When we take a good long look at market systems we'll see what you might do under these circumstances to manage your trading. Right here we'll stick with the fact that the exchange value of anything can change. If the exchange value of something is going to be a useful quantity to know about, we need a way to deal with changes in it.

Put it this way: If it matters to you how much you weigh, then you want to be sure that each day when you step on the scales you'll be able to read off a weight that's related in a reasonable way to the weight that you read off the day before. In particular—and allowing for water retention, getting a haircut, and other minor factors—you want changes in your weight to be related to your getting fatter or thinner. And if you've neither gotten fatter nor thinner, you'd like the scales to register the same weight as before. If this weren't so, then the scales would be of no use to you. Similarly, if the exchange value of items were to change from day to day, you'd like these changes to have some reasonable basis. Otherwise, the notion of exchange value would be no use to you in trying to plan out your own activity, for example, how many gallons of milk to have ready to trade.

Adam Smith made two attempts to provide a reasonable basis for changes in exchange value. One is the labor theory of value; the other is the law of supply and demand.[4]

**THE LABOR THEORY OF VALUE** As I said before, Adam Smith wanted to show that land was not the only source of wealth. In the world that confronted Smith, labor stood out as one of the other sources of wealth. He reminded us that most things of value for us get their value

---

[4]See Smith, op. cit., Book I, chapter 5. I will not be discussing Ricardo's version of the labor theory of value, which is nonetheless important for a full historical account. See David Ricardo, *Principles of Political Economy and Taxation* (New Yok: Dutton, 1933).

—or increase their value—because they've been worked on. A sweater is no good to us when it's still on the sheep. It has to be sheared off, combed, spun, dyed, and knit. Then it has its maximum value. All the operations which bring it to its valuable state involve labor.

Now, you might ask why labor as a source of value got such big notice only in 1776. If labor was important then, it must have always been important. Indeed it was, and some writers had given it notice. But prior to Adam Smith's time, those who labored were not significant holders of wealth and power. The only sort of labor that was truly valued was the exercise of craftsmanship and artisanship. Very often, the rest of the labor was performed by slaves or by what we would call "sharecroppers." Laborers were thought of as dependent, secondary sorts of persons. For example, during the seventeenth century in England, it was thought by nearly everyone that no person who worked for another person ought to be allowed to participate in the political process. Why not? Because if you worked for someone else you were thought to be dependent on him, and it was supposed that in voting you would express *his* will, not your own. Therefore, since those who labored were thought to be secondary (somewhat like tools), they were often left out of account when it came to theorizing about wealth. The proposal that labor is an important source of wealth came along at exactly the time that those who labored were just beginning to gain a bit of dignity, a bit of wealth, a bit of power.

We must see, then, how Smith uses labor as a central feature of his theory of value. First, we notice that if labor is indeed the major source or contributor to the value of things, then it's a kind of common denominator of value. To use a metaphor that became standard for defenders of the labor theory of value: Every valuable object contains bound up in it the labor that contributed to its value. Well, if labor is a common denominator, we ought to be able to express the value of anything in terms of the labor that was required to produce that value. Then we could say that the real value of anything was equal to the amount of labor involved in its production.

When sketched out in this way, the theory might seem promising; and, in fact, Smith doesn't go much beyond such a sketch. When the theory is examined closely, though, difficulties start to appear. Let's first look at the problem of quantification and measurement. Remember, for a theory of exchange value to be useful, it must give us information about what quantity of something is to be exchanged for some quantity of something else. The labor theory of value proposes that in every exchange we can think of equal quantities of labor being exchanged. So, if the total amount of labor bound up in a bushel of wheat as it sits in the market is equal to the total amount of labor bound up in three pounds of lamb chops, they ought to trade equally for one another. We now have to determine the quantities of labor. Unfortunately, this isn't very easy to do. Adam Smith himself admits some of the worst difficulties. You can ask, for example, whether an hour spent planting a garden is equal to an hour spent writing this book, and not quite know how to answer. Planting the garden requires digging, tilling, raking, and seeding—a lot of sweat. Writing this book requires wiggling the fingers in appropriate ways, and it can be done, believe me, while lounging around in bed. Is an hour's work at one equal to an hour's work at the other? Or do we have to measure effort expended, or difficulty, or the pleasantness or unpleasantness of the job? Adam Smith stops short of giving us a precise way of measuring labor. I think we can see why.

A second problem is that there are things we could bring to the market for which people would give a lot of lamb chops and other things that aren't worth a gnawed-down bone. This doesn't seem to have much to do with the amount of labor bound up in them. We might find a really tasty weed growing rampant in the lawn—a weed worth some lamb chops. All we'd have to do is pull up the weed and carry it to market. On the other hand, we might find a plant that was incredibly hard to grow and tasted awful. We couldn't trade any of it no matter how hard we'd worked to raise it. So the exchange value and the amount of labor bound up in the produce seem unrelated—at least in this case.

So we find, at the very least, that if we want to hold on to the labor theory of value, we're going to have to improve it. Will it be worth our time? Adam Smith thought it was. There are several reasons for this. First, as you remember, labor was coming into better repute in Smith's time. He seems to have had the feeling that hard work ought to be rewarded—just as ingenuity and enterprise ought to be rewarded. All three of these contribute to a world where products are more plentiful; hence a world in which life is easier. The labor theory of value reflects a determination that work be recognized and rewarded.

Second, it seems that the sorts of things we find in the market will depend on the amount of labor required to get them there. Some things just might not be worth the effort to produce, given what they'll bring in return. From this we might conclude that a person calculates the labor involved in producing something as the value of producing it. (When we get to the theory of supply and demand, we'll see some of the consequences of this.)

Third, and perhaps most important, the labor theory of value seems to offer a connection between use value and exchange value. To see this, we first have to go back to some of the things we said about explanation and rationality in the first chapter. We saw that the things people do make sense in a context of plans and projects which constitute their lives as they conceive them and live them. We can ask why people bargain and trade.

Obviously they do so to get what they want and need. Then, of course, we as philosophers (that is, as insatiably curious) can ask why they want what they want and need what they need. These latter questions push us right to the concept of use value. That is, we would have to find out what value the various objects of trading had for the people who traded them. You can't tell from what a person traded for why it was traded for. For example, three people might end up with a bushel of wheat apiece (each at the price of three pounds of lamb chops). One might want the wheat to make bread, a second to make whiskey, and the third to scatter as a sacrifice to the goddess Demeter. Their trading activity is identical. The use value of the results of their trading is very different. If we are only interested in the trading activity as such, then we don't care why any of them wanted a bushel of wheat. Furthermore, the different uses to which the wheat was put might have no effect at all on the price of wheat. All this seems to make the use value of wheat irrelevant to its exchange value. We are left wondering how they're connected.

But suppose people bring their labor to the market. For the person who's not already wealthy, labor is the main marketable resource. For such a person, labor defines the basic outlines of life. It largely determines how he spends his days and weeks: for example, nine to five, five days a week, then the weekend. Furthermore, at the time Adam Smith was writing, the Protestant ethic was reaching its peak. That is, the life of labor was related to an overall system of religious values. It was believed that God put people on earth to work diligently: "Idle hands are the devil's playground." The upright person was the sober, hard-working person. So, offering one's labor in the market was definitive of the worthwhile life. What better grounds for trying to make labor the measure of value?

Thus, despite the difficulties in making labor the measure of price and despite the apparent lack of a strict relationship between the amount of labor bound up in a product and the price of that product, the labor theory of value retained its attractiveness.


**SUPPLY AND DEMAND**    Keeping in mind the reasons why Adam Smith might have been drawn to the labor theory of value, we can move to an examination of the other part of his account of exchange value: the laws of supply and demand.[5]

We can start at the extremes: Suppose there is something that everyone needs, and there is so much of it everywhere that it takes no work to get it. If someone brought it to market, no one would ever trade for it,

[5]See Smith, op. cit., Book I, Chapter 7.

because they'd already have plenty. In other words, the supply of this stuff would be so great that it would have no exchange value. Of course, it could have enormous use value. As an example think of breathable air. In Adam Smith's time this was available everywhere (except, perhaps, at the bottom of the coal mines). Nature provided it in abundance, so no one could market it, despite the fact that it's absolutely necessary for human life.

At the other extreme would be something that everyone, or nearly everyone, wanted or needed, but which was so scarce that hardly anyone was able to get any. Someone who brought some of this stuff to market would be able to make a really good trade—many lamb chops would be offered for it.

Now for a different set of extremes: Suppose there is something that is in relatively good supply. It's not as abundant as air, but it's readily available. But everyone wants it and wants a lot of it. Despite the fact that it's in such good supply, someone bringing it to market might be able to trade it at good terms. At the other extreme from this, of course, we can imagine something which is very, very scarce, but which no one wants. Anyone bringing this to market would be disappointed, for despite its scarcity it will not be tradable.

These extreme cases are: Large supply—no demand; small supply—large demand; large supply—large demand; and small supply—no demand. Demand, of course, means the willingness of people to trade for whatever is in question. It's easy to see in these extreme cases that the size of the supply and the size of the demand radically affect a person's ability to trade a given item in the market. In the most extreme cases, in fact, it's impossible to make any trade at all. If the supply is so great that everyone has enough, no one will trade. If there is no demand, no one will trade. The economist is interested in the cases between the extremes, where trading will take place. The laws of supply and demand are supposed to tell the economist about the exchange values of things brought to the market. They are supposed to give an account of the price of any one thing in terms of another.

We have to remember that a theory of price must tell us what *quantity* of one thing will be traded for some quantity of another. Furthermore, if the theory is going to be of any use, it must allow us to predict what these quantities will be. It should come as no surprise, then, when economists say that there has to be a mathematical relationship between supply and demand on the one hand and price on the other. Later on we will take a good look at some of the simple mathematics of the theory of price. For now we'll just note that Adam Smith gives the foundations for the mathematics of price theory when he formulates the relationship of supply and demand to price in this way: As supply increases, price tends to decrease; as supply decreases, price tends to increase; and as demand increases, price tends to increase; as demand decreases, price tends to decrease. These relationships appeal to our common sense. They seem right—especially when we compare them to the extreme cases.

One interesting thing about the laws of supply and demand expressed in this way is that they give us the outlines of a whole picture of the world. This is especially true if we ask why these laws should work and what their consequences are for the people who live by them. Let's see what the picture is. After all, if the laws of supply and demand work in *our* world, we're talking about a picture of ourselves.

**WE MEET THE RATIONAL ECONOMIC MAN**

I have to think of myself as a supplier of some things (maybe just labor) and a demander of other things. I will supply things that are valuable to others and demand things that are valuable to me. Now, what is the rational way for me to go about this? Well, if the laws of supply and demand are working, then I must have decided that the rational thing to do is to try to gain as much value as I can while giving up as little value as I can. Furthermore, everyone else in the market must have decided the same thing. We have already seen this sort of rationality at work. When you were wondering whether to buy a lottery ticket, you were trying to figure out how to come out ahead. You decided not to buy the ticket (I assume) when I showed you that the trade of a dollar for a ticket was likely to make you come out behind rather than ahead. The trade was not worth making. The value that you could rationally expect was less than the value that you would have to expend. The rule of rationality involved here is: *Act so as to get the most value you can for the least value expended.* Someone who acts on the basis of this rule has come to be called a "rational economic man." who may be you or me. It's important to see that the laws of supply and demand and the picture of the rational economic man go hand in hand. Either one leads to the other.[6]

**THE THEORY OF UTILITY**

In our brief look at Adam Smith's theory, we've seen two important points relating to value:

1. Economists must find measurable quantities as the basis for a theory of price.
2. It is possible to distinguish use value from exchange value, thus creating the problem of the relationship between the two.

[6]The concept of the rational economic man, otherwise known as "economic man," "the economizer," or "homo economicus" is found throughout economic theory from its beginnings. No one owns the copyright on the concept. The necessary connection between a market based on supply and demand and the rational economic man is either assumed or insisted upon by all classical and neoclassical economists including the Austrian school.

In the two centuries since the *Wealth of Nations* was published, economists have been working hard on the first of the two points. In order to understand the foundations of contemporary economic theory, we're going to have to follow the line of thought which leads to contemporary concepts of value and price.

The key word throughout will be "utility." Adam Smith used it as a synonym for "use value." The later philosophers and economists called Utilitarians tended to use it as the general word for value. We'll find that we have to break some of our habits concerning the word "utility" and the related word "utilitarian." For instance, my wife is a potter, and potters have the habit of contrasting "utilitarian" pots with pots that have no obvious use but are created for their beauty. A coffee mug or a pitcher would be a utilitarian pot; a ceramic plaque or a sculpture would not be utilitarian. This contrast between what is useful in a day-to-day sense and what is not useful seems to be an important part of our ordinary sense of the word "utility." Well, I'm afraid you're going to have to forget all that for a while. The word "utility" as used by the utilitarian economists is the general word for value whether that value is usefulness, beauty, or anything else. For a while, we'll just accept that use of the word without even asking why it was ever adopted. Furthermore, we'll swallow a companion piece of vocabulary—the opposite of utility: "negative utility, or "disutility." The disutility of anything would be what makes it something to be avoided.

**BENTHAM'S**          Jeremy Bentham was the earliest important thinker
**CALCULUS**           after Adam Smith to develop the theory of utility.
He first used it to try to assess the relative merits of various types of penal systems. The idea was to weigh up the utilities and disutilities of one system, and compare them with the utilities and disutilities of the other possible systems. The system with the highest net utility was supposed to be chosen. Bentham soon generalized the theory of utility for use in evaluating anything at all that we might do. Thus, his theory was meant to tell us which of two courses of action we should carry out. We are meant to weigh all the utilities and disutilities of the two courses of action and carry out the one having the greatest net utility. Thus, our old rule of action: "Act so that you get the most value for the least value expended" is rephrased as: "Act so as to maximize the net amount of utility."[7]

But how in the world are we supposed to do this "weighing," "determining net utility," and so forth? Clearly, we are meant to go through

---

[7]Jeremy Bentham, *An Introduction to the Principles of Morals and Legislation,* (New York: Hafner Library, 1948) especially chapter 4.

some process of adding and subtracting, but it isn't clear yet how the quantities to be added or subtracted are to be found. Somehow, the concept of utility has to be made precise so that the calculation of utility will be possible.

Bentham's attempt to make the concept of utility precise sets the terms for the development of utility theory over the next century and a half. He asks us to reflect on why we choose one thing over another and suggests that we do so because the consequences of one are better than the consequences of the other. For instance, think back to the choice of buying or not buying a lottery ticket. The consequences of not buying one seemed better than the consequences of buying one—once the risk was figured in. But, if choices are made on the basis of their consequences, then either these consequences have utility, or they lead to further consequences which have utility. In any case once we involve ourselves in this process of means and ends, we have to find the eventual ends which give utility to all the means. Otherwise, the process would go on forever, and we could never make a decision on the basis of utility. Bentham suggests that there is a common end toward which every action is directed. That end is happiness. To be more precise, and to allow for cases in which acting to produce the maximum net utility involves producing the least disutility rather than the greatest utility, the principle of utility is best phrased; *All actions are directed toward the gaining of pleasure or the avoidance of pain.*

If this were an investigation of value in general, we would have to stop here to look at a whole raft of problems that arise when utility is identified with happiness, and happiness with pleasure and the avoidance of pain.

This explicit requirement for a quantitative theory allows us to leave aside many puzzles about pleasure. We'll be able to leave the philosopher free to worry about whether pleasure is always and necessarily a good thing, whether the good life is the life of pleasure, and even whether we really know what we mean by the word "pleasure" in the first place. What's clear is that we use the word "pleasure" enough so that doing away with it would be a nuisance. It's entirely another question, though, whether any concept of pleasure can be used successfully in quantitative economic calculations. That's the question we have to look at here.

Any quantity useful to the economist will have to be measurable with a decent amount of precision: There will have to be some reliable way to determine the quantity; when we measure the same quantity more than once (to check ourselves out) we ought to get the same answer; and, however the quantity is measured, it will have to give us a way of comparing the answer we get for one person with the answers we get for other persons. For example, we know how to measure boards with a steel measuring tape. We lay the tape down on the board with the end of the tape at one end of the board, and we notice the mark on the tape at the point where the board ends. We're confident that if we were to lay the tape down the same way on the same board later on, the board would end at the same mark. We're also confident that if we measured another board in the same way, and it ended at the same mark as the first board, then the two boards would be the same length: That is, were one to be laid on the other, their ends would correspond.

All this seems absurdly simple (until you come to build your cabinets) and hardly worth talking about. But you have to see that measuring boards is absurdly simple because you have a nice set of rules for using your tape measure. Without these rules, which give you a "recipe" for measuring, you wouldn't know how in the world to measure boards. The same sort of thing can be said for all other measuring devices: scales, surveyors' transits, graduated beakers, quart bottles, thermometers, etc. What the economists found out was that it was impossible to find rules for using devices for measuring pleasure.

We can begin to see why they arrived at this judgment if we look at some of Bentham's suggestions. He gives us several aspects, or "dimensions," of pleasure to consider: among them "extent," "duration," and "intensity." Let's begin by seeing what it would be like to measure the extent of pleasure. Seems easy enough: The extent of pleasure, says Bentham, is given by the number of people who experience it. All we have to do is pick out the people who are experiencing the pleasure and count them up; that tells us the extent of the pleasure. The measuring system used here is simply a counting system. The basic rule for applying a counting system tells you *what* to count. "How many pumpkins are left in the basement?" someone asks. "Twenty-six," say I—because I can tell pumpkins from other things and one pumpkin from another, and consequently I know what to count and what not to count.

Well, when determining the extent of a pleasure, how do I know what to count? It might depend on the degree of precision I'm after. Suppose I want to know the extent of pleasure "yielded" by a particular movie. The sensible thing to do seems to be to count the number of people who enjoy it. Of course, this assumes that "enjoying something" and "getting pleasure from something" are the same, an identification that a very careful philosopher might question. But we might well decide to ignore distinctions at that level of finickiness. We now would have the task of identifying those who enjoyed the movie. They're the ones to be counted, but how are they to be recognized? If the movie is *My Little Chickadee*, we probably couldn't go far wrong by counting everybody who laughs. On the other hand, if the movie is *Wuthering Heights* we probably ought to count everyone who cries. And what about those who neither laugh nor cry? Are we sure none of them got pleasure from the movie? Certainly not; a quiet contemplation of the artistry of the movie might be a pleasure too.

Another long philosophical discussion has to be omitted here. The multiplicity and complexity of behavior and circumstance relevant to judgments about pleasure have thwarted every attempt to find a precise usable measure of the extent of pleasure. Anyone is welcome to go on trying, but economists have long since given it up as a bad job.[8]

We press on to Bentham's second dimension of pleasure: duration. One pleasure is said to be of greater duration than another if it lasts longer. Here the appropriate measuring device seems to be the stopwatch. All we have to do is decide when to start the watch and when to stop it. Well, we might say that if we're to measure the duration of the pleasure of a particular activity, we surely can't start the watch until the activity starts. But what if some people receive pleasure in anticipation and begin to savor the future enjoyment long before it starts? Shouldn't we be clocking that too? Obviously, deciding when to start the watch will involve some very complicated judgments.

If starting the watch is a problem, stopping it is a worse one. When you get pleasure from a movie, how long does the pleasure last? Suppose you reflect back over the movie a few days after seeing it, and the memory brings you pleasure. Or suppose you discuss the movie with friends— again with pleasure. We say of some things we experience that they "stay with us our whole lives." Once we start the watch on these experiences, should we keep it running until we die? It ought to be clear that precise measurement by stopwatch (or calendar) is out of place here. In fact there's a suspicion that "duration of pleasure" is nothing more than a metaphor—except perhaps in the exceptional case where the "pleasure" is a particular, identifiable feeling. In any case we're just not dealing with anything that can be measured precisely.

We ought to be about ready to give up the attempt to get a calculus of pleasure. The hope of getting precise measurements seems misguided. But first we have to look at the dimension of "intensity." Determining the intensity of pleasure (and later the intensity of preference) has been a key issue in the history of the theory of utility. Here again, our ordinary way of talking makes it look as if judgments of intensity make perfectly good sense—and so they do, if we keep them at a rough-and-ready level of precision. It makes good sense to say that although we liked two movies,

---

[8]This only begins to show the problems involved in identifying and counting pleasures. Furthermore, it does no good to classify pleasures in terms of kinds, for the same problems arise with respect to the kinds. The literature in recent philosophy on these matters is very extensive. Some starting points are: Gilbert Ryle, *Dilemmas* (Cambridge University Press, 1954) chapter 4; Ludwig Wittgenstein, *Philosophical Investigation* (New York: Macmillan, 1953); P. F. Strawson, *Individuals* (London: Methuen, 1959).

one gave us more pleasure than the other. When we ask how much more pleasure, though, the troubles begin. It's hard to know even how to begin to make the quantitative judgments that are asked for. Usually we don't need the precise quantities and don't care about them, but then we're not usually trying to ground a precise economic theory in a quantitative theory of pleasure. Everyone trying to do the latter job has found the situation hopeless.

Things get worse than hopeless when we try to move toward a comparison of the intensity of one person's pleasure and that of another person. In this case the information you have about your own pleasures is bound to be different from the information you have about the pleasures of anyone else. So there is no hope of using the intensity-measuring device in the same way to compare the intensities of the two pleasures. Imagine Tweedledee and Tweedledum finishing a game of tennis. Tweedledee says "I got more pleasure from the game than you did." "Contrariwise," says Tweedledum, "I got more pleasure from the game than you did." They could (and would) argue forever. Or better, if they wanted to argue forever, they needn't have any fear that they'd accidentally stumble on a solution which would end all possibility of argument. No one has ever come up with a satisfactory way of settling such disputes. This problem is called "the problem of interpersonal comparison of utilities," and in one form or another it has plagued economics since Bentham. We'll see it in some of its other forms.

Well, so much for Bentham's calculus of pleasure. You can try to fix it up if you like. As I said, economists have long since given it up as a bad job. To go back to our old analogy: If you need a few boards to throw across a puddle, you won't need to measure with a steel tape. Long enough is precise enough. But when it comes to cabinet-making, you need to measure well. The economist is aspiring to the precision of the cabinetmaker, and the measurement of pleasure won't get him there. But the failure of Bentham's calculus leaves us with the problem of finding a quantitative measure of utility. It seemed clear to the post-Bentham Utilitarians that utility was equivalent to happiness, but with no hope of equating happiness with pleasure, some other measure of happiness had to be found.[9]

---

[9]On the dependence of all the social sciences on hedonism see: Gunnar Myrdal, *Objectivity in Social Research* (New York: Random House, 1969); also see Roberto Unger, *Knowledge and Politics* (New York: The Free Press, 1975) chapters 1–3. We may wonder about the ability of psychology to give us an empirical account of pleasure to help us here. A recent attempt to incorporate some findings of psychology into the base of economic theory is: Tibor Scitovsky, *The Joyless Economy* (New York: Oxford University Press, 1976). The difficulty with defining pleasure empirically is a classic one. Once defined we must then ask why pleasure is connected with value. Scitovsky becomes involved in this difficulty in an interesting way.

**MARGINAL UTILITY**     The search for a measure of utility went on. All the while economists were confident that such a measure would be found. They began to develop theories which presupposed the quantitative theory yet to be found.

First, it was noticed that the utility of things changed with the amount that a person had. The simplest case is the one in which a person becomes more and more glutted with something until the next bit is hardly worth having. Or, we can think of the difference between the poor man so hard up for cash that five dollars is all that stands between him and starvation and the rich man who lights his cigar with a five dollar bill. The general relationship between quantities of money and utility is best shown on a graph. We will measure quantities of utility in the vertical direction—from zero on up—and quantities of money in the horizontal direction—from zero on out. So:

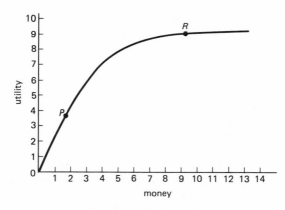

**Figure 1**

I assume that you have a basic understanding of graphs of this sort from your high-school mathematics. They'll start to appear thicker and faster as we go along. None of them will be very complicated. Remember, though, that any line drawn on the graph is called a curve; and any curve represents the relation of the quantities measured on one axis and the quantities measured on the axis drawn at right angles to the first. So, in Figure 1, the curve *PR* represents the relationship between utility and money. Because it goes to the right and gets less and less steep as it goes, it shows us that the amount of utility per quantity of money decreases as the amount of money increases. The poor man is located somewhere around point *P*, and the rich man somewhere around point *R*.

Our ability to draw this graph clearly depends on our ability to get a quantitative measure of utility—whatever it might be. Furthermore, if all the points on the curve are going to make sense, then utility and money have to be divisible into very small units. It's always assumed that this is so. We can then start to think about very small parts of the curve: very small increases of money and very small increases of utility. We can see from the graph that at the left, where the amount of money is small, a little increase in money will result in a significant increase in utility. As we move to the right, the same little increase in money will result in a much smaller increase in utility. So, on one part of the curve (around $P$) we have the situation:

and on another part of the curve (around R) we have this situation:

The quantity of money is the same, but the resulting utility has changed. This change in the increase of utility per given amount of money is called the *diminishing marginal utility* of money. The word "marginal" is included to signify that we are talking about the ratio of tiny amounts of money and utility at various points on the curve. The developments in the theory of utility embodied in the graph include not only the discovery that utility varies with amount of money or goods but also the discovery of a sophisticated way of talking about utility, that is, in terms of marginal utility. This opens up the possibility of using some very high-powered mathematics. We'll stick to simple graphs.

Now let's step back and see what Figure 1 means from a broader perspective. We're concerned only with the general shape of the curve and not with the exact quantities it passes through. The curve slopes off to the right, getting flatter and flatter. If the curve ever became exactly horizontal, that would mean that there would be a point of satiation— where the next quantity of money would yield no utility at all. It's usually assumed that the curve never does become quite horizontal.

First we ask what the graph is supposed to represent. We know that it appears to be a mathematical snapshot of situations familiar to us all. It says that every beer won't taste as good as the first. It says that if you feed a kid ice cream cones long enough she'll begin to get sick of them. It says that the more money you give someone the less he'll care about getting more. Of course we could go on and on. The curve of Figure 1 is meant to be the abstract summary of all the situations we can point to where the marginal utility of something decreases with the increase in the quantity possessed. It's meant to be a shorthand way of expressing a general truth.

A general truth about what? Is it a general truth about human nature? Is it a summary of what we have observed about the people we happen to have observed? These are extremely important questions, for we want to know if the theory of marginal utility applies to us and whether or not to believe it.

As often happens it will help us to get a case to compare with the one at hand. We'll analyze the effectiveness of a liquid fertilizer on roses. On the horizontal axis we'll represent a number of milliliters of fertilizer applied to each rosebush. On the vertical axis we'll measure the number of blooms. Suppose we find the following:

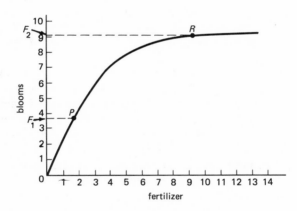

**Figure 2**

In other words if we apply no fertilizer, the bush produces no flowers. The number of flowers goes up with the quantity of fertilizer. But as we get to bigger doses of fertilizer, the number of blooms per additional milliliter gets smaller and smaller. Wow. We've discovered the principle of the diminishing marginal flower production of fertilizer. We also notice that the curve in Figure 2 is identical to the curve in Figure 1. The relationship between fertilizer and blooming seems to be the same as that between money and utility.

Are roses secretly rational economic men, with fertilizer as their money? Have we discovered something about their value system? Are they expressing their pleasure with the fertilizer by blooming? I certainly hope you don't think so. I hope you think that we've discovered a biological, nutritional relationship between fertilizer and blooming in roses, a horticultural law, if you like, based on the observation of what roses do when they're fertilized.

Back in Figure 1 we ought to ask the same question: What does the curve represent? A scientific economist would have to say that it must represent an economic law, based on the observation of human behavior. Or does it represent a discovery about human value systems? Perhaps both?

If you were a horticulturalist interested in the maximum production of roses, Figure 2 would be a big help to you. It would tell you how much fertilizer to put on each rosebush. Suppose you had some fertilizer in hand and wanted to decide which of two rosebushes to put it on: a Peace rose or a Rambler rose. You check your records and find out that you've already put some fertilizer on them. The amount put on each is shown by the distances $F_1P$ (for the Peace rose) and $F_2R$ (for the Rambler rose). Given the relationship shown by the curve *NPR,* you might well decide to fertilize the Peace. That's the way you could do the most good with your fertilizer—in terms of maximizing the number of blooms per unit of fertilizer.

You're also a philanthropist with some money to give away, and you're a utilitarian. You look again at Figure 1. If you're guided by it in the same way you were guided by Figure 2, then you'll give the money to the poor man. That's the way you'll get the most utility for your money. But then you begin to think: Maybe this is all too simplistic. Even leaving aside the fact that we don't yet know how to measure utility, there may be considerations left out of Figure 1 that are important to the decision. Is it fair to give money to one man and not the other? Does the poor man care where his money comes from? Maybe where the money comes from is as important to him as the quantity. And what about the rich man? Maybe if you give money to the poor man, the rich man will be unhappy because he was proud of the previous gap in wealth—which you propose to close up. There may be factors like envy and relative status to take into account. In addition you might find other considerations which would make you hesitate simply to give money to the poor man. It's not obvious that the considerations I've mentioned or the other ones that you might come up with can be represented on Figure 1. It's almost certain that they aren't in it as it stands.

Finally, you might come to worry about whether or not the curve in Figure 1 is even the right one. For example, compare the following curve with that of Figure 1:

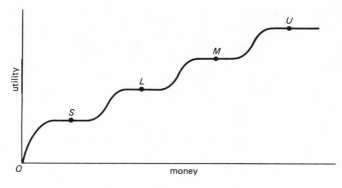

**Figure 3**

What could this figure represent? Try this: The marginal utility of money does not change smoothly. There are some things that require a substantial amount of money in a lump. Until you have the whole lump the change in utility of the money is gradual, but once you have the whole lump the utility of the money jumps greatly.

To get a foot planted in the real world, think of Figure 3 this way: Someone is poor and lives in the slums (*S*). In order to get out of the slums into a lower class neighborhood (*L*), he has to amass quite a lump of money. Once he gets the lump together, he gets out of the slums and his level of utility increases greatly. Then he needs another big lump of money to get into a middle class neighborhood (*M*) and if he gets there, yet another lump will allow him to move to the posh upper-class neighborhood (*U*). Now, as the philanthropist, you look at Figure 3 and try to decide whether to give your money to someone at *S* or *L* or *M*. Let's suppose that if you spread it evenly among them, none of them will be able to make the jump to the next level. You've got to give the money in a lump to one of them. You notice that the amount of utility you produce for your money will be the same no matter who you give the money to. So, a decision will have to be based on some considerations not represented in Figure 3. You might think about what these considerations could be. What you *do* see in a comparison of Figure 1 and Figure 3 is that it's very important for you to have the graph drawn right. Adding to this the fact that a decision will probably have to depend on considerations not represented on the figures, we can say that if decisions about the distribution of money have to be made, considerations of utility maximization will probably not be sufficient to determine the right decision.

This point holds not only for philanthropic distribution but for any method of distribution which might be considered by a society. For example look back at Figure 1 again. Suppose that the money possessed by the poor man and the rich man is all the money there is. We ask if there is a way to redistribute the money so that the total utility is increased. Sure there is. Look at the modification of Figure 1 which we call Figure 4.

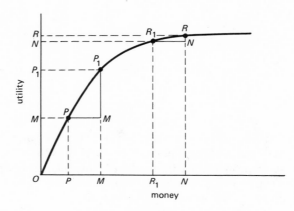

**Figure 4**

We take away an amount of money $(N-R_1)$ from the rich man and give it to the poor man. So we make $N-R_1 = M-P$. This puts the rich man at $R_1$ and the poor man at $P_1$. The amount of utility lost by the rich man is $R-N$, and the amount gained by the poor man is $P_1-M$. $P_1-M$ is greater than $R-N$. Now we see why Robin Hood was a hero instead of a villain. He was a wise utilitarian decision-maker who redistributed money from the rich to the poor in order to increase total utility. Again, you may have the feeling that this is far too simplistic—even for Robin Hood. In particular someone is going to have to explain the difference between stealing, on the one hand, and redistribution, on the other. Some people think there's a big difference; other people can't see that there's any difference at all.

When first developed, these methods seemed to form part of the foundations of a scientific economics—especially an economics which would help us to make decisions about, say, the best use of national resources to produce the most utility. We can't forget, though, that we have a number of unanswered questions about these methods. At the present moment the abiding question is how we are ever going to measure utility. If we don't answer that question, we don't even know how to draw the graphs. Furthermore, to use the graphs to talk about increasing and decreasing utility among several people, interpersonal comparisons of utility must be made; otherwise, we can't even begin to say that giving a quantity of money to one person would produce more utility than giving it to someone else.

Economists have been fully aware of the problems of measuring utility for two hundred years. Despite that, they have stuck with utility as their main value concept. It's easy to see why. No other value concept seems to offer any hope of leading to a quantitative theory of value: one that can be fit into a scientific, mathematical economic theory. In fact, the theory of utility looked to be *so* central to economics that economists went right on developing their theories *as if* the problem of measurement had a solution—perhaps right around the corner. The principle of diminishing marginal utility that we've been playing around with is just one among many examples of economic theorizing which assume that utility is measurable. You might think that all this theorizing on the assumption that a key problem can be solved is foolhardy. After all, what happens to all your theory if the problem turns out to be insoluble? But I really don't think that the economists were foolhardy. First of all, it seemed to them, as I've said, that there was no choice but to go on talking about utility. And second, we all seem to make common sense judgments about how happy we are, what makes us happy, when we are well off, when we are better or worse off, whether or not we are better off than someone else, and so forth. All these judgments seem to presuppose that we can measure something like utility—at least roughly—and that we can make interpersonal comparisons. It's tempting to think that what can be done roughly through common sense could be done precisely if we were only clever enough to come up with the right theory.

Because of the problems with the concept of utility, though, another term began to appear in key places: "welfare." "Welfare" began to be used as the general term for human well-being. It was the welfare of its citizens that a society ought to have been worried about. Money and goods were thought to be the instruments of welfare in that whatever a person's welfare was, money and goods were the means for achieving it. The concept of welfare in this general sense has all the problems that attach to the concept of utility. The word "welfare" has come into our common usage in a narrower sense, especially in the phrases "welfare state," and "going on welfare." It's easy to see how the narrower use is connected to the general one. The problem of measurement is still with us.

## CHAPTER THREE

# Utility
# as Preference

During the second half of the nineteenth century and the first half of this century, a way of understanding utility was developed that looked really promising. It fit very nicely with the mathematics that economists wanted to use, and it seemed to get around some of the problems of measurement. We pick up the story where Bentham's calculus was rejected as a failure. Economists began to feel that a theory of human value in general was going to be very difficult to find, and that furthermore, as economists, all they really needed was a theory of *economic* value. They began to confine their investigations to the ways in which people budget their resources (including their time and effort). They focused on the choices that people make when they are confronted with alternatives in the marketplace.

The theory they developed will be easier to understand (and question) if we work with another set of diagrams. One small word of apology: I'm going to present this as if the full theory with all its subtleties just popped into existence all at once. In fact, many theorists contributed to the development of the theory over a long period of time. But I assume that we're more interested in finding a workable theory of utility than we are in its historical development.

**INDIFFERENCE MAPS**     We start with a single person—call her *O*—who is faced with a choice between two things. These could be any two things: wheat and milk, work and leisure, a home in the country and a townhouse in the city, or whatever. We'll let them be aspirin and bourbon. *O* starts out with some aspirin and some bourbon, packaged up in what we'll call a *bundle*. We then imagine ourselves offering *O* other bundles of aspirin and bourbon in trade for the bundle she has. Some of these bundles she'll accept in trade; others not. If she accepts a new bundle in trade for the one she has, we'll say that she prefers the new bundle to the old one. Conversely, if she refuses to accept the new bundle in trade for the old one, we'll say that she prefers the old bundle to the new one. Sometimes we'll find that we offer her a new bundle, and she finds that she doesn't care whether she has the new bundle or the old one. They're equal for her. In this case we'll say that the two bundles are indifferent. (This is a mild butchery of the English language. We should say that *O* is indifferent as to whether she has one or the other, but saying that the bundles are indifferent will make for shorter sentences.)

We then make some assumptions about *O*. We assume that, for her, more of something is always better than less. So, for example, if she started with a bundle with all aspirin in it, and if we offered her a bundle with *more* aspirin in it, she would be sure to prefer the new bundle; the same with bourbon. We also assume that everything has diminishing marginal utility for her. In other words, she fits the curve in Figure 1 of the last chapter when either aspirin or bourbon is put in place of money. Third, we assume that she has no trouble comparing bundles and deciding between them. This means that for any two bundles of aspirin and bourbon, either one is preferred to the other, or they're indifferent. We can now put all these assumptions into a diagram.

We put *O* at the corner where the two axes cross, measure quantities of aspirin on the vertical axis *A,* and measure quantities of bourbon on the horizontal axis *B.* We then have the outlines of Figure 5—with the curves in the middle yet to be explained.

Now, how do those curved lines get onto Figure 5? Well, start out by noticing that any point on the diagram represents a particular bundle of aspirin and bourbon. For example, point *P* is the bundle containing 100 grains of aspirin and 1 liter of bourbon. Point *Q* is the bundle containing 200 grains of aspirin and 2 liters of bourbon. Previously we assumed that more was always better than less. On the diagram, this means that every

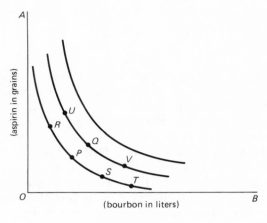

**Figure 5**

bundle farther out from $O$ is preferred to any bundle closer in. So, for example, $Q$ must be preferred to $P$. Just put a ruler down through $O$ heading into the space between $OA$ and $OB$. Anything farther along the ruler is preferred to anything closer in.

We now start to offer all those trades to $O$ that we talked about. She always has some bundle, and we offer her a new one in exchange. We keep doing this until we've offered her *all possible* trades; that is, we make her compare every point in the space $AOB$ with every other point. Now let's face it; we really couldn't do that. It would take forever. But for now we *imagine* that we do it.

Every time we offer an exchange and find out that for $O$ the two bundles are indifferent, we connect the bundles with a line. So, suppose that $P$ and $R$ are indifferent; $R$ and $S$ are indifferent; and $S$ and $T$ are indifferent. Then there will be a line connecting $P$ and $R$, one connecting $P$ and $S$, and one connecting $S$ and $T$. The total effect will be a continuous line which eventually connects $P$ and $T$. We'll call such a line an *indifference curve*. Just as there is an indifference curve through point $P$, there is another one through $Q$. In Figure 5, this latter curve goes through $U$ and $V$, telling us that $Q$, $U$, and $V$ are indifferent. In fact, there's going to be an indifference curve through every point in $AOB$. When we've drawn every indifference curve (which takes forever), we end up with what we'll call an *indifference map*. Just so we can keep a clear view of things, we'll stick with the two indifference curves drawn in Figure 5.

We can ask some questions about them. First, why are they drawn so that they curve in toward $O$, then out again, instead of as straight lines or lines curving the other way? This is because we put in the assumption that aspirin and booze had diminishing marginal utility. On that assumption, the curves have to be the shape they are. Second, can any two indifference curves like the ones through *P* and *Q* ever cross or even touch each other? No. It's easy to see why. For any two bundles, either one is preferred to the other, or they are indifferent. Furthermore, one bundle can't be preferred to another bundle and also be indifferent to it at the same time. You can't say "I'd rather have *Q* than *P*, but I don't care which I have." That would be a self-contradiction. To say that you'd rather have *Q* is to say that you *do* care. Now, suppose that there is some bundle *W* which is on the indifference curve through *P* and also on the indifference curve through *Q*. That would mean that there would be a point, *W*, where the two indifference curves touched or crossed. Since *Q* is farther out from *O* than *P* is, *Q* is preferred to *P*. Since *W* is on the same indifference curve as *P*, *Q* must be preferred to *W*. But *W* is on the same indifference curve as *Q*, so *W* and *Q* are indifferent. That would mean both that *Q* is preferred to *W*, and *Q* and *W* are indifferent. And that's a contradiction and shows us that no two indifference curves can ever touch or cross.

If an analogy would help, think of putting everyone exactly six feet tall on one line, and everyone exactly five feet tall on another line. Six feet tall is taller than five feet tall, so no one exactly six feet tall can be exactly five feet tall. Consequently, the line containing the six footers and the line containing the five footers can never cross or touch. If I'm taller than you are, we can't be the same height, and no one my height can be your height.

Now let's add a few more interesting lines to our diagram. We'll put them on Figure 6.

**Figure 6**

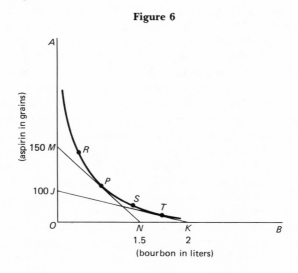

The curved line *RPST* is the same indifference curve through *P* that we had in Figure 5. Line *MPN* is a straight line drawn tangent to (touching) the curve *RPST* at *P*. If you look in one of your old math books, you'll find that there can be only one straight line tangent to a curve at any given point on the curve. This tangent to *RPST* will help us see what's going on at *P*. Imagine that *O* is trading along the indifference curve *RPST*, exchanging the bundle *R* for the next bundle, then the next, then the next, and so on until she gets the bundle *S*. All the time she will be giving up some aspirin to get some more bourbon. Then, for lack of anything better to do, she could start trading back along the curve to *R*. This would involve giving up some bourbon to get some more aspirin. At any point along the way, when any two bundles are exchanged, a certain amount of aspirin is being traded for a certain amount of bourbon, or vice versa, depending on which way *O* is moving along the curve. The straight line *MPN* tells us the *rate* at which bourbon is being traded for aspirin (or aspirin for bourbon) when *O* has the bundle *P* in hand. *M* is at 150 grains of aspirin, and *N* is at 1.5 liters of bourbon, so *at the point P* aspirin and bourbon are being exchanged at the rate of 150 grains of aspirin for 1.5 liters of bourbon—or, if we do the long division, at the rate of 100 grains of aspirin for 1 liter of bourbon, or 1 grain of aspirin for .01 liters of bourbon.

As *O* moves up and down the curve *RPST*, the rate of exchange of aspirin and bourbon changes. This reflects the fact that the marginal utility of one is increasing as the quantity in the bundle goes down, and the marginal utility of the other is decreasing as the quantity of *it* in the bundle goes up.

Now let's put this together with some of what we learned in the chapter on Adam Smith. There we saw that the exchange value of one thing in terms of another is the *price* of the one thing in terms of the other. This price, of course, is the rate at which one can be exchanged for the other. Since in Figure 6 the tangent to the curve *RPST* at *P* tells us the rate at which aspirin and bourbon are being exchanged at that point, we can call *MPN* a price line. The price at which *O* is just willing to trade aspirin for bourbon changes with respect to the amount of bourbon and aspirin she has—again reflecting the diminishing marginal utility of each. So the price line at *T* is *JTK* which tells us that at *T*, 1 grain of aspirin is trading for .02 liters of bourbon—just twice as much bourbon as was traded for aspirin at *P*. *O* has less aspirin, so is willing to give up more bourbon for extra aspirin. There will be a new price line at every point on *RPST*.

The two price lines *MPN* and *JTK* tell us two of the prices at which *O* is *just* willing to trade aspirin for bourbon in *just* such a way that the new bundle she gets and the old bundle she gives up are indifferent. Our normal thoughts about price make these seem to be very special—lucky price situations. We think of prices as sometimes being too high—so we're not willing to trade, or of prices being low enough so that we can trade a bundle we have in hand for a bundle which we prefer. We can represent these thoughts on *O's* indifference map. I'll draw Figure 7 so the new price lines don't get confused with the old ones.

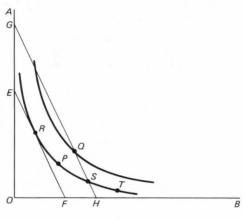

**Figure 7**

We will now think of *O* as coming along with her bundle of aspirin and bourbon and finding that the price at which she can trade one for the other is set. She has to take the price as given. This, of course, is the situation we all are in when we want to buy something and find the price marked on it. We want to represent the fact that the price of aspirin in terms of bourbon (and bourbon in terms of aspirin) remains the same no matter what bundle *O* happens to have in hand. So we will draw a price line which has a fixed direction (the price is set) and think of ourselves being able to move that price line anywhere we want to on the map *without changing its direction.* To change the direction of the price line is to change the price. Alternatively, you can think of drawing a lot of parallel price lines so that every bundle has a price line going through it.

*ERF* is the price line which goes through the bundle *R* and is tangent to the curve *RPST.* *GQSH* is the price line exactly parallel to *ERF* and which goes through the bundles *Q* and *S*. First let's look at *ERF*. We'll suppose that *O* had the bundle *R* in hand. Will she trade that bundle for any other at the price *ERF?* No. To say that she has the bundle *R* and is forced to trade at the price *ERF*, if she *wants* to trade, is to say that the only bundles available to her are the ones that lie along *ERF*. But of all the bundles that lie along *ERF*, *R* is the one that is most preferred, so she'd be silly to trade it for any of the others. Given any price line, the most preferred bundle on that price line is the one which is also on the indifference curve tangent to that price line. Remember, the indifference curves are nested; and any curve farther out contains bundles that are all preferred to any bundles on curves closer in. So, every point on *ERF* except *R* is on an indifference curve closer in than *RPST*, and that's why *R* is preferred to any other bundle on *ERF*. This gets clearer when you see a contrasting situation. Look at *GQSH*. This represents the same price as *ERF* because it is exactly parallel to *ERF*. But the bundles on *GQSH* are different. Let's suppose that *O* has the bundle *S* in hand to start with, instead of the bundle *R*. The price is the same as it was in the previous case, but now she has different quantities of aspirin and liquor. Since she has the bundle *S* in hand, and since the price *GQSH* is set, the only bundles available to her are the ones along *GQSH*. Will she trade the bundle *S* for another bundle? Yes, in this case she will. Look at the bundle *Q* (our old bundle *Q* from Figure 5). We know that bundle *Q* is preferred to bundle *P*—it's farther out. We also know that bundles *P* and *S* are indifferent—they're on the same indifference curve. That means that bundle *Q* is preferred to bundle *S*. And *Q* is available to *O* at the price that's been set. She can trade along the line *GQSH* to get the bundle *Q*. So we find that when *O* has the bundle *S* to start with, and the price is set as we (arbitrarily) set it, the price is right for trading bourbon for aspirin. But when she has bundle *R* to start with, the price is wrong for trading bourbon for aspirin. Notice that when she starts with the bundle *S* she will trade bourbon for aspirin, but not aspirin for bourbon. All bundles on *GQSH* below *S* are on indifference curves closer in than *RPST* —the indifference curve she starts on.[1]

**MEASURE AS ORDERING**  We'll interrupt the story of *O* right here, for the time being, and ask whether it has helped us in our search for a theory of utility which, in turn, will help us with a theory of price. First, what could "utility" mean in terms of the diagram? Well, it seems to have disappeared in favor of the concept of preference. We *could* say that if two bundles are on the same indifference curve, then they have the same utility. On that basis, I suppose, if one bundle occurred on a curve farther out, then it would be said to have a greater utility than any bundle occurring on a curve closer in. The problem with saying these

[1]Indifference maps were invented by F. Y. Edgeworth in the nineteenth century. Contemporary discussions of their construction and use can be found in: I. M. D. Little, *A Critique of Welfare Economics*, (Oxford University Press, 1950); Paul Samuelson, *Foundations of Economic Analysis* (New York: Atheneum, 1970); J. de V. Graaff, *Theoretical Welfare Economics*, (Cambridge University Press, 1957). Samuelson's preferred method of index numbers will not be discussed here. Within the limits of this book, it would add nothing to what we can do with indifference maps.

things is that we have to be very clear about what we can mean by "the same as" and "greater than" on the basis of the information given in the diagram. The diagram doesn't tell us anything about quantities of utility. It only tells us about quantities of aspirin and bourbon packaged up in bundles, and which of those bundles $O$ prefers. The vertical axis is marked off in grains; the horizontal axis in liters. Are we supposed to talk of grains, or liters, or grain-liters of utility? Of course not, and there are no other units represented on the diagram. If we were really desperate to establish units of utility on an indifference map, we might try the following: We get a ruler and lay it down on Figure 5 so that the edge goes through $O$'s corner. We find that we can place it so $O$, $P$, and $Q$ are on the same straight edge. We now measure the distance between $O$ and $P$, and $O$ and $Q$. We find that $Q$ is twice as far from $O$ as $P$ is. It doesn't matter whether we use the centimeter or the inch scale of the ruler. If some line $a$ is twice as long as line $b$ in inches, then $a$ has to be twice as long as $b$ in centimeters. So we choose, say, the centimeter scale, and begin measuring the distances of various bundles from $O$. But we immediately get into trouble. $T$ is much farther from $O$ than $P$ is, but they're on the same indifference curve. We decided that any two bundles on the same indifference curve would be said to have the same utility—same utility, different distances from $O$. Therefore, the distance from $O$ can't measure the utility. That's strange. We've been saying all along that a bundle farther out was preferred to bundles closer in. Was that wrong? No. On an indifference map "farther out" and "closer in" are not to be measured by a ruler. They are to be measured by passing over the indifference curves one by one, starting at $O$ and saying "first curve," "second curve," "third curve," etc. The indifference curves can be passed over in order so that we can always tell whether one is higher in the order (say, twentieth rather than nineteenth) or lower in the order (say, third rather than fifth). So, "farther out" and "closer in" *do* make sense, after all—even though we can't measure them with a ruler. They make comparative sense.

The difference between the way that Bentham wanted to measure utility and the way indifference maps measure utility is very like the difference between constructing a family tree on the basis of the ages of the members of the family and constructing it on the basis of generations. Ages are quantities; if you know that "great-grampaw" Ephesus is 100 years old and your cousin Sam is twenty-five, then Ephesus is four times as old as Sam. But if you know only that Ephesus is a member of the eighth recorded generation of Herpins and Sam is a member of the eleventh generation, all you know is their order in the lineage.

Since the indifference map gives us an ordering of the bundles on it, we could easily transfer this information into a list of bundles. We can make the list vertical down the page and adopt the convention that "higher up on the list" is equivalent to "farther out from $O$ on the map"; and if two bundles appear on the same line of the list, that means that they were on the same indifference curve. So, all the information about utility in Figure 8:

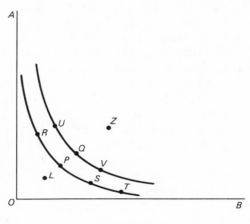

**Figure 8**

is translated as:

| | |
|---|---|
| $Z$ | (most preferred) |
| $U{:}Q{:}V$ | (next most preferred) |
| $R{:}P{:}S{:}T$ | (etc.) |
| $L$ | (least preferred) |

A list of this sort is called a preference ordering, or *preference ranking.* Since it is set out in terms of "first place," "second place," that is, in terms of ordinal numbers, it is also called an *ordinal ranking.*

The information about utility given us in an ordinal ranking is much less than the information Bentham hoped to convey in his calculus of pleasure. He wanted to convey quantitative information, and, as we've seen, preference rankings don't do this. In consequence, we don't know yet how to make interpersonal comparisons of utility. Thus, suppose we had $O$'s indifference map and someone else's indifference map, and suppose we had free aspirin and free bourbon to give out. On the basis of what we have learned about indifference maps and preference rankings so far, we still wouldn't be able to decide how to distribute the aspirin and bourbon in order to produce the most utility. We have no way to compare two distributions with respect to *quantity* of utility. When we discuss the market system, we'll see if this gap can be filled in.

**THE RATIONAL**                    The indifference maps give us the most precise ac-
**ECONOMIC MAN**                    count we have had so far of the "rational economic
man" (a sexist formulation that $O$ will rightly object to—but that's the
term in common use). In spelling out this account I'll introduce some new
specialized terminology. This is always a pain in the neck, but I have the
hope that you'll want to go on from this book to more sophisticated ones.
Understanding the terminology will help you do this.

All these characteristics of $O$ as rational economic man are either
assumptions we have made in order to draw the indifference maps, or
consequences we have been able to read off the maps once we've drawn
them. Here's the new list of characteristics of the rational economic man,
with a few comments on each item.

1. *More is always preferred to less.* For all practical purposes, this defines
"goods" or "commodities" as opposed to waste products. Commodities
are things that you would always pay some price to get. Waste is what
you'd always pay some price to get rid of. For example, you pay to have
your trash taken away. "Being a commodity" or "being waste" isn't
intrinsic to things. They are relative to the place things have in someone's
life. For a while you might pay the garbage man to haul away your
garbage. But if you start a compost pile, you might even end up collecting
the neighbors garbage. Garbage will have become a good for you. More
garbage will now be preferred to less.

2. *The marginal utility of any commodity diminishes as the quantity increases.*
You might well wonder if this is true for all commodities and for all
people. You'll have to think of real people in real situations to decide
whether you're going to be happy with this characteristic of rational
economic man. It might help to think of how this characteristic actually
appears on the indifference map. The shape we have chosen for the
indifference curves tells us that the price of a commodity A in terms of
a commodity B decreases as the quantity of A in hand increases. Of
course, the same is true with A and B switched around. Another way to
put this is that the more you have of something, the more of it you will
be willing to give up to get something else you want. The advantage of
this way of expressing the matter is that you can translate talk about
"utility"—as in "diminishing marginal utility"—into talk about changes
in the rate at which you would be willing to trade one thing for another.

3. *All the bundles on the indifference map are connected.* Here, "connected-
ness" or "connexity" is a technical expression. It expresses the assumption that $O$ can decide between any two bundles on the map no matter
where these bundles *are* on the map. When faced with the choice between
any two bundles, $O$ will be able to say either that one is preferred to the
other or that they are indifferent.

The main reason for insisting upon this characteristic of the rational economic man is that it insures that the indifference map is even and continuous. There are no holes in it. From a mathematical point of view this is a big advantage. But you begin to worry about this characteristic when you try to put it in terms of the real world. We are asked to think of everything as a commodity and to establish a rate of exchange between every pair of things. This isn't difficult when the two things are aspirin and bourbon. We might even be able to handle more abstract cases: Someone tells us that we are ruining our health by carousing every night. We might come to see that we had established a rate of exchange between fun and health. Then we could decide whether we were really serious about that rate of exchange. We might find that carousing was worth the threat to health or that it wasn't worth it. In either case, health and fun would be connected—in the technical sense.

Similarly, when the highwayman says "Your money or your life!"—we usually opt for life. The highwayman is asking us to connect money and life, and it seems that we can do it. On the other hand, what about peace, prosperity, freedom, the lives of others, and so forth? When choices are put at this level of abstraction, it's far from clear that we can compare the alternatives and express a preference. Sometimes we behave *as if* that's what we're doing. But that is another matter.

Furthermore, we may have moral beliefs that tell us that we shouldn't compare some things and calculate our preferences. A case that's often brought up is the one in which a father is asked to choose between two of his children. One can live, but the other must die. It might seem wrong for the father to decide. But if he doesn't decide, he just leaves the decision to someone else, and this seems wrong too. The economist could also point out that very often failing to decide is just one way of making a decision. If you fail to decide whether to swim out to save a drowning man, that can be equivalent to deciding not to save him.

At any rate, if you think that there are some things that cannot or should not be compared, you must refuse to put them on the axes of an indifference map. The rule of connexity says that anything put on one axis of an indifference map is comparable to anything put on the other axis. Of course, if you find that some things cannot be measured, you know right off that they can't be put on the axes of an indifference map, for any point on the map represents a bundle containing certain *quantities* of two things.

4. *Preference and indifference must be transitive.* Transitivity is another technical concept, but you use it all the time. For example, if you know that Kareem is taller than Wilt, and Wilt is taller than Red, then Kareem is taller than Red. The relationship "taller than" is transitive. Transitivity

of preference and indifference are expressed this way: For any three bundles, if bundle A is preferred to bundle B, or they are indifferent; and if bundle B is preferred to bundle C, or they are indifferent; then bundle A is preferred to bundle C, or they are indifferent.

You can think of transitivity as requiring that the choices of the rational economic man have to be consistent. You're really trying to rule out the case where someone prefers A to B, prefers B to C, but prefers C to A. What would a person with those preferences choose, if asked to choose between A, B, and C? How would we write down his preference ranking? How would we draw his indifference map? All these questions are impossible to answer—because the person is inconsistent. We might even say that the person has irrational preferences. There's one advantage, though. We wouldn't have to worry about whether to give him A, B, or C. Whatever we gave him would be preferable to whatever else we might have given him. On the other hand, he's impossible to please, since whatever we gave him would be worse than something else we could have given him. It's to avoid this kind of crazy situation that we demand that the rational economic man have transitive preferences.

5. *The most preferred bundle available is chosen.* This is the new formulation of the rule of choice previously expressed as "Act so as to maximize utility"; or, originally, as "Get the most value for the least value expended." In terms of the indifference maps, the rule would be expressed: "Act so as to reach the available indifference curve which is farthest out from $O$."

It might seem that this rule is just another way of saying that more is preferred to less—so we don't need it. But no, we do need it. Remember that we were talking about bundles containing various quantities of things. So two of $O$'s bundles might differ in that one had more aspirin and less bourbon than the other, and $O$ might prefer that bundle. So a preferred bundle would have *more* of *one* thing and *less* of the other. This would make "more is preferred to less" ambiguous as a rule of choice. The ambiguity is taken care of by determining the rate at which $O$ would be willing to trade one thing for the other, and then adding the rule that she should choose the preferred bundle. At least in the context at hand this rule seems to make good sense. When you think about it, we have been assuming all along that *"$O$ prefers $Q$ to $P$"* means "Given the choice between $P$ and $Q$, $O$ would choose $Q$." This is the way in which the rule of choice is already built into the the indifference maps and preference rankings.

We now have a clear picture of the "rational economic man." In addition we have a promising new version of the theory of utility. We need to take one more step in the development of the theory of utility; then we'll sit back and try to evaluate what we've found out.

**ELEMENTARY GAME**    The following addition to utility theory will give us
**THEORY AND RATIO**    a deeper sense of the resources of the concept of
**SCALES**    utility, and, in addition, it will allow us to see the
concept of utility in action—in situations where we might want to use it
ourselves. This advance in utility theory is called the *theory of games.* The
last time you saw it, I was using it to convince you not to buy a lottery
ticket. We will look only at the very basic aspects of the theory, but one
of the good things about game theory is that knowing the basics lets you
see the possibilities of the theory. You'll be in a position to understand
some of its most interesting discoveries.

When I discussed the lottery ticket, I showed you how to calculate the
expected gains and the expected losses of the outcomes of choosing to
do one thing or another—buy a ticket or not. These expected gains and
losses were expressed in dollars and cents, but I had to explain to you
that the actual dollars-and-cents figures might not have any literal meaning for the one-shot purchase of a lottery ticket. We found that the
expected result of buying a ticket was a loss of ten cents, when you knew
full well that if you bought a ticket you would either win a lot of money
or lose a dollar. The reason why it was still worth calculating these
expected gains and losses was that in a case where a decision involved the
risk of winning or losing, your evaluation of the outcome of buying or not
buying a ticket had to include the evaluation of the *chance* you had of
winning or losing. So, one of the factors in the expected gains and losses
was the probability of winning or losing. The resulting numbers (0 for
not buying a ticket: –\$.10 for buying one) could then be listed in order
of size, and the rule of choice I gave you was to choose the outcome with
the highest number. You can see that what I was actually doing then was
showing you how to construct a preference ranking. I was trying to get
you to be the rational economic man. The concept of rationality I developed then was exactly the same one we developed in the last section.

So let's look again at a preference ranking to see what can be done with
it. Here is the ranking in column a:

| a | b | c | d | e |
|---|---|---|---|---|
| A | 5 | 212 | 100 | 1 |
| B | 4 | 100 | 37.8 | .378 |
| C | 3 | 68 | 20 | .2 |
| D | 2 | 50 | 10 | .1 |
| E | 1 | 32 | 0 | 0 |

In the usual way, A is most preferred, and E is least preferred. In
column b, I've numbered the items up from the bottom. When I do this,

it's easy to see how I could recommend that you choose the item with the highest number. It's also easy to see that I could give you the same recommendation no matter what the numbers happened to be, just as long as I made sure that as I went up the ranking I made each number bigger than the one below it. So, all the other columns give the same result as column b: an item with a higher number is preferred to an item with a lower number.

Now, if we look at columns c and d, we may be able to see an interesting way of adding to our ability to "measure utility." Think of it this way: All of a sudden, with the switchover to the metric system, radio weather forecasters are telling us the temperature in terms of two temperature scales. If scale c listed temperatures on the Fahrenheit scale instead of preferences, then scale d would be a list of the *same* temperatures on the Celsius scale. We know that the choice between the two scales rests only on their relative convenience. You might also know that neither the Fahrenheit nor the Celsius scale measures quantities. Look at the craziness that would be involved if quantities were being measured: 10° Celsius is equivalent to 50° Fahrenheit. If these were measures of quantities, we could determine what temperature to call "twice as warm" as 10° C (50° F). Twenty quarts of milk, after all, is twice as much milk as ten quarts of milk. Quarts measure quantity. But degrees of temperature can't measure quantities, because, as we see in columns c and d, 20° C, which seems to be twice 10° C, is equivalent to 68° F, which is certainly not twice 50° F. But 20° C and 68° F are the same temperature, as the weather forecaster will tell you some fine spring day. So temperature scales measure in a different way than do quarts, liters, yards, and meters.

I suspect this is all familiar to you. We learn about temperature scales in elementary school. But moving to a more general understanding of scales such as the Fahrenheit and Celsius scales, we can notice one more thing. Any two scales related in the way that the Fahrenheit and the Celsius scale are related are always equivalent to some scale in which the topmost entry in the scale is arbitrarily called "1," and the bottommost entry is called "0." All the other entries can then be put on the scale as fractions of the distance between 0 and 1. Thus, scale e is the result of putting all the temperatures in either c or d on a scale from 0 to 1. What we find is obvious: 10° C is 1/10 of the way between the freezing point (0° C) and the boiling point (100° C) of water; 50° F is 1/10 of the way between the freezing point (32° F) and the boiling point (212° F) of water. That, after all, is what we mean by saying that they are the same temperature. Any scale that can be transformed into a scale from 0 to 1 in this way—preserving not only the order of the entries but also their places as fractions of the total scale—is called an interval scale, or *ratio scale.*

If we were to find a way to measure "utilities" on interval scales, then we would (a) have less information than Bentham wanted from his calculus, for we would not be measuring quantities, but (b) have more information than is available in a merely ordinal ranking, for we would also know where each item was located on the scale. It might be advantageous to have the additional information. Is there a way to get an interval ranking of a person's preferences?

Yes there is. I won't go into all the ins and outs of it here, but we can take a quick look at the basic method. Suppose someone is willing to take chances and thinks that gambling is all right to do, but no great source of enjoyment in itself. Then, in just the way we asked 0 to compare bundles, we could ask this person to compare bundles—say, the bundles G and H. Suppose he prefers G to H. We then put G at the top of the scale, at 1; and we put H at the bottom of the scale, at 0. We then find a bundle K which the person prefers to H but which he doesn't like as much as G. This puts K in between G and H on the preference ranking —but *where* between G and H? Try this: We give the person a choice between bundle K and the chance to gamble: he gets G if a coin comes up heads and H if it comes up tails. We all agree that there's a 50 percent chance of a head coming up and a 50 percent chance of a tail coming up. Suppose he says that bundle K and the chance to gamble on G and H are indifferent. This makes his preference ranking look like this:

G
K;     (G if heads, H if tails)
H

We know from our decision about the lottery ticket that the expected gain of a fifty-fifty chance at, say, a dollar is half a dollar. So we can see that if G is assigned a utility of one then a fifty-fifty chance at one has to have an expected gain of one-half. But K and the gamble are indifferent. Thus, if the gamble is at one-half, then K must be at one-half—that is, K is half the way along the scale between G and H.

It turns out that you can always cook up some gamble at the right odds to locate a bundle between two other bundles. So, by asking enough questions and offering enough gambles you can get all the bundles you please located on an interval scale. Hence you can get an interval measure of utilities—or of preferences, if you'd rather look at it that way.

Game theory tells us that it can give us a method for making rational decisions any time we can express our preferences for the outcomes of the various choices on an interval scale. We could do so when you were trying to decide whether to buy a lottery ticket, so we used a simple version of the theory there.

*Game theory* is called game theory because it can help us choose between various strategies in games or in other situations which are like games.

One of the most interesting discoveries by the game theorists is that there are some games in which we can work out the strategies as a succession of moves from the beginning of the game to the end and say exactly what the outcome of each of the strategies will be. For instance, Tic-Tac-Toe is one such game. The strategies for each of the players can be written out in words in this way: "Start with $X$ in a corner; then if $O$ is put in the middle, $X$ in the opposite corner; then if $O$ is put in a third corner, $X$ in the fourth corner; . . . and so forth." There are many different strategies just as there are many different squares in which the players can put their $X$'s and $O$'s on their successive moves. You can tell beforehand how each of these strategies will come out. The one I started to write out comes out as a win for $X$ if he doesn't do anything stupid. Some come out as a win for $O$; some come out a draw. Anyone who has played a lot of Tic-Tac-Toe knows that if you don't make a mistake, you can't lose. Two good players always draw, unless one of them does something stupid. The game theorist puts all this more precisely by saying: "If two perfectly rational economic men play Tic-Tac-Toe, then the best that either can do is draw; and the worst that either can do is draw."

Since we can know beforehand what the outcome will be for any strategy, we can abbreviate $X$'s strategies as $X_1$, $X_2$, $X_3$, and so forth, and $O$'s strategies as $O_1$, $O_2$, $O_3$, and so forth; then match them up with their outcomes. We know that we can state the utilities of the outcomes as: Win for $X = 1$; loss for $X = 0$; draw $= \frac{1}{2}$. Then we can write down all this information in a matrix:

|        | $O_1$ | $O_2$ | $O_3$ |
|--------|-------|-------|-------|
| $X_1$  | 0     | 0     | 1/2   |
| $X_2$  | 1/2   | 1     | 0     |
| $X_3$  | 1     | 1/2   | 0     |

**Figure 9**

Each box is the outcome of a strategy by $X$ and a strategy by $O$. So the matrix tells us that, for instance, if $X$ adopts strategy $X_2$ and $O$ adopts strategy $O_2$, $X$ will win.

Of course the matrix for Tic-Tac-Toe is much larger than the small part that I've bothered to write down. However, it's small enough to write down on a piece of paper. In contrast, the matrix for chess is enormous

—so enormous that no one has been able to figure out how two perfectly rational men would make out if they played without making any mistakes.

There are four reasons why I've bothered talking about game matrices here even though I've only scratched the surface of a discussion of them:

1. They are an important development in the theory of utility.
2. Many people think that economic activity is enough like a game so that these techniques could be useful in understanding it.
3. I want to discuss a very simple game matrix in a later chapter.
4. The rule of rational choice that goes along with the game matrices has become rather famous in philosophy and political science as well as in economics; so you're apt to run into a mention of it one of these days.

The rule of rational choice in question is: "Maximize your minimum gain." All this means is that you may find a strategy that avoids the risk of a disastrous result—no matter what your perfectly rational opponent might do. In Tic-Tac-Toe, this means that you may be able to find a strategy that guarantees that you won't lose. Look at the piece of matrix given in Figure 9. If some strategy such as $X_3$ shows nothing but ½ and 1 all the way across the row, then you know that if you adopt this strategy you can do no worse than draw. If your opponent is also rational, he will be looking for a column which has nothing but O and ½ in it. If he finds one, then he has found a strategy that will guarantee him no worse than a draw. You'll find that if both you and your opponent are rational economic men, and if you both find a strategy that guarantees you a draw, then the box in the matrix at the junction where your chosen row and his chosen column meet has ½ in it. In other words, if you're both rational, you'll always draw. Furthermore, if you deviate from this policy of maximizing your minimum gain, your rational opponent will beat you some of the time, but never lose.

It would be nice to think that we could apply this straight off to the stock market or the horse races. Unfortunately, neither the stock market nor the races will give you a matrix which has a guaranteed winning strategy in it.[2]

Now, finally, with some of the basic contributions of game theory as part of our understanding of the theory of utility, we can step back to try to gain a perspective on the whole thing.

[2]The classic in game theory is John Von Neumann and O. Morgenstern, *Theory of Games and Economic Behavior* (Princeton: Princeton University Press, 1944). See also Luce and Raiffa, op. cit. I think the best introductions to game theory are Anatol Rapoport, *Two-Person Game Theory* (Ann Arbor: University of Michigan Press, 1966), and *N-Person Game Theory* (Ann Arbor: University of Michigan Press, 1970). For preference rankings and their correspondence to indifference maps, see Jeffrey, op. cit. The general method of calculating ratio rankings is also described by Jeffrey. The primary sources are Von Neumann and Morgenstern, op. cit., and F. P. Ramsey, "Truth and Probability," in The *Foundations of Mathematics and other Essays* (New York: Harcourt, 1931).

**DOUBTS ABOUT**
**REVEALED**
**PREFERENCE**

To see the consequences, the attractions, and the drawbacks of the theory of value behind indifference maps and preference rankings, we have to understand how economists think of themselves and their work. Much in the way that I've said I'm a philosopher, not a missionary, economists insist they're scientists, not preachers. They want to provide an economic theory that's based on facts—the kind of theory that physicists, chemists, and biologists provide. When economists look at the work of the physical scientists, they see that their success seems to depend upon the ability to find mathematical relationships. Equations such as Newton's laws, the laws of thermodynamics, and laws concerning chemical combination help us understand how our world works. They show us the relationship between one state of the world and another. These states of the world follow one another in an orderly way, mathematically describable. In one state of the world, King Kong is hanging onto the top of the Empire State Building; in a succeeding state of the world, he's on the pavement below. We can relate these states of the world to one another. We can calculate how fast King Kong was going when he hit the sidewalk. We have equations which relate the height of his fall to the speed at which he'll hit the ground. Furthermore, we can become more and more confident that these equations are adequate. We test them either by experiment or by watching to see if natural events proceed in the way that the equations say they will. The economist would like to have similar equations and similar means of testing them.

The desire to be scientific has consequences for the theory of value. Just as it's not the physicist's job—as physicist or even as engineer—to tell us whether we *ought* to build a bridge or a particular steam engine, the economist claims that it's not his job as economist to tell us what values we ought to have. Just as we can ask the engineer how to build a bridge, once we've decided that we ought to build one we also should be able to ask the economist what will happen if we pursue certain values, once we've decided what those values are. The economist would like these parallels between himself and the natural scientist to be maintained.

From this point of view, the techniques of indifference maps and preference rankings look very promising. No one has told $O$ what her preferences for aspirin and bourbon ought to be. But once she has expressed these preferences, the economist can tell her how she ought to choose if she is to be a rational economic man. From the point of view of economics as a science the economist wants values given as data: good hard facts to build a theory on. Furthermore, as I keep emphasizing, the facts have to be mathematically relatable.

Well, what's available to the economist? There aren't (and probably couldn't be) any hard facts on pleasure and satisfaction. Happiness is notoriously hard to identify—let alone quantify. But what *is* available to the economist is the behavior of the people like *O* who make choices between bundles in the marketplace. In these choices people reveal their preferences, so the theory of value behind the indifference maps is called the theory of revealed preference. On the basis of these *revealed preferences* the economist constructs the indifference curves. On the basis of the curves *O*'s future behavior can be predicted assuming that she's a rational economic man. For instance, the economist can predict the trading activity she'll engage in when she has a certain bundle of aspirin and bourbon in hand and is faced with a set price for aspirin and bourbon.

Another important feature of the revealed preference approach, from the point of view of the economist-as-scientist, is that all the choices are left up to *O*. Whatever values are expressed on the indifference map are *her* values. No one is making decisions about what she should want or prefer. She is master of her values, sovereign of her wants and preferences; so the theory is called the theory of *Consumer Sovereignty.* Of course the notion of consumer sovereignty has attractions beyond the ones mentioned. In our political tradition, the freedom of individuals to make their own decisions is very important. The theory of consumer sovereignty seems to fit very nicely with these political beliefs.

Thus, when we ask what *O*'s values are, the economist says "Well, as far as values are any of my business as an economist, just look at *O*'s revealed preferences. That's all the information we have about her values." But suppose we're concerned about *O*'s welfare—and remember, traditional economics hoped to be able to help us make decisions about welfare. If we're going to be confident that the indifference maps will help us with *O*'s welfare, then we have to be confident that her revealed preferences are a good indication of what her welfare would be.

At this point the economist could become impatient with us and remind us that the theory of revealed preference is the best way we've found so far to make sense out of the notions of utility and welfare. If we're going to contrast some other notion of welfare with the theory of revealed preference, then it's up to us to show what that new notion of welfare is.

This way of proceeding seems to put the burden of proof on us to come up with a theory of welfare, but I think that if we're cagey we can turn the tables enough to have the burden equally shared. That is, we might be able to force the economist to tell us why in the world we ought to think that the theory of revealed preference is an adequate theory of welfare —or of value in general, for that matter. We can at least try. If we fail, then the worst result we can get is the confidence in the theory of revealed preference that the economist wants us to have in the first place.

Let's go back to *O*'s indifference curve. This curve shows how *O* behaved when offered a lot of choices between bundles of aspirin and bourbon. Suppose we ask why she behaved like that. We could ask a biologist about $O$'s behavior. The biologist might be able to start us down a chain of explanations including metabolism, hormonal activity, etc. But it's clear that the kinds of explanations we found in chapter one and the ones that we normally seek and provide in our everyday lives are very different from the ones a biologist would give us. The explanations in chapter one referred particular actions to plans, projects, and conceptions of what kind of person you wanted to be.

We'll try out some of the sorts of explanations we found in chapter one on $O$. We have to keep in mind, though, that the economist as scientist might refuse to have anything to do with these explanations. The economist can note his interest in $O$'s indifference map as data. Why this is her indifference map is none of the economist's business. On the other hand, we think that if we knew more about $O$ we could decide better whether her indifference map was a good basis for determining her welfare. So we press on. "Why," we ask, "is $O$ indifferent between precisely those bundles that appear on the indifference curve?" One answer might be: "They are pure preferences. No reason, that's just what they are." This answer would make the economist happy, confident that nothing important is left out of $O$'s indifference map. But $O$'s preferences might be reasoned preferences. When asked why the pattern of her choices produced *that* indifference curve she might tell us that she needs the bourbon for a party and aspirin for the hangover afterward. She might go on to talk about being a good hostess; how she won't let her guests drive home drunk; how she has aspirin on hand in case they get a headache, and so forth. In short, she explains her preferences by describing a life context within which the preferences fit. This life context will embody what $O$ thinks is worth having, doing, and being. That is, it will embody her values. Whether her indifference curve is rational or not can be decided in the context of these values.

You might notice that $O$ could be a rational economic man with respect to aspirin and bourbon (that is, have connected transitive preferences, etc.) and still not be rational with respect to the appropriateness of her preferences to the broader life context into which they're supposed to fit.

Now we can imagine a different situation for $O$. We have the same indifference map we had before, but now we find that $O$ is an alcoholic and an aspirin junkie. Her preferences for aspirin and bourbon reflect her search for the optimum high. Furthermore, she's good at it: She really does know what's the right combination of aspirin and bourbon. She's the rational economic man, *and* her preferences fit with her broader aims. Now, ask yourself honestly if you'd want to use her indifference map for aspirin and bourbon as a basis for her welfare. I'd be inclined to think that she'd be better off if she had entirely different preferences. Of course, if

I suggested that to her she might come back with "Don't mess with my consumer sovereignty!" She'd have a point. It certainly seems that if for example, I prevented her from getting any aspirin and bourbon I would be acting against her will, denying her the freedom of choice. But I think that most of us feel that consumer sovereignty has its limits. Sometimes we feel it right to constrain people's choices. If we could ever get O dried out, she might even agree. What's certain is that all known societies have believed that certain choices ought to be constrained. This is reflected in every known legal system—even the legal systems of the freest societies. Paradoxically, ardent prohibitionists are often ardent advocates of free enterprise and consumer sovereignty.

It's also certain, though, that there are grave dangers in constraining choices. I don't think I need to go into them here. It's because of these dangers that the theory of consumer sovereignty has its great attraction. Most of us resist having values imposed on us.

We now see that we have to choose whether or not to connect O's indifference map directly to her welfare. This choice doesn't have to do with anything that appears on the indifference map itself. It rests on complicated judgments about why O is behaving as she is—revealing the preferences that appear on the map. We could grit our teeth and refuse to make these judgments; that is, we could let consumer sovereignty reign supreme as our only indicator of welfare. I leave it to you to decide whether such a refusal would reflect your best thoughts on the matter.[3]

**PREFERENCE OVER TIME** We now move to a different difficulty with using the indifference maps as an indicator of value or welfare. Here, we imagine that on Tuesday we ask O all the questions necessary to construct her indifference map for aspirin and bourbon. On this map, let's suppose, bundles R, P, S, and T are indifferent. On Wednesday we offer O bundle R and she says "I'd much rather have T." "But," we say, "R and T are indifferent." "No they're not," she says. "Aha, then you're irrational!", we say, "You've contradicted what you said yesterday!" "Well, I've changed my mind," says O.

At this point we could accuse O of being fickle and not knowing her own mind. What use are indifference maps going to be for predicting behavior and determining welfare if they can change from day to day? However, I think we ought to hesitate before we accuse O of irrationality. Changing your mind isn't always a bad thing to do. Obviously if you find

[3]The "limits of consumer sovereignty" raise an age-old problem within liberalism: individual liberty vs. social cohesion. The classic liberal position is in John Stuart Mill, *On Liberty* (many editions). For a contemporary liberal view see: Norman Bowie and Robert Simon, *The Individual and the Social Order* (Englewood Cliffs, N.J.: Prentice-Hall, 1977).

out you are wrong about something, it would be irrational *not* to change your mind. More important, there is the sense of yourself as someone who learns, develops, broadens, deepens—in a word, as someone who changes all the time. When *O* says "I've changed my mind," she may or may not be irrational. Against a background of people growing and developing as they become older and wiser, the burden of proof is on those who want to accuse her of irrationality. They have to show what was wrong with her changing her mind. She has a new pattern of choices that raises havoc with her old indifference map. This doesn't by itself make her irrational even if over a considerable period she never has an indifference map with nice transitive preferences on it. She may be in a period of exploration, trying out new things, exploring new alternatives, accepting some, rejecting others once they've been tried. Such a period might be one of the most important in her life, but while she's in it, she's certainly not going to look like the rational economic man. And maybe this sort of thing ought to be going on in our lives all the time. Is it wrong to learn, grow, and develop? While we're in such a period, our indifference maps are likely to be a poor guide to our welfare.

But the economist has another question. How in the world is anyone going to be able to make sound economic decisions in the state of changeableness that we've imagined. Long-range planning and investment require a certain stability, things we can count on. Otherwise, every decision would be a shot in the dark. How could we ever derive a theory of price from indifference maps on which the indifference curves were wiggling around like snakes—even slithering across one another?

Before you dismiss the economist, pointing out that this is not your problem, think of how you would ever live a stable, predictable life if patterns of behavior were chaotic. A government needs to know what its citizens want and need. If these wants and needs changed on a daily basis, the government would never be able to decide how to provide the conditions for its citizens' welfare.

It may be that the right course is to avoid the extremes of absolute stability on the one hand and chaotic change on the other. Perhaps a way has to be found to accommodate personal growth and development against a background of basically stable wants and needs. Maybe that's what we try to do all the time anyway. It doesn't seem to be easy. Two things are certain: The usefulness of indifference maps and similar devices is questionable in these circumstances—economists themselves express worries about this; and if we do try to accommodate growth and development in our concept of welfare, the scheme of values that we employ will go well beyond what the theory of revealed preference and the concept of the rational economic man can give us.

There's a related problem which is really pressing right now. One of the most serious issues facing us is the problem of how to leave the world for future generations. If we want them to lead good lives, we have to know what they will need and ensure that it's available for them. From the point of view of utility theory as we have seen it develop, this would mean guessing at the preferences that future generations will have. It's not easy to see how to do this, especially if we have a concern for their consumer sovereignty. The problem of future generations raises all the problems we have seen in the theory of utility in the most serious possible way. Yet we can't avoid the problem of future generations. We make decisions every day which go far toward shaping the world that future generations will live in. On what basis *should* we open and close options for future generations? If it's on the basis of our own revealed preferences, then that's like taking the Golden Rule in its silliest interpretation: Doing unto others as we would have them do unto us—whether they like it or not.

**CAN WE DRAW THE MAPS?**    Here's another fundamental worry about revealed preference and interval preference rankings. Indifference maps and interval rankings were constructed on the basis of a lot of information that we imagined dragging out of $O$ and others. We asked $O$ to compare many, many bundles in order to construct her indifference curves; then, to construct interval rankings, we sought not only comparisons between bundles but also comparisons between bundles and gambles. For the purpose of laying out the maps and rankings for our mythical $O$, we could easily imagine collecting this information. When it comes to doing it for real people in a real world, imagination isn't enough. The fact of the matter is that no economist has enough information about any person to construct an indifference map or an interval ranking. Furthermore, it's difficult to see how such information could actually be obtained. Most of the choices offered between bundles would be hypothetical ones—with nothing really at stake. It seems questionable whether or not such hypothetical choices offer the guide to genuine preferences that the economist wants and needs. Upon offering a person hypothetical choices, all the economist would find out is how the person reacted in a bizarre word game. Why assume that these same preferences would be expressed in a genuine choice situation? The assumption becomes especially questionable when we remember all the complicated reasons a person might have for expressing a given preference in a real world situation.

On the other hand, if the economist confines his attention to actual choices, another difficulty arises. The number of choices, trades, and exchanges that a person actually makes is very small compared to the number represented on the indifference map. Furthermore, since any person starts out with a given set of resources, only some of the bundles on the map will be available. Perhaps all the economist needs to care about is the small area of the indifference map where the actual choices are located. But even in this small area the leap from a few real choices to the smooth, continuous indifference curve that the economist wants is a very long one. How is this leap made? Well, the economist takes the few actual choices, trades, and exchanges observed; assumes that the chooser is a rational economic man; and draws the curve on that basis. Without the assumption that the chooser is a rational economic man, there is no way in the world to decide between drawing one indifference curve or drawing any of an infinite family of others.

But this way of proceeding leads to another problem. One of the choices may have been a mistake. It happens, you know. You buy something, and the minute you get it home you realize you never should have bought it. You certainly don't want an economist to be thinking of your welfare in terms of *that* choice. You want to say that the choice you made was irrational and to be disregarded. Maybe you'd better rush out and make some good trades to try to cover up the bad one.

**THE COMMON SENSE OF "UTILITY"** All through this discussion of utility there has been a common sense belief lurking behind the scenes. We really seem to know—at least sometimes—when someone is better or worse off. Doesn't this mean that we can calculate utility after all? I don't think so. I think we have a fuller and more complicated sense of our lives than the utilitarian economists have been able to capture. In deciding whether someone is doing well or doing badly, we have one of two things in mind: (a) a general conception of what's worth having, being, and doing; or (b) the person's *own* conception of what's worth having, being, and doing. We make comparisons between these conceptions and the way people are making out in terms of them.

Now, the economist will rightly argue that he never meant to provide the total theory of value that we seem to be talking about here. His concern is only with economic value. Economics, based on the observation of economic behavior, is a separate, self-contained field of study.

Unfortunately, our economic activity is not a separate, self-contained part of our lives. The values we pursue economically are necessarily connected with all the other values that give shape to our lives. So if the economists want to talk about our welfare they have to show us one of two things (both of which they've tried):

First, they could try to convince us that *all* our values could be translated into the language and technique of revealed preference. Knowing some of the problems with that theory even in its narrower economic forms, we might be very skeptical of this alternative.

Second, they could try to show us that our economic values, as expressed in the theory of revealed preference, could be made to fit well with all our other values. They could try to convince us that a life as a rational economic man is a necessary part of a life as a person rational with respect to the overall plans, hopes, and aspirations that define our lives as a whole. Maybe they could do this; maybe not. But, what seems clear to me is that a large part of the burden of proof now falls on them.

Anyway, our final judgment on the economists' conception of value, and the way it works out in the broader context of our lives as we live them, will have to wait at least until we've examined the market system.

## CHAPTER FOUR

# Two Alternative Theories of Economic Value

I have been suggesting that a satisfactory theory of value ought to relate our economic activity to the broader concerns of our lives. In other words economic value ought to be related to our conception of what, in general, is worth being, doing, and having. I don't stand alone in this. Adam Smith's concept of use value was an attempt to integrate exchange value, or price, with the wants and needs of those who buy, sell, and trade. The concept of use value is meant to explain *why* people trade: They trade for what is useful; and the usefulness of anything could then, in turn, be explained by spelling out the plan of life within which it fits.

As we've seen, the development of the theory of utility seems to have moved us away from the concept of use value, so that revealed preference becomes the only facet of economic value considered. The *reasons* for the preferences which are revealed are then thought to lie outside economics —a situation which is satisfactory from the economist's point of view but which leaves us wondering how the pursuit of economic value is related to our overall welfare.

In this chapter I want to give you a brief look at two theories which explicitly attempt to preserve the connection of economic value with value in general. Both these theories show us how we might try to derive a theory of value from a theory of human nature. The interesting thing about putting the theories side by side is that the underlying conceptions of human nature are very different and lead to very different views about how the world ought to be.

**LUDWIG VON MISES** The first of the two theories is that of Ludwig Von Mises. Von Mises' name may not be familar to you, but he is an important intellectual ancestor of people whose names might very well be familiar: Ayn Rand, John Hospers, and William F. Buckley, Jr.[1] Von Mises' claim is that we can derive economic theory from the very nature of human action. To see what this means, we can start by going back to one of the difficulties we found in drawing indifference maps. I said that no economist ever really had enough data to draw anyone's indifference map and that the only way that indifference curves could be drawn for a person was by assuming that the person was a "rational economic man." Von Mises would agree with the assumption (but not the drawing of indifference maps) and would push on to the key question: "Why assume that a person is a rational economic man?" His answer to that question is that it is perfectly correct to make this assumption because being a rational economic man is the basic characteristic of human nature.

Von Mises asks us to think of human beings as creatures with wants, needs, and intelligence. All human action is directed toward satisfying these wants and needs. Furthermore, it is an axiom of human nature that the effort a person will expend in action is directly proportional to the intensity of the wants and needs. Thus, as a need becomes more and more satisfied, the energy a person is willing to expend to satisfy it becomes less and less. According to Von Mises, this is the basis of the principle of diminishing marginal utility. The total picture that we get from this is that of human beings as "economizers," getting the most they can from the least expenditure. This is a familiar picture to us by now. Von Mises adds to Adam Smith's picture by telling us that economizing is the defining characteristic of human motivation: the defining characteristic of rationality.

Our instinct might now be to look around to see if the human beings in our experience fit the picture Von Mises paints. But, according to Von Mises, this would be a bad mistake. This is not a picture we can derive from an observation of human beings; it is a picture we *must* accept in

---

[1]The most complete statement of Von Mises' theory is in Ludwig Von Mises, *Human Action* (New Haven: Yale University Press, 1949).

order to understand human beings in the first place. Again recall the situation with the indifference maps.

All this leaves me scratching my head—a little puzzled about whether I ought to accept it or not. Assuming that you're in the same boat, let's try to go a bit deeper by examining the theory from another point of view. This will give us our first look at how scientific theories are constructed and tested out. As usual we try an analogy, one that Von Mises himself uses.

When we investigate phenomena in the physical sciences, we assume that there are reasons for the occurrence of each physical event. This assumption is the underpinning of our scientific activity. If we didn't make it, our scientific investigations would always threaten to be useless; and physical events would threaten to be incomprehensible. In other words we have to be confident beforehand that we can find the reasons why things happen in nature. Otherwise we might think that the search for reasons was a waste of time. But the scientist is committed to the assumption that there are no mysteries that are bound to remain mysteries forever. There are reasons for everything, he assumes, and these reasons can be found if science is clever enough. The assumption that there's a reason for everything is classically phrased "Every event has a cause." But there are other suitable ways of saying the same thing which take into account the fact that physicists, for example, don't talk about causes within their theories. It's well known that the assumption can never be proven. Still science depends on its acceptance as a presupposition of all its activity.[2]

Von Mises is telling us that a parallel assumption must be made when we try to explain human action. I can buy that; and I would guess that the parallel assumption might be that what a person does has reasons behind it.

Of course we have to be careful about the *kinds* of reasons there are for people doing what they're doing. First of all, there's a whole set of explanations which have to do with accidents, mistakes, inadvertencies, and other ways of going astray. All these explanations serve to remove an action from the realm of a person's plans, projects, and rational calculations; and place it as something whose reasons lie elsewhere. So any assumption about the reasons for human action has to take into account the fact that some of the things we do are done by accident, by mistake, or in some other way don't reflect *our own* reasons.

The presence of slip-ups makes explaining human behavior a good bit

---

[2]A readable discussion of the development of science's ability to explain can be found in Paul Snyder, *Toward One Science* (New York: St. Martin's Press, 1977).

harder than explaining the behavior of pendula and electrons. They don't make mistakes, have accidents, or mess up through inattention. It's not at all clear that Von Mises' theory can account for slip-ups.

But even were mistakes and so forth taken care of, we would still have to account for all the sorts of reasons there are for doing things.

Von Mises wants to say that correct explanations of human action are of only one sort: explanations which fit a specific pattern, namely: The person did (      ) in circumstances (      ) as the most economical means to satisfy the want or need for (      ). The blanks are to be filled in by the facts of the situation: The person is identified; the action is specified; the circumstances are spelled out; the want or need is stated. Now, as one among many possible schemes for explaining what people do, this pattern makes perfectly good sense. It's the pattern that fits the things we do when we're economizing—calculating how to get the most benefit at the least cost. But it no longer seems parallel to "Every event has a cause" or its equivalents. It seems parallel to some particular theory of why physical events occur, for example to "Every event in nature obeys Newton's laws of motion." If we believed that Newton's laws explained everything, we would surely have a program of scientific investigation mapped out for us—the program of finding out the equations of motion for everything. But we'd end up embarrassed, because some things don't seem to be explainable on the basis of Newton's laws.

The simple mechanical explanations we get when we use Newton's Laws have their limits. Different explanations, in terms of more powerful theories, are needed for investigating very large-scale or very small-scale phenomena. The big advances in physics in the twentieth century have come about because new theories have been developed which extend our understanding beyond the range of Newton's mechanics. These new theories don't plunge us into mystery. They don't force us to abandon the assumption that an explanation can be given for everything that happens. In fact they extend our ability to find reasons.

Similarly, when I say that Von Mises' pattern of explanation in terms of economizing is only one among many possible schemes for explaining human action. I'm not trying to get you to abandon the assumption that reasons can be found for what people do. What I think we ought to consider, though, is the range of explanations we actually use in order to understand ourselves and others. We whisked through a small sample in chapter one.

If you're attracted to Von Mises' pattern of explanation, then you have to think that all explanations except for those that spell out a person's economizing are unsatisfactory. Such an attraction ought to interest you. It points directly to your conception of human nature, just as Von Mises says it should. Humans are by nature economizers, says Von Mises. On the other hand, if you think that people don't always act as economizers, then you must hold another conception of human nature.

You'd think that the choice between theories of human nature would depend on the facts of the matter. But Von Mises tells us not to base our theory of human nature on facts. The theory of human nature—and the consequent theory of value—laid out in terms of human beings as economizers has to be assumed to be true, says Von Mises, before we go on to examine the facts. Thus, if we disagree with his theory of human nature —possibly because we see economizing as only one kind of reason for acting—then we have to hold back from agreeing with Von Mises' theory of value.

One thing has to be made clear, though. I phrase it in terms of Converse's law, which is: In the social sciences there is no such thing as refutation; only embarrassment.[3] What this means for our purposes is that there is no point where you *have* to give up your theory of human nature. Anyone attracted to Von Mises theory can say to us "All those other explanations that you come up with are faulty. You only give them because you haven't yet come up with the *real* explanations: the ones in terms of Von Mises' pattern." So a committed Von Misan could always approach the world of human action in search of explanations in terms of the pattern. If he didn't find them he might be embarrassed but never finally refuted, for he could always say that the explanations he's looking for are there, but he just hasn't happened to find them. The upshot of this is that if the portrait of human nature Von Mises presents—the portrait of the economizer—seems obviously the right one to you, then you can hold on for dear life, secure in the knowledge that you will never be shown to be wrong once and for all. Of course, the same is true of any other theory of human nature which anyone else might want to hold onto.

It would really be cheap of me to end a discussion of Von Mises without emphasizing a feature of his world picture which accounts for a good part of the charm of his theory. The world of economizers is a world of independent human beings making their own decisions and acting as they think best to satisfy their wants and needs. Everyone has responsibility for him or herself and is meant to make his or her way through life on the basis of his or her own ability and diligence. Any interference with individual human action is a violation of human nature, a tampering with human beings as they are at their best. Some people will succeed, and some fail; but success and failure are the responsibility of the individual. If successful, a person is to be admired; if a failure, it's his own fault. This picture of the world appeals to those people who live in a tradition of independence and self help.

[3]Converse's law was formulated by John Converse in 1977.

In summary we can say that if Von Mises' basic conception of human nature is accepted, then he has indeed connected economic value with value in general, for *all* human activity is economic activity: That is what his pattern of explanation tells us. Trading is an especially important part of human activity, of course, because it's the main way in which economizers can fulfill their wants and needs. Because of the importance of freedom and independence, this trading must not be restricted or regulated by an agency outside the market. Trading must be the free consequence of the activity of individual economizers.

**KARL MARX**     We now move on to a very different conception of human nature. While Von Mises gives us the picture of the individual economizer working alone to satisfy wants, Marx gives us the picture of groups of people working together for the mutual achievement of their destiny as human beings. According to Marx the source of all value is the mutual recognition and appreciation of people by one another. People are not isolated individuals but necessarily members of groups. Human history is the story of the progress of human beings toward a world in which human values can be fully realized.

The full scope of Marx's theory is far too great to present in this book. In addition it's one of those theories in which everything fits with everything else, so it's hard to present isolated pieces. Nonetheless we can get a decent idea of his theory of value. Just as this theory of value is here offered as a contrast to the utilitarian theory of value, later we will look at other parts of Marx's theory to provide additional contrasts.[4]

The best place for us to start is back at Adam Smith's distinction between use value and exchange value. Marx says that Smith was on the right track in making this distinction. It shows us something important about how values must be pursued in a society based on the division of labor and trading activity. The use value of something is its value in a qualitative way; that is, it refers to the place of the thing as a contributor to the overall quality of life of some person or persons. Exchange value is value in a quantitative way; that is, it refers to what a thing will fetch in a market. In any society which has to try to live with both these kinds of value at the same time, there's the real danger that the two kinds of value will not match up right—at least for many people. For example, the relative prices of things may not reflect the contributions they could make

[4]There is no single, compact source for Marx's theory of value. This account is culled from *"The Economic and Philosophical Manuscripts of 1844"* in Lloyd Easton and Kurt Guddat, eds. *Writings of the Young Marx on Philosophy and Society* (New York: Doubleday, 1967); the first eleven chapters of *Capital* (New York: The Modern Library, 1936); *Value, Price, and Profit* (New York: International Publishers, 1935); *Grundrisse,* Martin Nicolaus, Tr., (New York: Vintage, 1973); and *Theories of Surplus Value* (New York: Beckman Publishers, 1970).

to the quality of life of some or all persons in a society. In fact, it's Marx's claim that *no* system in which trade and exchange are the means by which things are distributed among people will be able to get use value and exchange value to match up. In a capitalist society—which we can think of as a society in which some people own the productive facilities such as factories, industries, and other corporations, and all the rest of the people work for these owners for a wage—the gap between use value and exchange value will exist for the workers. The owners will be able to set prices in such a way that the workers will be forced to trade their labor in a disadvantageous way; the value they produce will be more than the value that they receive as a wage. The difference between the value that a worker produces and what he receives in return is called "surplus value." We will deal with it more fully in our examination of market systems.

Just as did Adam Smith, Marx believed that labor was the central concept in our proper understanding of human value. The roots of this belief go right to his overall conception of human nature and human value. Human beings are aware of themselves as human beings; so they must think of themselves as persons among persons. If they want to fulfill themselves as persons they must be recognized by others as persons of worth; they must be respected and appreciated by others. That's how they find a place of dignity in the human world. In order to be recognized and respected by others, a person must act in the world—make changes in it which can be recognized and appreciated by others. In general, these changes will be intended to make the world a better place, more beautiful, more suitable for the same kind of activity by all people. Marx calls such human activity "creative productive activity." At its best this activity expresses the special contribution each person has to make to the lives of others. In other words, creative productive activity should be social, done with others in mind and capable of being respected and appreciated by others. The primary things of value in the world are human beings and their creative productive activity. Anything else has value only insofar as it's necessary for creative productive activity.

Creative productive activity is the basic form of labor; so one's value is in one's labor. This may seem strange to those of us who think of our life as workers merely as a means to leading our life as consumers. Marx thinks that this is a terrible reversal of a worthwhile human life. He tells us that we ought to eat in order to work rather than working in order to eat. He says that the reversal of the worthwhile human life is forced upon us by our lives in the capitalist system, a system which doesn't allow most of us to fulfill ourselves as creative productive persons. Instead of being respected for what we do, we try to become respected for what we consume: what kind of house or car we have; where we can afford to travel.

Since labor is the primary value, Marx tries to work out a theory of price on the basis of the labor theory of value. If we remember the difficulties we saw in Adam Smith's attempt to do the same thing, we might imagine that the same difficulties crop up in Marx's theory. Marx worked about seventy-five years after Smith, so it's no surprise that his theory is a good bit more sophisticated. However, there's still serious disagreement about whether or not Marx successfully worked out a satisfactory theory of price on the basis of the labor theory of value. Without engaging in the debate about this—which, again, I leave to your future studies—we can pick out two interesting and important points.

First, it's clear that if a theory of price is to be built on the labor theory of value, then labor itself is going to have to be measurable. It must be expressed quantitatively. It must be representable on one of the axes of an indifference map. This quantitative representation of labor is called "labor power." Labor power is what is offered in the labor market and which receives a wage in return. But now, with the distinction between labor, which has a use value, and labor power, which has an exchange value, we can see how a gap can open up. The value of labor is qualitative and related to a person's self fulfillment; the value of labor power is quantitative, and subject to the laws of supply and demand. The two "values" of what a person does may bear no relation to one another.

Second, Marx thinks that the misfit between the use value and the exchange value of a person's labor can never be satisfactorily eliminated in a system where labor is traded, bought and sold. So the only way to be sure that people will be free to fulfill themselves by engaging in their own special creative productive activities is to abolish the system of trading—and the theory of price that goes with it. This, of course, means the abolition of the capitalist system in favor of a system in which the only value is qualitative. In such a system there will be no prices, no quantitative measure of value at all. Values will be incommensurable which means not only that they will not be measurable, but also that there can be no quantitative interpersonal comparisons of value. So all the utilitarian apparatus we have seen will be totally irrelevant. In order to make sure that everything is properly distributed, we will have to have a full appreciation and respect for what a person needs in order to engage in creative productive activity—and allocate things on that basis.

Well, this picture of a good world is certainly different from that of Von Mises or even that of the utilitarians. The basic conception of human nature which it rests on is, after all, very different. We have to ask whether people are (or could be) as Marx paints them. Here again there are difficulties in just going out and looking at the next few people we happen to run into. It's an integral part of Marx's theory that in the course of our history as a species we go through stages. At each of the stages before the last one, people are stuck in a system which prevents them from living a life of free creative productive activity. At some stages there are slaves; at other stages people must sell their labor as labor power in an exchange system. In order to make out in any of these systems, people will have to modify their activity—and even, to a large extent, their conceptions of themselves. From inside any system it looks as if the thing to do is to conform to the requirements of the system. In consequence, our conception of ourselves as—at best—creative productive beings will only develop gradually and by stages. So we shouldn't be surprised if the people around us at any given time don't act like the creative productive beings Marx describes.

Marx himself thought he could show how the normal workings of history were bound to result in the realization of a world of creative productive human beings free to fulfill themselves. Again there are enough problems with his theory about how this was going to happen that many people doubt his claims.

Well, where does this leave us? With yet another theory to think about, yet another theory of human nature to compare. I think if we're wise we'll do best to reserve judgment on all the theories until we've gotten a lot farther along in our investigations.[5]

[5]The classic critique of Marx's theory of value is that of Böhm-Bawerk, published with the equally classic reply of Hilferding in Paul Sweezy, ed. *Karl Marx and the Close of his System*, by Eugen Böhm-Bawerk and *Eugen Böhm-Bawerk's Criticism of Marx*, by Rudolf Hilferding, New York, 1949. Böhm-Bawerk states the so-called "transformation problem" which concerns the consistency of Books I and III of *Capital*. The thought that there is such a problem depends on (A) a misunderstanding of Marx's theory of value, (B) a misunderstanding of Marx's methodology in *Capital* and (C) a disagreement about the role of competition within capitalism. See also Joan Robinson, *Economic Philosophy* (New York: Doubleday, 1962), and *An Essay on Marxian Economics* (New York: St. Martin's, 1967). A seminal work on Marx's theory of value is Franz Petry, *Der Soziale Gehalt der Marxschen Werttheorie* (Jena Fischer Verlag 1916).

## CHAPTER FIVE

# Property

We often hear that possession is nine-tenths of the law. I'm not sure what that means, but what *does* seem clear is that laws about possession constitute about nine-tenths of the laws we have. It's always been that way. Roman law was one of the first systems of law worked out in great detail. Some parts of Roman law are still imbedded in modern legal systems. In Roman law virtually everything except international law is thought of as part of the law of *meum et tuum,* that is, the law of what's mine and what's yours.

The basic picture we have to think of is a dispute among people over some object, a piece of land, or something of the kind. Several people claim that it's theirs, and the job of the law is to resolve the dispute. So the law needs some method for deciding which claim is to be honored. Obviously, mere possession isn't going to be decisive. We can see what that would lead to: a constant battle for possession. The whole point of having laws about what's mine and what's yours is to avoid these battles.

Once possession is ruled out as the sole ground for what's mine and what's yours, we have to start talking about ownership or property, that is, about *rightful* possession. Who has the right to this or that? Who has the rightful use of this or that?

It's easy to see that every society must have a firm understanding of such rights. In fact, it's seemed to some people that every society must have the *same* understanding of the rights of property—or at least should have. On the other hand, we know that the rights of property vary from society to society—and even from period to period in the same society. What are we to make of all this?

First, we have to establish a basic fixed point from which to begin. Within any group of people who live in close enough contact so that disputes about the rightful possession of anything might break out, there has to be some way of resolving the disputes. Furthermore, if the people are going to live in tolerable harmony, the method for resolving disputes has to be satisfactory to them. If we keep these two conditions in mind as conditions that any theory of property must fulfill, then we're ready to examine a few theories.[1]

**OUR OWN SYSTEM OF PROPERTY**
First, let's look at the system of property in our own (American) society. Or rather, let's look at some pieces of it, since the whole system is vast and complicated. Begin by thinking of owning a book—the one you're reading. Your ownership of it has two aspects: how you got it and what you may do with it. In our society, there are two ways in which you could have come to own the book: It could have been given to you, or you could have bought it. According to our system of property, if you got it any other way, it's not rightfully yours. Now, granted that you have it, what may you do with it? Well, you may read it, write in the margins, prop up the legs of a table with it, start a fire with it; but also sell it, give it away, throw it away, or lend it to somebody. These are all rights you have with respect to the book, and these rights along with others define your ownership of the book. On the other hand, the copyright laws limit what you may do with the book. They say that you may not photocopy big chunks of it, reprint it without permission, and so forth. When you've considered all these rights and prohibitions, then you know what it means for the book to be your property.

Next, let's take a look at your car. If it's really yours, then you have a title to it in your name. You need no title to the book, so immediately we suspect that the rights and prohibitions with respect to the car will be different from those with respect to the book—and so they are. For example, there are strict rules about what I must do to get rid of a car. I'm not supposed to just abandon it somewhere for instance. Furthermore, my use of it is subject to proper licensing procedures, and that isn't

[1]There are several good introductions to Roman Law including Barry Nicholas, *An Introduction to Roman Law* (Oxford: Oxford University Press, 1962).

true of the book. In addition if I lend you a book, I'm not liable for the damage it does to you and others. Not so with the car. In consequence of these and other considerations, we're forced to see that the rights and prohibitions which add up to ownership of the car are different from those that add up to ownership of the book.

From here we can move on to ownership of houses and real estate in general. Titles are involved here, as they are with cars, but the system of rights and prohibitions is even more complicated. Just to ask what a person may do with his or her house and ground is to open up a Pandora's box containing zoning laws, laws of eminent domain, mineral and water rights, rights of air space, and on and on until you have to hire a lawyer. Then, on top of all that, if a house is designated as a historic building even more rules apply—for example, no one can change the way it looks.

We could push farther and ask what it is to own a business. Then we'd be faced with all the laws about incorporation, partnership, stockholding, directorship, and the like. Until we understood at least a major part of the law with respect to these things, we wouldn't understand what it is to own a business, a corporation, a company. I don't know about you, but I surely don't have the necessary legal knowledge to be able to spell out what ownership means in these cases.

So, in a society as complicated as ours, it's almost impossible for the average person to understand all the aspects of ownership—at least in detail. We all operate with a rough, workable understanding of what it is to own something, and when we get into trouble we hire a lawyer. We might ask, though, if there is some basic core to the concept of property in our society, some features of ownership as we know it that are common to all kinds of ownership. These might serve as a foundation to our understanding of property.

In fact, the rules about how one can come to rightful possession of something serve as part of the core. We're pretty clear about the difference between buying and stealing, and between giving and lending. Insofar as we can keep these differences straight we'll have a grasp of the basics of our concept of property. In addition, it seems basic to our concept of property that individuals or freely associated individuals are the primary owners of things. This is why we say that we have a system of private property.[2]

---

[2]The classic formulation of the theory of property within liberalism is that of John Locke, *Two Treatises of Government,* ed. Peter Laslett (Cambridge: Cambridge University Press, 1964.) Locke says that by property he means people's "Lives, Liberties, and Estates"; and that "The great and chief end therefore, of Men's uniting into Commonwealths, and putting themselves under Government, *is the Preservation of their Property*" (pp. 368, 369). His full analysis of property occurs in chapter 5 of the second treatise.

**REGULATION AND**  In a system of property where the primary owners
**RESTRICTION**  are private individuals, one finds out who owns a
given thing by finding out who has come to possess it in a rightful way.
We can think of what we'll call a "pure system of private property." In
such a system, once one owned something one would have the right to
do *whatever you like with whatever you own.* No restrictions; no regulations;
no permits required. If you owned a house you could sell it, give it away,
tear it down, turn it into a glue factory, or whatever. Nobody would have
the right to complain. The same thing would be true for everything else
you owned.

Now, even where the ideal of private property is very strong, "pure
systems of private property" soon get modified. In any system we find in
the real world, restrictions and regulations are placed upon what we can
do with what we own. Our quick look at our own system showed us how
complicated the system of regulations and restrictions can become.

People who are ardent defenders of private property are dismayed
every time a regulation or restriction is added to the system of property
rights. In fact, the real purists go so far as to say that any regulation,
restriction, or change of rights "destroys" private property. This may be
excessive. We still think of our own system as a system of private property
even though the regulations and restrictions on what we can do with what
we own are quite extensive. The best way to see why it's still possible to
call our system a system of private property is to go back to our old notion
of "burden of proof." We can say that there is a system of private property when primary owners are individuals, and the burden of proof is on
any person, group, or agency that wants to regulate or restrict the right
of the owner to do what he pleases with what he owns. In the absence of
good reasons to the contrary, the owner has the basic rights. This is what
it means for him to be the primary owner.

The questions that immediately pop up are: "What would count as a
good reason for regulation or restriction?" and "Who can legitimately
decide about regulation or restriction?" There are two approaches to
these questions. The first is for us to go back along the path of our own
history to see how and why movement away from a pure system of private
property has occurred. We could then evaluate the ways in which various
taxes have been established; how rules of corporate ownership were
arrived at; where our real estate laws came from; why licensing procedures were set up; and, in general, how we, as a society, have inched away
from allowing people to do whatever they pleased with whatever they
own. We would find this examination of history a long task. Furthermore,
we'd have to keep asking whether our forebears had done the right thing
when they regulated this or restricted that property right. So, while I
don't want to discourage your understanding of economic history, I'll

move to a second approach to the two questions. In the usual philosopher's way, I propose that we step back and try to gain a perspective on
what all the fuss about private property is about.

First, we have to notice that there are many, many systems of property
to choose from. (Soon we'll see some that are very different from the ones
we've already looked at.) At the moment we're thinking about choosing
a pure system of private property or one of the systems of private property which contains some regulations and restrictions. We're trying to see
what reasons might be good ones for choosing a particular system over
another, and we want to see who might legitimately urge a change in
property rights. By focusing on systems of private property, we have
assumed that we will treat them as the normal situation, so the reasons
for choosing one system over another will appear as reasons for deviating
(or deviating farther) from a pure system of private property.

We have to notice that every system of property—even pure private
property—is a system instituted within a group of people. For there to
be a possibility of a dispute about who owns what, there have to be at least
two parties to the dispute. And theories of property are devices for
dealing with disputes. Now we ask, "Does my doing what I please with
what I own affect others in the group? Suppose I convert my house into
a glue factory. Are my neighbors going to be happy about that? Do they
have good reasons for restricting my right to do anything I want with my
house? If I have concern, respect, or friendship for them, would I agree
that there are things that I ought not to do with my house?"

Following along this line of complicated questioning, we get to the
basis for the regulation and restriction of private property. After a while
it becomes clearer what limits might be reasonable. For example, you
don't have to have a license to use a ballpoint pen. Your use of it has only
the remotest possible effect on others. On the other hand, you have to
have a license to use an automobile because others seem to have a legitimate concern that your use of it may affect them deeply. Thus they want
to be sure that you have the basic ability to use a car so as not, for
example, to make tire marks happen on their chests.

We must keep in mind that almost every reason offered for regulation
is subject to dispute, and someone deeply committed to pure private
property won't want to accept any of them. But once it's recognized that
property rights are always defined for people living with other people,
*and* it's conceded that people other than the owner might have a legitimate concern about how property is used; then the good reasons for
regulation and restriction begin to appear. If you look back at our own
history, you'll see that this is what has happened to us over a period of
time. The people we live with advance claims that our property rights
ought to be modified; then the political process decides whether these

claims ought to be recognized in law. Our system remains a system of private property because the burden of proof continues to rest on those who think that there ought to be a new restriction or regulation.

**THE FEUDAL ALTERNATIVE**    When we look at "mine" and "thine" more broadly, we see that the alternatives to private property are unlimited in number. For instance, we could have a system of property under which everything belonged to your Aunt Gertrude's cat. Everyone else's use of things would then depend on their being able to show how the cat granted them rights of use.

Here we go again. You ask me why I keep introducing stupid alternatives. I nimbly reply that I do it to try to show what can be taken for granted and what can't. Of course no one has every seriously advocated a system of property under which the whole world belongs to Aunt Gertrude's cat. But ask yourself "Why not?" What rules out some theories of whom or what the world belongs to? What makes some theories okay and others silly? I can imagine telling an alien being that I own my house because my wife and I signed some papers, pay some money to the bank every month, and so forth—and have him laugh in my face. What a ridiculous thing to base ownership on. There's nothing particularly persuasive about my claim to own my house to anyone unfamiliar with titles, mortgages, banks, and the whole way of life of which they are a part. Outside the realm of habitual familiarity, the whole business might look absurd. So, as we go through these alternative theories of property, try to get a feel for the kind of life that goes along with them and the kind of reasons someone might have for thinking that they're not silly, but entirely satisfactory.

An alternative to private property which is part of our own heritage is the system of property associated with medieval feudalism. Actually, we'll be talking about a system of *landed* property, and land is only one of the things that can be owned; but, since at that time landed property was thought to be fundamental, we'll be talking about the most important part of the system. Furthermore, need I say it, we'll simplify somewhat. As usual you're invited to examine the (literally) gory details on your own.

At any rate, in days of old when knights were bold and maidens knew no grief, the king owned all the real estate and let it out in fief. This theory of property was a direct consequence of the theory of the divine right of kings. The claim was that the king had dominion over all his lands as the trustee for God. Men other than the king could have the rightful possession and use of lands only by being granted the land by the king. Thus, for any piece of land, the presumption was that it was the king's land; and if anyone else claimed the land he would have to produce the documents proving his right to it. Here we get to the point of looking at a simplified view of feudalism.[3] We see a system in which the burden of proof of ownership or right to use is exactly opposite from what is familiar to us. The consequences of the difference are easy to see. Take taxation: In a system of private property, anyone proposing a tax has the burden on him, for he is proposing to restrict people from doing what they want with their property (usually money). But where the king is the primary owner of everything, he can claim the use of what is (after all) his; in taxing, he's simply taking back part of what belongs to him anyway. If someone objects to the tax, it's up to him to show that, for example, the tax violates the conditions of the grant under which he has the rightful use of his land.

Some version of this basic situation prevailed throughout Europe in the period before the Renaissance. During and after the Renaissance several things happened which led to deep dissatisfaction with the system of property in which the king was the primary owner of everything. A class of people appeared who were very wealthy (hence powerful) but whose wealth did not depend primarily on the possession of land These people were merchants, traders, bankers, craftsmen, and—a bit later—manufacturers. It seemed to them that their wealth came to them as the result of their own effort—their own enterprise—and there was no reason why a king, emperor, or pope should have primary ownership of it. Furthermore, if their wealth allowed them to acquire land, this land seemed as much an earned result of their enterprise as the money that bought it. Pressures by these people led to the explicit change to a system of private property in one part of Europe after another. So, when you look at the theory of private property in this light, you can see why there is such an emphasis on the method in which property is acquired as the basis of ownership. I think that the theory of private property which we know so well appears in the best light when we think of the Renaissance merchants and bankers asserting their claims against those of the feudal kings, emperors, and popes. Even nowadays, when private property is defended, it's often defended by contrasting it with the old medieval system of property—even though that old system has been gone for a long time.

In addition, when we think of the Renaissance merchant asserting his right to the primary ownership of the fruits of his enterprise, we can get a feeling for the apparent oddity that first generation and second generation Americans are conspicuous defenders of pure private property. They are still close to the adventure of immigration which was undertaken in the spirit of enterprise and the search for the new life. They look at America as the land where a person's own effort can produce success, and

[3]For a more complete account of economics within feudalism, see Henri Pirenne, *Economic and Social History of Medieval Europe,* (New York: Harcourt, 1937).

they hate to see restrictions placed on what they feel is the climate of opportunity that a system of private property provides. They are our equivalent of the hopeful, enterprising Renaissance merchant.

**POSSESSION BASED ON UTILITY: GODWIN**
So far we've seen two different systems of property which we can identify in the real world, past or present, even though it's not likely that we ever have or ever will see them in their pure form. Now let's move to a theory of property that's the creature of a philosopher's imagination. It spells out a system of property which will never find a home in the real world—or, at least, I'll bet the family fortune that it won't. Still, it's worth looking at. It connects with what we've said about utility, and when we see why it would never work, we'll know a lot better why some theories of property are sensible and some absurd.

The theory was put forward by William Godwin, an English philosopher who lived about the same time as Jeremy Bentham.[4] Like Bentham, Godwin was a Utilitarian. He tried to develop a purely utilitarian theory of property. Remember, the main function of a theory of property is to specify what is mine and what is yours. Godwin says that the possession and use of anything ought to be determined on the basis of the utility it will have—depending on who has it. In a rough and ready way this is easy enough to understand. "Who gets the car tonight?" Well, Harry has a date to go to the drive-in; and Clem is going downtown to hang out on the corner. You can take the bus downtown, and you don't need a car to hang out on the corner. On the other hand, drive-in movies are a drag without a car, so Harry should get to use the car. What Godwin adds to this familiar situation is the claim that the *reasoning* makes the car Harry's car. The total utility is greater if Harry has the car than if Clem has it. Therefore, it is Harry's car.

The first thing to notice is that in this theory the rightful possession and use of anything has nothing to do with how it was acquired. So this theory differs markedly from the theory of private property. Second, it's clear that the rightful possession of anything is likely to be temporary. The car might be Harry's tonight, but there's no guarantee that he'll ever see it again. For all succeeding time the car might produce more utility in the hands of someone else. We're not used to this kind of temporariness and would probably find it disturbing. Maybe we could get used to it; maybe not.

The third consideration is the real killer. It's one thing to decide who

---

[4]Godwin's theory of property can be found in William Godwin, *Enquiry Concerning Political Justice,* abridged and edited by K. Codell Carter (Oxford: Oxford University Press, 1971) Book VIII.

should have the car on Saturday night on the basis of its usefulness to Harry or Clem. It's another thing to try to generalize this for everything that could be possessed and used and to calculate the utility for all possible possessors and users. In other words, in some contexts at some times we could make reasonable decisions. In general, the problem of measurement would be a disaster. All the problems of utility theory that we have seen would arise in the most difficult way. This is enough to make Godwin's theory of rightful possession an idle dream.

Why even bother with it, then? Well, there's the case of Clem and Harry and the family car. We have the feeling that the use of the car ought to go to the one who needs it most. And think of all those things lying around in someone's garage that you could really use. Isn't that a waste? In other words we can understand the ideal of a world in which everything belongs to just that person who can make the best use of it. Oftentimes families or neighbors operate on this ideal. Things get passed around to those who need them most. Godwin is telling us that we ought to generalize this basic feeling. He asks us to imagine a world in which everything was distributed for the best. There's something reasonable about that.

So let's make one more try to save the theory from the jaws of the measurement problem. We'll see if we can make it work on the basis of utility as revealed preference. Imagine everyone shuffling things around among themselves until everything is in its right place. This will be indicated by the cessation of the shuffling. Notice that we can't talk of people *trading*—as if they were in a market. To talk of them trading would mean that there was private property, and the whole point is not to make use of that system. So, in effect, they all sort through what's available, revealing their preferences by what they take. Now suppose two people both reveal their preference for the same item. Who gets to keep it? If they were in a trading situation, this would be decided by the accident of what they already owned; but here this is impossible. They don't own anything. They can't trade. And, in short, there is no way to resolve the dispute. So there's no way to specify rightful possession. In consequence it's easy to see that Godwin's theory can't make use of the theory of revealed preference. Quite simply this is because the theory of revealed preference presupposes a prior theory of rightful possession. Without such a theory the trading behavior which reveals the preferences cannot take place.

**SOCIAL PROPERTY**　　While Godwin's theory seems impossible to put into effect, it does have a tempting side to it. Somehow, we feel, things ought to be put to their best use and not wasted. This feeling is also one of the main roots of the so-called socialist theories. Now socialism, fully worked out, has many facets, which we will encounter one by one as we proceed. At this point we need to know about the socialist theory of property. We can understand it best by going back to the notions of primary ownership and burden of proof.

To start, we have to think of the difference between making a decision as an individual and making a decision as a group—the difference between *me* making a decision, and *us* making a decision. When *I* make a decision, I may as well make it on the basis of my own good. When *we* make a decision, then the decision ought to reflect the good of us all. But who are "we?" Obviously that varies. "We" could be a family, a tribe, or a biosystem containing aardvarks and ants, llamas and lungworts. This is to mention only a few of the ways in which we could be part of a "we." Both the kinds of decisions we make as a group and the way in which we make the decisions will vary with the group involved. We as a family might tend to make decisions by talking things over until we reach agreement. We as a nation tend to make decisions by voting. We as part of a biosystem might have to guess at how, say, ants and lungworts might like matters to turn out. But, just as long as we can understand what it is to decide as a group, we can get to the basics of the socialist theories of property. For the socialist, we as a group are the primary owner of everything. If individuals want special individual rights of possession and use, then the burden of proof is on the individuals to show that they ought to be granted these rights. As you can see, this just reverses the situation that exists in a system of private property. There the individual is the primary owner, and the burden of proof is on the group—collectively— to show that there ought to be regulation or restriction.

Some advocates of private property say that the socialist systems of property are just like the old system in which the king owned everything. This needn't be so. In the old system the king could say "I am the state." In socialism people can say "We are the state." Now, depending on how socialists as "the state" make their collective decisions, they could end up with anything from autocratic king-like rule on the one hand to the peaceful consensus of the Quaker meeting on the other. It all depends on how the group understands itself as a "we." Respect for individuals could be very strong, or individuals could be crushed beneath a dictatorial regime, or any of the possibilities in between. Again we run into something I keep warning about. Economic systems, including the systems of property which are basic to them, have to be looked at in the light of the conception of human nature that stands behind them. We have to keep asking "How do those people think of themselves and others?" Socialist systems *and* systems of private property can vary widely on the basis of how the people living in them think of themselves and others.

While we're talking about socialism in contrast to private property:

People are often confused about which present-day nations are socialist, and which have systems of private property. If you too are worried about this, then you might keep the following considerations in mind: First, you're not likely to find a pure system of *any* kind in the real world. Defining pure types can aid our understanding, but we shouldn't suppose that we'll ever find one. Second, every nation has a history. At the roots of the way it is now is the way it used to be. The way people think of themselves, the way they think things ought to be, and the way they think decisions ought to be made are all the results of traditions and events from their past. Because of this it would be odd to find two systems exactly alike. Third, socialist systems and systems of private property can shade off into each other so that it's almost impossible to tell the difference between them. At the one end you start with individuals as the primary owners, but over a period of time they as a group have argued successfully for regulation and restriction. This might have happened as, little by little, people saw how private property had to be modified to promote their harmonious existence as a group and to reflect more accurately their concern for each other as persons. Perhaps there were other reasons for the successful modification of property rights. At the other end you start with the group as the primary owner, but, over a long period of time, individuals have successfully argued that they ought to be given rights of individual possession and use. This might have happened because the group came to realize that if individuals were to develop their talents and enjoy productive lives, they had to have individual control over certain things necessary to them. Perhaps there were other reasons for enlarging the sphere of individual rights to possession and use. But whatever the actual reasons, it's easy to see the possibility of two societies, beginning from opposite ends of the theoretical spectrum, gradually converging to the point where, from a practical point of view, their systems look virtually identical.

Well, you ask, if this convergence takes place, why all the fuss about distinguishing them so radically? Two reasons. First, the convergence need not take place. A society might retain a place very close to the pure system fundamental to it. And second, the fact that at a given moment the two societies have converged to the same practical system does not mean that their systems will remain the same in the future. They are on two different historical paths that may diverge. Remember, because of what I've been calling "the burden of proof," their internal dynamics of change differ. In the private property societies, the group as a collective body has to generate the muscle to overcome the presumption of individual rights. In the socialist societies, individuals must generate the muscle to overcome the presumption of social control. These different dynamics could well lead to different futures. We live at a time when we have the chance to watch—and participate in—these processes ourselves.[5]

**MARX ON "MINE"**    The last theory of "property" we'll look at isn't a
**AND "THINE"**    theory of property at all. How about that? It *is* a
theory of "mine" and "yours"—the basic concepts of this chapter. The theory comes from Karl Marx.

We're going to have to think of "mine" and "yours" in a sense in which those words don't mean "property of." This shouldn't be a problem. We use them in a non-property sense all the time. We can distinguish between *my* parents and *your* parents, *my* favorite music and *yours, my* nose and *yours.* In none of these cases need we be talking about property. (Although, with transplants becoming more common, we might yet be buying and selling noses.) There are many ways to be related to something so that you call it yours. Owning it is only one of those ways. Marx wanted to point us toward the meanings of "mine" and "yours" that have nothing to do with property.

When we talk about *our* parents or *our* children, it's easy enough to agree that we shouldn't think of them as our property. They're ours in some other way. Similarly with our friends: Someone might be my friend and your friend at the same time. Does this mean joint ownership? Not usually. So our normal use of "mine" and "yours" when people are involved doesn't generally refer to them as property. On the other hand, we shouldn't forget that slavery is part of human history and that in many cultures the institution of marriage is a property relationship—most often with a woman (or women) as the property of a man. If you object to these kinds of ownership, then you can see one of the points that Marx was getting at.

But the fact that we can talk about our friends, our children, and our parents without talking of them as property doesn't seem to help us much when we move on to other things. What is Marx getting at when he says that objects can be mine, yet not be my property?

We need an example, and we need to recall his theory of value. First the example: Rembrandt painted a masterpiece, "Aristotle Contemplating a Bust of Homer." The painting was sold, "changed hands" I don't know how many times, and eventually was bought by the Metropolitan Museum of Art in New York. We go to look at it. You ask me "Whose

[5]Galbraith discusses the convergence in *Almost Everyone's Guide to Economics,* op. cit. While the convergence thesis has often been discussed with respect to the USA and the USSR, it is probably time to discuss it with respect to the Republic of China.

painting is that?" I say "Rembrandt's." But he sold it, and furthermore he's been dead for years. The painting is the property of the Met. Nonetheless it's Rembrandt's by virtue of artistic creation. No one else can claim it in the way that he could. To think of it as an item of property is to think of it as an article of commerce rather than as a work of art. Ownership is irrelevant to it as a work of art, and once we think of it as a work of art it can be mine and yours—and everyone else's—in addition to being Rembrandt's. It becomes an item of value in the sense of value we saw in the last chapter. It can fit into the creative, productive life of each of us. To say that it's mine is to say that it's of value to me, that I recognize its value. It can be mine and yours at the same time just as surely as someone can be my friend and yours at the same time. At the same time there will still be a special sense in which it's Rembrandt's. He created it, so it fits into his creative, productive life in a way that it never can fit into ours.

Marx wants us to think of all things in the way we've been thinking about the painting. That is, he wants us to integrate them into our system of value, and speak of them as ours only as "ours" expresses the value relations that things have to us. We must not think of them as property.

A system in which "mine" and "yours" are thought of in this way is called by Marx "the higher form of communism." It must be contrasted with socialism. In socialism we as a group are the primary owners; in the higher form of communism there is no ownership at all. When Marx talks about the abolition of property, he means that eventually there will be no ownership of anything at all. Socialism, where "we" are owners, is only a way-station to what Marx advocates.

Terrific, but what about rightful possession and use? Just as we worried about Marx's theory of value because we couldn't get a theory of price from it, we now have to worry about his theory of "mine" and "yours" because it's not clear how to tell who should have what at any given time. The problem doesn't seem too severe with art. Art should be where we can all appreciate and enjoy it. We have the same feeling in our own society, so we have museums and put sculpture in public places.

Other kinds of things are more difficult. In order to know how to allocate them we have to appeal to Marx's principle: "From each according to his abilities; to each according to his needs" and focus on the second part. We're supposed to be related to other people in such a way that we respect and appreciate them. We're supposed to have a concern for their fulfillment as creative productive beings. The claim is that if we're related to them in this way, we'll know what they need and be eager to see they are provided with it. If something has value for all, then it ought to be available for all. If it fulfills a special need of a particular person, then that person ought to have the use of it.

So here again we have to move back to the conception of ourselves that underpins the theory of mine and yours that we're talking about. Marx is asking us to imagine a world very different from the one we're used to. We have to ask ourselves whether such a world is really one of the human possibilities or just another idle dream. Granted that it seems strange to us from our perspective, could we and should we work toward the realization of such a world? I don't know, but thanks to Marx we at least have this alternative to contemplate and to contrast with our own world.[6]

**SUMMARY**                       Where does this leave us?

First, systems of property are devices for making determinate decisions about what's mine and what's yours. They specify rights of possession and use. They tell us how we may acquire things and how we may get rid of them.

Second, there are innumerable possible systems of property, depending upon who or what is considered to be the primary owner, what regulations govern what the owner can do with what he owns, and where the burden of proof lies for those who would like to modify the system of rights of possession and use.

Third, some of the possible systems of property are silly, unworkable, or otherwise not very attractive. But even unworkable theories might reflect some of our feelings about how a system of property should work. Godwin's theory is an example of such a system.

Fourth, in our world, systems of property generally fall into one of two families. The first family contains systems of private property. In these systems individuals are primary owners; rules of rightful acquisition are specified to determine ownership; in the pure system the owners have the right to do whatever they please with what they own; the burden of proof lies with those who would introduce regulations and restrictions. The second family contains the various types of socialism. In these systems, the primary owner is a group—a society, tribe, family, nation; the possession and use of things are determined by the group on the basis of their judgment about what is good for it; the burden of proof falls on those who want to modify the rights of possession and use to accommodate the advantages of individual ownership.

Fifth, Marx presents us a system in which there is no property. The words "mine," "yours," and so on are to be used to express our relation to persons and objects with respect to their value. The workability of

[6]This account of Marx's theory comes from the 1844 Manuscripts (op. cit.) especially the sections "Money and Alienated Man," and "Private Property and Communism"; and *Grundrisse* (op. cit.) pp. 495 ff.

Marx's system is an open question; but at least it makes us see more clearly that any system of property will necessarily be imbedded in an underlying theory of what human beings are, could be, and should be.

Now, with a basic understanding of rationality, value, and property, we can get right into a study of the dominating economic institution of our time: the market system.

## CHAPTER SIX

# The Market

We will now build up an understanding of the market on the basis of what we've learned so far. We'll start with a two-person situation. One of the persons is $O$, who we already know; the other could be anyone so we'll call him $X$. We might as well build our basic picture in terms of the theory of revealed preference. Later on we'll see how some other theories of value fit with the market.

This is only one of a number of ways to present the basic features of the market. While the picture will be filled out as we go along, it will never become as complex as those provided by economists themselves. This is only partially the result of our keeping the mathematics relatively simple. As we go along, the question may arise as to whether the criticisms presented apply to the more sophisticated, mathematically elegant formulations of market theory. I think they do. This is because the criticisms are aimed at assumptions which all versions share. Sometimes it's a bit difficult to locate the assumptions, but they're always there. Some of them are necessary in order to bring the mathematical apparatus to bear in the first place; some others are required as assumptions for and conditions on existence proofs; still others turn out to be information assumptions (which I touch on later). I quote Professor Galbraith in my defense: "In the case of economics there are no important propositions that cannot be stated in plain language. Qualifications and refinements are numerous and of great technical complexity. These are important for separating the good students from the dolts. But in economics the refinements rarely, if ever, modify the essential and practical point. The writer who seeks to be intelligible needs to be right; he must be challenged if his argument leads to an erroneous conclusion and especially if it leads to the wrong action. But he can safely dismiss the charge that he made the subject too easy. The truth is not difficult."[1]

**A BASIC PICTURE OF TRADING**     First, we'll draw an indifference map for $O$ (Figure 10); then we'll draw one for $X$ (Figure 11), but we'll draw $X$'s upside-down.

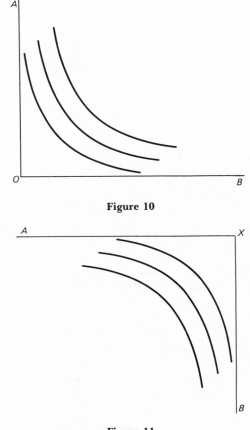

**Figure 10**

**Figure 11**

[1]From John Kenneth Galbraith, "Writing, Typing, and Economics," *Atlantic Monthly,* 241 (April 1978), p. 105.

In each case we'll measure quantities of apples on the vertical axis and bananas on the horizontal axis. Now we push Figures 10 and 11 together to get Figure 12:

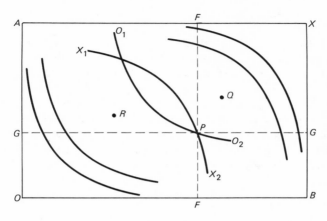

**Figure 12**

*OA*, which is the same length as *XB*, will represent the total number of apples that *O* and *X* have between them; and *OB*, which is the same length as *XA*, will represent the total number of bananas they have between them.

*O*'s indifference curves look just the way they did in chapter five. *X*'s would look just the same as *O*'s if you were reading this standing on your head. *X*'s preferences are measured out from *X*, just as *O*'s preferences are measured out from *O*; thus the indifference curve of each has the proper shape.

Each point on Figure 12 represents a certain number of apples and bananas that *O* and *X* might have. So, *P* is the point where *O* has the bundle containing *OG* of apples and *OF* of bananas; while *X* has the bundle containing *XG* of apples and *XF* of bananas. Of course, if you put the two bundles together, they add up to all the apples and bananas they have between them. We'll imagine that the two of them start out with the bundles represented by point *P*. *O* has a lot of bananas and not many apples; *X* has a lot of apples and not many bananas. We'll further imagine that *O* and *X* are rational economic men. What's more, each of them is looking out for his or her own interests and has no concern for the interests of the other.

Let's ask whether either of them could be better off than they are at *P*. That is, could either get to a higher indifference curve than the one at *P*? Sure they could. First of all, if *O* can manage to swipe some apples and bananas from *X*, she can get to, say, *Q*. For *O*, *Q* is on a higher line than $P$ is, so she's better off than she was at $P$. But $X$ isn't going to stand for that. *For him*, $Q$ is on a *lower* line than $P$ is. Remember, his indifference curves get higher as you move out from $X$. On the other hand, if $X$ is the thief, then the situation is just reversed. He can get to, say, $R$ by stealing apples and bananas from $O$; but clearly she isn't going to stand for getting robbed either.

So, if neither is going to stand for theft, can either become better off than they are at $P$? This would have to be a case in which they were *both* better off. Well, suppose we set them free as rational economic men to trade apples and bananas just as they wished. They start at $P$. $O$'s indifference curve through $P$ is $O_1PO_2$; and $X$'s indifference curve through $P$ is $X_1PX_2$. These two indifference curves close off a lens shaped area. Every point within that lens shaped area is on one of $X$'s indifference curves higher than $X_1PX_2$; and also on one of $O$'s indifference curves higher than $O_1PO_2$. Here is an enlargement of the area around $P$:

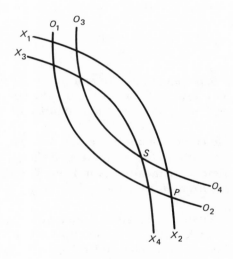

**Figure 13**

S is on $X$'s indifference curve $X_3SX_4$ and on $O$'s indifference curve $O_3SO_4$. $O_3SO_4$ is farther out from $O$ than $O_1PO_2$, and $X_3SX_4$ is farther out from $X$ than $X_1PX_2$. So both of them are better off at $S$ than they were at $P$. Furthermore, they can get to $S$ if $O$ trades some of her many bananas for some of $X$'s many apples. By trading freely they can both become better off.

What's more, if they're both rational they won't stop trading when they get to $S$. There's still a lens-shaped space between $O_3SO_4$ and $X_3SX_4$, and if they move into that space they can both be even better off than at $S$. In fact, they should both keep trading until there is no lens-shaped space to move into. This will happen at point $T$ (Figure 14) where $O$'s indifference curve and $X$'s indifference curve just touch each other.

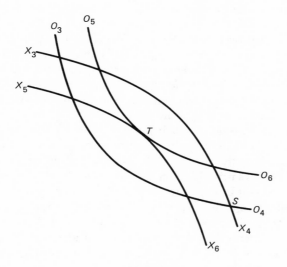

**Figure 14**

When they reach $T$ they'll stop trading. There's no way they can get to a higher line without pushing the other to a lower line. As rational economic men they'll see that there is no trade to be made which is acceptable to them both.[2]

**THE INVISIBLE HAND**    Now we can go back and look at Adam Smith's claims for the market economy. We've already seen the basics of his theory of supply and demand. We've seen that the market is meant to establish the exchange value of various commodities. This exchange value is the price of the commodities. On the basis of this fundamental idea of the market, Smith tried to convince us that the best way to organize our activity is to let people trade freely with the resources that they

[2]Point $T$ is said to be a "Pareto optimum," that is, one of a family of points at which neither trader can become better off without the other becoming worse off, given the initial resources. The ultimate source is Wilfredo Pareto, *Cours d'Economie Politique* (Lausanne: F. Rouge, 1896).

have. If people trade freely with an eye to their own individual well-being, the well-being of *everyone* will be promoted. Total well-being will reach the highest level possible—given the initial resources. Smith's way of putting this is that if each person pursues his rational self-interest, then the wealth of the nation will be maximized "as if guided by an invisible hand." Free enterprise and free trade can't be topped as a method of providing maximum wealth for all. I'll call this the "efficiency claim" for the market.

We're in a position to see what this "invisible hand" really is. We have the saga of $X$ and $O$ to examine. We've seen that if $X$ and $O$ each start out with a bundle of resources (in our example apples and bananas), and are allowed to trade freely, they'll reach a point which is on the highest indifference curve either of them can reach without stealing from the other. They start at $P$; they end up at $T$.

If $X$ and $O$ are going to reach point $T$, then they must find the price at which they ought to trade. In the figures as we've drawn them, $O$ will be trading bananas for apples, and $X$ will be trading apples for bananas. There are two ways in which $O$ and $X$ could settle on a price. If they both had Figure 14 to look at, they would both immediately see the price which would lead them to $T$. It's given by the price line tangent to their indifference curves at $T$. They would know that neither of them ought to settle for a different price. But normally when we trade we don't have indifference maps in front of us, so we have to search around for the right price. If $X$ and $O$ are equally clever bargainers, they will agree on the price given by the price line tangent to their indifference curves at $T$. They will be led to $T$ "as if guided by an invisible hand." But the invisible hand is nothing more than their mutual rationality, their mutual unwillingness to trade at a bad price, and their willingness to trade when the price is right.

Another way to think of the "invisible hand" is to remember the idea of a strategy, from our brief look at the theory of games. Bargaining is a game that $X$ and $O$ are playing. If they both use their best rational strategy, they'll find that they've agreed on the price that will land them at $T$. Against a rational opponent, neither can get a better bundle than the one at $T$. So the "invisible hand" turns out to be a metaphor for the pursuit of minimax strategy by fully rational competitors. Of course, if one competitor is a better bargainer than the other, she has a good chance of getting a better result. But she can get it without deviating from the strategy which would get her to $T$ against an equally clever opponent.

**THE EFFICIENCY**   Now we can see that Adam Smith's claim that the
**CLAIM**   free market is the most efficient system comes down
to the claim that the result $T$ is the best result that can be reached by

rational competitors—given the bundles they had to start with. Any other result is worse for at least one of them. The strength of this claim is even clearer if we contrast the free bargaining situation with situations in which the price of bananas and apples is not decided by $X$ and $O$ but is set beforehand.

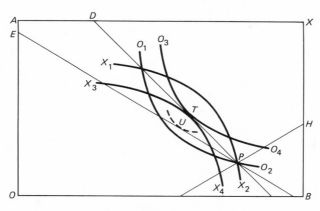

**Figure 15**

In Figure 15, the line $DP$ is the price line which represents the price $O$ and $X$ would agree on if they were allowed to bargain freely. Trading at this price they'd land at $T$. Line $EP$ represents a price which is set arbitrarily and line $HP$ is yet another price which could be set arbitrarily. First we look at line $HP$. At this price no trades would take place. They start at $P$ and can only trade along the line $HP$: that's what it means to say that the price $HP$ has been set. But surely $X$ won't be willing to trade out to the right along $HP$. Any bundle on $HP$ in that direction is worse for him than $P$. And $O$ certainly won't be willing to trade to the left of $P$ on $HP$. Any bundle along $HP$ in that direction is worse for her than $P$. So if they're both rational, they'll never trade.

$HP$ is rather a sad price. It makes $X$ and $O$ stick at $P$ when at another price, say $DP$, they could both be better off than they are at $P$. If you agree that $HP$ is a sad price, then you're likely to agree with Adam Smith that we ought to let $O$ and $X$ bargain freely to set their own price.

Now let's look at price $EP$. They'll never trade to the right of $P$. Every bundle along $EP$ to the right of $P$ is worse than the one at $P$. However, they will trade to the left of $P$, because each of them can reach higher indifference curves than the ones going through $P$. In fact, they'll trade until they reach a point $U$ at which one of $O$'s indifference curves is just tangent to *EP*. At that point *O* will stop trading. She's reached the highest indifference curve she can at the price *EP*.

We can see that *X* will be happy that the price *EP* has been set. At that price he gets to *U*, which is even better for him than *T*. But *O* isn't quite so happy. Sure, she reaches *U* which is better than *P*, but if the price *EP* hadn't been set, and if she and *X* had been able to bargain freely, she could have gotten to *T*, which is better for her than *U*. In setting the price *EP* we've favored *X* to the detriment of *O*. That can't seem quite fair to *O*. She might even point out that another way to reach *U* would have been for *X* to have stolen some bananas and apples from her before they started to bargain freely.

Given all this, the way to express Adam Smith's claim for the market is to say that the most efficient, *fair* way to manage initial resources held by rational individuals is to let them bargain freely. Now, if we look back at the *Wealth of Nations,* we won't find Adam Smith appealing to fairness in his defense of the market. I don't think this is because he's indifferent to fairness. He just thinks that it will take care of itself. And this attitude is typical of many later defenders of the market, too. They think that the operation of the market is bound to be fair, so that all we have to worry about is its efficiency. Let's see what would allow them to think this.

First we remind ourselves that the claim that the market is most efficient means that when *O* and *X* start out with particular bundles of apples and bananas, then the best bundles they could end up with are the ones they'd have after trading freely and rationally. To decide whether or not this claim is correct, we have to compare the bundles they hold after free trading with other bundles they might have held. Now how are we going to compare the bundles? What can it mean to say that one set of bundles is best? Well, the easiest answer is that one set of bundles is better than the other if it yields more total utility, and this is the answer that Smith would probably give. As we saw, the wealth of nations must be measured in terms of utility.

This brings us right back to many of the problems we ran into in the chapters on utility. If the utilitarian is going to convince us that free trading is bound to lead to the best combination of bundles for the traders, he's going to have to convince us that:

1. All traders are rational economic men.
2. Utility has a quantitative measure.
3. Bargaining activity is an accurate measure of utility. (That is, use value and exchange value are linked up in the proper way.)

Only on these assumptions could we be sure that the result reached by free trading was bound to be the best result. We've seen reasons to doubt each of these assumptions.

But even if we granted all the assumptions, we'd still have to worry about whether or not the "best result" reached by free trading was a fair result. The utilitarian would have to find an additional argument to meet these worries. The classic argument he finds for this purpose is based on the principle of diminishing marginal utility: Someone who has a lot of something will be willing to give up quite a bit of it in trade for something else he wants. Similarly, someone who hasn't much of anything at all is supposed to be willing to work harder than the person who has a great deal of what he wants. The total consequence is supposed to be that differences in assets and resources will tend to even up.

I think we have the right to be skeptical about the claim that the market is bound to reach the best result. We have plenty of worries about the quantitative theory of utility we'd need in order to accept the claim. Furthermore, if our worries about fairness are supposed to be calmed by the appeal to the principle of diminishing marginal utility, then we have to remember our discussion in chapter two.

**FAIRNESS AND THE**          The market theorist has another line of argument
**MARKET**                    in support of free trading. He can begin by telling
us that it's high time that we explained exactly what we mean by "fairness." So far we've used the term as if the intuitive examples showed exactly what it meant; but we can't get away with that any longer.

Apparently, when we worry about whether the result of free bargaining and trading will be a fair result, we're worrying about whether the distribution of the commodities traded will be a *just* result. It then becomes important to say exactly how we're going to determine the justice or injustice of a distribution of commodities. But the minute we start talking about the justice or injustice of the *result* of bargaining, the defender of the market stops us in our tracks. "Hold on," he says, "There's no reason to wrestle with the problem of just distribution. You've forgotten some important things about the process of bargaining itself. For one thing, given your example in which $X$ and $O$ start at point $P$, you can be sure that $T$ is the only "just" result that they can obtain if they're both rational economic men. We've already noticed that fixing prices to get them to $U$ instead of $T$ has the same effect as stealing apples and bananas from $O$ and giving them to $X$; *then* letting them bargain freely. But stealing from $O$ is surely unjust; hence anything equivalent to stealing from $O$ is unjust. Consequently, point $T$ is better than point $U$ not on grounds of utility, but on grounds of justice. Furthermore, if you don't let them bargain freely, you're robbing them of their freedom to act as rational economic men. So, on grounds of both freedom and justice, point $T$ must be better than point U; and this judgment requires neither a comparison of quantities of utility nor an examination of the resulting distribution. Finally, if, in the course of bargaining, $X$ and $O$ *do* happen to end up at $U$ rather than at $T$, this simply shows that $O$ is irrational. So we ought to let *that* result stand too, since it would be unjust to penalize $X$ for $O$'s stupidity. Any result reached by free bargaining is the best result and ought not to be disturbed. Freedom and justice demand this."

And so, a conception of freedom and a conception of justice are used in order to push aside any problem of comparing a point like $T$ with a point like $U$. Indeed, on the conception of freedom and justice invoked by the market theorist, the argument seems a pretty good one. It even has the advantage of fitting in with the theory of revealed preference; there's no need to compare points with respect to quantity of utility.

If we want to quarrel with this argument, we're going to have to do one of three things: disagree with the conception of justice, disagree with the concept of freedom, or restate our worries about the theory of revealed preference. We'll question the conception of freedom in a later chapter. Here I'll sketch out the major issues concerning the concept of justice. I won't go into a long discussion of justice, because fine discussions of this issue are available to you elsewhere.[3]

**JUSTICE: A SKETCH**     The basic conception of justice used in defense of the market is that it is unjust to take from one person to give to another. This conception, in turn, can rest on one of two more general principles: (1) It is wrong to treat people differentially, or (2) Every person has the right to what she possesses and it is unjust to violate this right. Now, we might worry a bit about (2) on the basis of what we saw in the chapter on property. There are many, many different conceptions of rightful possession. But (1) does seem to state one of our fundamental feelings about what's just and what's unjust.

On the other hand, critics of the market have always based their arguments on a principle of justice that appeals to another feeling that we have: namely, that certain inequalities among people are unjust, possibly demoralizing, and possibly a violation of the human dignity we feel to be important to all persons. They go on to spell this out. To these critics, the effort to achieve (at least approximate) equality seems important enough so that the operation of the market—and even the institution of pure private property—ought to be modified if necessary.

At one extreme we find the ardent defenders of the market and pure private property. At the other extreme we find egalitarian socialists. But

---

[3]An excellent starting point for thinking about economic justice is Bowie and Simon, op. cit. The reigning liberal work on justice is John Rawls, *A Theory of Justice* (Cambridge: Harvard University Press, 1971). An opposing view is found in Robert Nozick, *Anarchy, State, and Utopia* (New York: Basic Books, 1974).

many of us find that we have *both* basic feelings about justice and try to find some way to do justice to them both. In the give and take of politics over the last hundred years, many nations have evolved into what are called "welfare states," which can be looked at as systems which try to satisfy both basic feelings about justice.

Most discussions of distributive justice that you'll find are attempts to take up a position along the spectrum from pure private property market systems at one end to egalitarian socialist systems on the other. The one exception to this that I know of is Marx's theory, which is not on the spectrum at all. Marx clearly can't accept the concept of justice associated with market theory, since he rejects the concept of private property. Equally clearly he can't be an egalitarian, for the determination of equality presupposes commensurability of quantities of value, and Marx denies that values are commensurable.

I assume that you'll want to make your own decision about the conception of justice that you'll accept; if so, you'll find that the works on justice referred to in the appendix are well worth your time.


**EQUAL OPPORTUNITY**     One way to help focus your thinking about the justice of the market is to think about what might happen under conditions of extreme inequality. While we have the saga of X and O to help us, let's examine these extremes.

Imagine $X$ and $O$ with the bundles in hand which put them at $P$ (Figure 15). They're about to begin the process of bargaining. $O$ has just eaten a big meal and feels at peace with the world. $X$ hasn't eaten in a long time. He's been too busy getting his bananas and his apples together. As they're sitting at the bargaining table, $O$ notices that every time $X$ looks at his bundle of apples and bananas, he starts to drool. His stomach growls; his hand strays to an apple. $O$ thinks, "Aha, he's really hungry. Maybe if I take a tough bargaining position I can force the trading to take place at a much better price than the one that would get us to $T$." While she's thinking, $X$ eats an apple. They bargain on. $X$ eats a banana. $O$ smiles. The total number of bananas held between them shrinks. Point $P$ drifts slowly toward the corner $X$. Maybe at some stage $X$ cracks and trades off apples at a bad rate. Maybe he eats up all his bananas and apples and walks away.[4]

This scenario has serious limitations. In particular, I've set it up so that the bargaining game between $X$ and $O$ is the only game in town. I've not allowed for competitors to $O$, and we can't forget that possibility. None-

[4]An interesting discussion of "extinction games" occurs in Kenneth Boulding, *Conflict and Defense* (New York: Harper & Row 1962).

theless, the illustration shows us something important. If someone is forced to play a game (because it's the only game in town, for some reason), and if he's at a serious disadvantage in the game (because he can't hold out long enough, for example); then he can be forced to accept a result worse than the one he could have expected in the rational play of the game. If we think that $X$ and $O$ should end up at $T$ in the situation we've sketched, then we'll have to find some way to make $O$ trade at the appropriate rate. Why might we want to do that? Well, maybe we think that $O$ starts out with an unfair advantage. At any rate, if we can see that if $X$ doesn't get some help he's likely to be forced out of the game, we might think he ought to get the help he needs.

Market theorists are well aware of this possible problem; and they worry about it too. It's one of the main reasons why a fully developed theory of the market insists that there must be many buyers and many sellers of many commodities. It's important that nobody be faced with playing the only game in town.

Unfortunately, there are some real-world situations which look a lot like the simple one we've cooked up here. For example, if two people play poker with no betting limit, and if one is much richer than the other, then the poorer is likely to be forced out of the game—no matter what kinds of cards he gets. All you need to assume is that the richer person knows what the initial resources were and knows how to manage the betting. In this case you might think that the poorer person deserves his fate, since someone without resources shouldn't have been silly enough to get into the game in the first place.

Another situation which many people feel is paralled to our invented one is even more realistic. In the old days, before our present labor legislation was put into effect, workers demanding higher wages seemed to be at a disadvantage. If they went on strike, they had no source of income. There were no large strike funds as there are now and they seldom had savings, so their ability to hold out was severely limited. On the other hand, manufacturers could keep their shops closed for a long time, suffering only nominal losses which would soon be made up because of the wage bargains they could force on the workers. It's interesting to see why this can be looked at as an "only game in town" situation. In most cases where manufacturers managed to force workers back to the job, the manufacturers were the only substantial source of income in the area. The workers could only shop around for a new job at the cost of great sacrifice—a sacrifice so great, in fact, that there was really no alternative but to make whatever wage bargain they could with the one employer. To make matters worse, blacklists developed, so that workers who struck or made strong demands found that no one else would hire them.

In these cases, the United States as a political whole decided that the advantage held by the manufacturers in the wage-bargaining game was unfair. Labor legislation was passed which reduced the advantage. Such legislation can be justified without giving up the idea that free bargaining is a good thing. You only have to recognize, or insist, that free bargaining ought to take place among relative equals, neither of whom has a big advantage over the other. Only among relative equals will the right price emerge. At least, this is the line of thought that has been pursued in this country for a long time. The attempt is to get the result which would have been reached had the two bargainers been of equal strength and allowed to bargain freely. This might require favoring one of them: in this case by passing labor laws which change the rules of the wage-bargaining game.[5]

**DEALING WITH BARGAINING ADVANTAGE** At this stage you might ask whether all the extra bargaining advantages we've been talking about could be represented directly on the indifference maps. To go back to $X$, $O$, and the fruit, it's clear that $O$'s extra advantage is not represented in Figure 15. I just put in the extra features of the situation—$O$'s being well fed and $X$'s hunger—as additions to the story. It might seem that the extra information would simply change the shape of the indifference curves. But this can't be so if the curves only represent the rate at which the two people are willing to exchange apples and bananas. The curves say nothing about the intensity of their preferences —that is, how much they need apples and bananas. But $O$'s bargaining advantage over $X$ depends on the relative intensity of their needs.

There's a temptation to keep looking for elaborate ways to depict more and more complicated situations. This is all right if the more complicated pictures contribute to an understanding of the issues. But often the more complicated picture simply makes the same old issues appear in a new, more complicated way without contributing to their resolution. Here we're worried about a potential result of free bargaining. It looks as if there are situations in which one person can push the other right out of the game. Suppose that, in general, we're in favor of free bargaining as a way of arriving at prices. And suppose that we don't want to see players pushed out of the game—"extinguished," as they say. We have two possible strategies available: We can insist that if the bargaining situation is pictured in a complicated enough way, it will then show that bargaining will result in the best possible outcome; or we can concede that sometimes the bargaining process has to be helped along by modifying the conditions under which people bargain. If we accept the first alternative we have to try to improve the picture of the bargaining situation given

[5]The literature of the women's movement is important in this context, including that focused on the Equal Rights Amendment. A classic source is Karl Marx, "On the Jewish Question," in Easton and Guddat, op. cit. pp. 216–248.

in the indifference maps we've been using. For instance, we could add another resource to the maps by adding a third axis at right angles to the other two. This resource might be called "ability-to-wait," or "threat potential." $O$ would have a lot of this resource, and $X$ very little. We could then think of $O$ "spending" some of her waiting time to get a better deal on apples. The bundles each had in hand would contain apples, bananas, and ability-to-wait. Apples and bananas would change hands; ability-to-wait would just disappear little by little as a cost of bargaining. One thing we could be sure of is that the number of apples and bananas in $O$'s and $X$'s bundles at the close of bargaining would not be the number that was in their bundles at $T$. So, while the new picture represents the bargaining situation more completely, it doesn't change the nature of the situation. We can still ask which is the better point: $T$, or the new end point of bargaining on the (now three-dimensional) diagram. Our answer will still depend on how we feel about unbalanced bargaining advantages between people such as $X$ and $O$. It will still depend on the basic conception of justice that we hold. In fact, the same can be said for all the stratagems we might try in order to represent the bargaining picture more completely. We are always left with the same problem in some new and complicated form.[6]

The alternative strategy is to provide conditions which will even up bargaining advantages and prevent players from being extinguished. You'll find that you're familiar with some of these methods, although you may not have thought of them in the way that we'll think of them here.

Suppose you thought that prices ought to be set by free bargaining, but that severe bargaining advantages ought to be neutralized. That is, you want to be sure that the price agreed on will be the one that gets $X$ and $O$ to point $T$ on Figure 15. How could you manage this? Well, in the simple situation we've been looking at, you could feed $X$ a meal and then continue to keep him as well fed as $O$. You might even get $O$ to help feed $X$ as her contribution to the fairness of the bargaining. If this seems strange to you, think of the economics of public education as an analogy. We in this country have long recognized that education is generally an important factor in a person's success. We've also thought that providing an education to the disadvantaged is an important way of helping them to a fair start in the free market economy. As a nation we've felt strongly enough about this to subsidize education for all. In general, we can suppose that the cost of education is the same for each person. But to ensure a fair start we make people with initial advantages pay more of the total cost of education than the disadvantaged people. The usual device for doing this has been the real estate tax. People with a lot of valuable

[6]The notion of "threat potential" entered the literature through the work of Howard Shapley and J. F. Nash. See Rapaport, *Two Person Game Theory,* op. cit. chapter 8.

real estate pay a lot toward the schools. People with little real estate pay much less. But the poor get back educational benefits roughly equal to those received by the rich. It's as if, in Figure 15, we made $X$ and $O$ pay for the right to trade apples and bananas. Furthermore, they pay an amount proportional to their bargaining advantage: $O$ pays a lot; $X$ pays a little. Then we divide the total amount they've paid equally between them. Only then do we let them trade.

Any taxation scheme which taxes according to the ability to pay and redistributes without regard to what was initially paid is a way of equalizing bargaining advantages. Both the progressive income tax and the social security system are devices of this sort. They're familiar to us all.

As a last point, we can notice that in terms of the simple situation we've been looking at, an elaborate taxation scheme to equalize bargaining advantage would have the same effect as if we'd simply set the price that would land $X$ and $O$ at $T$, and then we had them trade at that price. If you wonder why, in our society, we have elaborate taxation and no authoritative price setting—even though in many cases these would have identical effects—then you ought to think back to the chapter on property. There we recognized that any system of property assigns a burden of proof. The burden of proof in a system of private property is on those who want to modify and restrict the individual's right to do as he pleases with what he owns. As a matter of historical development, arguments in favor of taxation have been accepted by the society as a whole, while arguments in favor of authoritative price setting usually have failed except in time of war. This has been true even though in many cases the two devices would modify the rights of property to the same effect.[7]

**ARROW'S PROOF AND THE PRISONERS' DILEMMA** The two-person saga of $X$ and $O$ has given us a limited look at bargaining and market situations. It's allowed us to see some of the major claims of market theory and to see how those claims might be attacked and defended. We can now look at two theoretical arguments which raise serious questions about the market's claim to guarantee efficiency. The advantage of these arguments is this: If a real world market system isn't working out to everyone's advantage, then it's open to the market theorist to attribute the lack of success to the irrationality of the participants or to some other accidental feature of the world that interferes with the smooth working of the market. The theorist can still say that *if* everyone were rational, and *if* conditions were made right; *then* the market would

---

[7]An interesting, if one-sided, discussion of "special tax—general benefit" schemes is found in James M. Buchanan and Gordon Tullock, *The Calculus of Consent* (Ann Arbor: University of Michigan Press, 1962). See also I. M. D. Little, op. cit.

work out right. The two following arguments both show us that *even if* all the conditions for the market are right, there's still a problem with the efficiency claim. Both the arguments are based on puzzles that have been known for centuries. Theorists in our own time have generalized these puzzles and pointed out their important consequences.

**PRISONERS' DILEMMA**  The first puzzle is called "The Prisoners' Dilemma" because of a shaggy-dog story in terms of which it's usually described. At any rate, we're asked to imagine two rational economic men playing a very simple game. We then use what we've learned about game theory to analyze the game. First we have to write down the pay-off matrix and see what it means.

$$
\begin{array}{c c}
 & B \\
 & \begin{array}{c c}
\text{talk} & \text{not talk}
\end{array}
\end{array}
$$

|           |          | B talk    | B not talk |
|-----------|----------|-----------|------------|
|           | talk     | 1/4, 1/4  | 1, 0       |
| A         |          |           |            |
|           | not talk | 0, 1      | 3/4, 3/4   |

**Figure 16**

On the outside of the matrix we label the two strategies that the two players (*A* and *B*) have available to them. Each can either talk or not talk. Inside the matrix we put the pay off each receives on the basis of what *A* does and what *B* does. We'll write down the pay offs to *A* as the first number in each box; then, after the comma, *B*'s pay off. So, for example, if *A* talks and *B* does not talk, the pay off to *A* is 1, and the pay off to *B* is 0. (Remember, we can express all the pay offs to the players as numbers between 0 and 1 because we're measuring utilities on an interval scale.) Of course, if *B* talks and *A* does not talk, the pay off to *B* is 1 and the pay off to *A* is 0. If they both talk, they both get ¼; if they both do not talk, they both get ¾.

Now, as disinterested spectators, we can see that they both ought not to talk. That's the way they'd both do best. But let's see what would happen if we made them make their own choice without knowing the choice of the other. That is, they choose independently and in isolation from each other. Of course we continue to insist that they both be rational economic men.

*A* looks at the matrix and says "What happens to me if *B* talks? Well, if I talk I'll get ¼, but if I do not talk I'll get 0. So in that case it's obviously better to talk. But suppose *B* does not talk. What then? Well, if I talk I'll get 1, but if I don't talk I'll get ¾, so in this case too it's obviously better to talk." The pay off for talking is better than the pay off for not talking in either eventuality, so *A,* being a rational economic man, talks.

The situation confronting *B* is exactly the same as the one confronting *A*. *B* goes through the same reasoning that *A* does; so *B* talks too. They each receive a pay off of ¼.

We're puzzled. There's a better result available to them both without either of them having to sacrifice anything, but they've missed it. Yet they've both acted as rational economic men. Is there anything they can do about this? Suppose *A* thinks about not talking. He says to himself "If we both don't talk we can each get ¾ instead of the ¼ we get if we both talk. Furthermore *B* is thinking along the same lines, so maybe he'll not talk. But if he doesn't talk I can take advantage of him by talking. So I'll talk. In fact, I'd better talk, because if I don't talk, *B* can take advantage of *me.*" *B* is no sucker. *B* thinks things out in the same way and talks too. Back they are at (¼, ¼).

It turns out that they can only get to (¾, ¾) if they each can guarantee that the other doesn't talk. This guarantee could be based on some sort of enforceable contract. But the presence of such a contract would mean that they weren't acting independently and in isolation any more. Alternatively, the guarantee could be based on firm mutual trust. But trust is no part of the rational economic man. As Adam Smith says: "It is not from the benevolence of the butcher, the brewer, or the baker that we expect our dinner, but from their regard to their own interest."

So the best result is not available to rational economic men acting independently. Now, what does this do to the claim of the market to be able to guarantee the most efficient result? Quite simply, it says that if "Prisoners' Dilemma" situations occur in the real world, then the market can't guarantee that it will reach the best result. Contract or trust might yield a better result than the market. So if the market theorist is going to make good his guarantee for the market, he's going to have to convince us that no "Prisoners' Dilemma" situations will arise.[8]

Will they arise? It's hard to tell for sure, but look at the following possibilities: First, a producer gets together with a consumer who has a continuing need for a product. They could deal day after day at the market price that happened to exist on the given day, or they could sign a contract for some amount of the product to be delivered over a long

[8]The Prisoners' Dilemma is the subject of an enormous amount of discussion. Any of the texts in game theory already cited will provide a starting point. Anatol Rapoport and Albert M. Chammah, *The Prisoner's Dilemma* (Ann Arbor: University of Michigan Press, 1965) offers interesting insights into the empirical significance of the Prisoners' Dilemma. Recent work on "meta-games" based on the Prisoners' Dilemma, that is, games played in which the players know that they face the Prisoners' Dilemma, do not help with the basic problem.

period of time at a single agreed price. If the market price went down over that long period, the producer would make out well; if the market price went up, the consumer would come out ahead. But in either eventuality the producer would be sure of selling a certain amount of his product, and the consumer would be sure of a constant supply. The needs of both are secured by the contract. Now, does this situation come up in the real world? *Most large-scale producers and consumers believe that it does.* Hence the prevalence of such contracts. They give up the freedom of acting independently in the market in exchange for the security the contract gives them. People who enter into such contracts are betting that a Prisoner's Dilemma situation is likely.

Now another case: A person wants a certain commodity and is trying to decide whether to buy it now or later. She judges that the price will be higher later than it is now, so she buys it now. Everyone else who wants the commodity reasons the same way. The price of the commodity goes up—and so does the price of everything else—in an inflationary spiral. We can easily imagine that all the buyers would have been better off if they had not contributed to inflation by buying when they did. So inflationary psychology may produce a Prisoners' Dilemma situation. This looks even more likely if you go through the reasoning of the individual buyer. She thinks: "Maybe buying now will help drive prices up. But all that means is that I'd better buy now. Maybe I can get in first; then others will have to bear the cost of the price rise. What's more, I can only win this way, because if the others don't buy now it will dampen the inflationary spiral, and I'll benefit from that too."[9]

While it looks as if inflation might be a good candidate for Prisoners' Dilemma reasoning, we have to be careful. The sketch just given is a gross abstraction. The same is true of the following related tale.

| | Consumer: buy | Consumer: not buy |
|---|---|---|
| Worker: strike | 1/4, 1/4 | 1, 0 |
| Worker: not strike | 0, 1 | 3/4, 3/4 |

**Figure 17**

[9]An analysis of inflation which fits well with the game-theory sketch provided is contained in Abba Lerner, *Flation* (Baltimore: Penguin Books, 1973).

The two players are now a worker who has to decide between striking for a higher wage or settling for his current wage and a consumer who has to decide whether to buy the commodity the worker makes. To make sense of the pay-off matrix, we concoct the following—always remembering the limited significance of the numbers.

If the worker strikes, and the consumer fails to buy, then the worker will receive a higher wage and be in good shape—hence the "1" for him in that box. The consumer will not have what he wants, and furthermore prices will go up to pay for the wage increase (cost-push inflation). Hence the "0" for the consumer in that box. If the consumer buys and the worker settles, then the consumer will get what he wants before the price goes up: hence the "1" for him in the "buy-settle" box. But prices *will* go up (demand-pull inflation), and the worker will be faced with higher prices at his old salary: hence the "0" for him in that box.

The "not-buy-settle" box is pretty good for both of them, (¾, ¾), because there will be neither cost-push nor demand-pull inflation. Careful wage bargains and buying strategies could keep life fairly good for them. The "buy-strike" box is less good for them. The consumer gets what he wants, and the worker gets a higher wage, but both inflationary pressures are present, making them worse off in the long run than they would be at "not-buy-settle': hence the (¼, ¼) here. The analysis of the strategies is obviously the same as it was for Figure 16—it depends only on the ordinal relation of the pay offs—so a rational economic worker and a rational economic consumer, acting independently, will end up in the "buy-strike" box.

Notice that if I've overestimated the bad effects of inflation and underestimated the good effects of immediate purchase and higher wage, then the (¾, ¾) and the (¼, ¼) should be reversed. In that case the worker and the consumer would still end up in the "buy-strike" box—this time less paradoxically. The total picture is that rational strategies by the worker and consumer will always produce both sorts of inflationary pressures, resulting in the familiar wage-price spiral. As a little exercise of your own, reflect that $W$ and $C$ might be the same person. Think of what the consequences of that might be.

Well, don't forget the degree of abstraction involved in setting up these little examples, a degree of simplification which often makes such examples more ingenious than helpful. Nonetheless, the examples are plausible enough to suggest that the market theorist has his work cut out for him if we're going to be convinced that Prisoners' Dilemma situations never arise.

In summary, the Prisoners' Dilemma shows us that two rational economic men, acting independently, need not end up with a best result. This means that if we are to be convinced by the market theorist that the market guarantees the best result, we need to be convinced that Prisoners' Dilemma type situations will never occur within the operation of the market.

**ARROW'S PROOF** There's a limit to how far we can go with two-person situations like the ones we've been using. The next theoretical argument will move us to many-person situations. In addition, the discussion of the Prisoners' Dilemma proceeded on the basis of interval rankings of utilities (though it needn't have). In the next argument we're firmly back with ordinal rankings. We'll be working with what is called "Arrow's Paradox"—after the economist Kenneth Arrow who worked it out in the 1950s.[10] An earlier version, limited to systems of voting, was worked out by the French mathematician and philosopher Condorcet in the eighteenth century.

The basic idea in Arrow's argument is that market and other related systems produce a joint result for many people. One way to understand this is to think of the system as starting with many *individual* preference rankings and constructing out of them one *social* preference ranking. Since we know how to translate back and forth between indifference maps and ordinal preference rankings, we could also think of the system as starting with many individual indifference maps and constructing out of them one social indifference map. Since Arrow conducted his proof in terms of preference rankings, and since it is easiest to follow in that form, we'll only refer to the version in terms of indifference maps as an occasional illustration.

You can easily see how the market can construct a social preference out of individual preferences. Consider the points *P, S,* and *T* from Figures

[10]The classic statement of Arrow's proof is in Kenneth Arrow, *Social Choice and Individual Values* (New York: Wiley, 1951). In subsequent editions of the book, and in other publications, Arrow provided several variants of the proof. The version used here comes from Kenneth Arrow, "Values and Collective Decision-making," in Peter Laslett and W. G. Runciman, eds. *Philosophy, Politics, and Society,* Third Series (Oxford: Basil Blackwell, 1967), p. 215 ff. Anyone really interested in this topic ought to follow the discussion of Arrow's proof through the pages of *The Review of Economic Studies, Econometrica, The Journal of Political Economy,* and *Economica* for the last twenty years. Among the most interesting work is that of A. K. Sen, *Collective Choice and Social Welfare* (San Francisco: Holden-Day, 1970); also worth reading by Sen are: "The Impossibility of a Paretian Liberal," *Journal of Political Economy,* Vol. 78 (1970); "Behavior and the Concept of Preference," *Economica,* Vol. 40 (1973); "Liberty, Unanimity, and Rights," ibid., Vol. 43 (1973); and "Rational Fools: A Critique of the Behavioral Foundations of Economic Theory" in Henry Harris, ed., *Scientific Models and Man* (Oxford: Oxford University Press, 1978). Sen and others have shown that Arrow's paradox can be avoided if we can make interpersonal comparisons of utility and, in general, can be assumed to be motivated by extended sympathy. So far as the "invisible hand" is concerned, this throws out the baby with the bath water. So much the worse for the invisible hand.

14 and 15. We know that for $O$, $S$ is better than $P$, and $T$ is better than $S$. The same is true for $X$, so each has the preference ranking $T/S/P$. It seems obvious that in this case the social ranking should also be $T/S/P$ since it represents their unanimous preferences. Social rankings can also be constructed when the individual rankings are not unanimous. For instance, in a system of majority rule, with three people choosing between two alternatives, you might have the following situation: Person $A$ prefers $T$ to $U$, person $B$ prefers $U$ to $T$, and person $C$ prefers $T$ to $U$. In that case the social preference ought to be $T$ over $U$, since a majority prefers $T$ over $U$.

Arrow found that he could generalize the problem of constructing social preferences out of individual ones by talking of "social choice functions." Anything is a social choice function if it starts out with individual preferences and specifies a social preference on the basis of them. So, as I've said, the market system can be expressed as a social choice function, and so can a system of majority rule (and in fact any voting system).

Now, among all the possible choice functions we could think of, there are some we wouldn't be happy with. For instance, we could imagine a rule of collective sado-masochism which told us that the society ought to prefer the alternative that all the individual members liked least. Arrow sorts out the social choice functions that we might find acceptable from the ones we wouldn't find acceptable by placing conditions on the way that the social preference can be derived from the individual preferences. The conditions will look familiar to us. They are all conditions which are important features of the market as it is thought of as an ideal.

The first condition merely states the rationality condition: "For any given set of orderings, the social choice function is derivable from an ordering." The important message in this condition is that we require both the individuals and the society to have rational preference rankings. All the individuals and the society must have preferences which are connected and transitive. The argument in favor of this condition is exactly the same here as it was when we discussed connexity and transitivity before. In effect, we're insisting that the individual preferences to be amalgamated into a social preference are the preferences of rational economic men. Furthermore, the society ought to be rational in the same way.

Next, we want a condition that reflects the common sense feeling that as some people begin to prefer something more than they did before, and everyone else feels the same about it as they always did, then this thing ought not to lose ground in the social ranking. It would be strange if something became more popular, yet sank in the social ranking or vice-versa. We need a condition which will rule out the sado-masochistic social choice functions—in addition to many others. The condition can be stated: "Pareto condition: If alternative $x$ is preferred to alternative $y$ by every single individual according to his ordering, then the social ordering also ranks $x$ above $y$." In terms of the saga of $X$ and $O$, this means that if they both have preferences $T/S/P$, then the social preference ranking *must be* $T/S/P$. Looked at in terms of an election, it means that if one candidate is unanimously preferred, then that candidate must win. We couldn't violate this condition without totally destroying our notions of consumer and voter sovereignty.

The next condition helps to tell us the way in which individuals may choose. "Independence of irrelevant alternatives: The social choice made from any environment depends only on the orderings of individuals with respect to the alternatives in that environment." What this means is that the individual preference rankings are simply ordinal, and so is the social ranking. This reflects the fact that in the face of all the difficulties there are in measuring utilities, we're better off with the notion of revealed preference. The effect of this condition is to make our choices depend only on the comparison of one "bundle" with another—the pattern of choice-making which allowed us to construct $O$'s indifference maps in the first place. This comparison of two bundles is to take place without reference to any third bundle which may or may not be available. An immediate consequence of this is that if one of the items in a preference ranking is pulled out of the ranking, the rest of the items cannot change position with respect to one another: That is, if we begin with the ranking in column a below, and if we remove B; then we must end up with ranking b, rather than any other like column c.

| a | b | c |
|---|---|---|
| A | A | A |
| B | C | F |
| C | D | D |
| D | E | E |
| E | F | C |
| F |   |   |

The theory of revealed preference meets this condition as do most normal voting systems. Orthodox market theory probably couldn't do without it for reasons that we'll see very soon.

The final condition is pretty obvious. It rules out social choice functions which make one individual's preferences decisive for the social choice. "Non-dictatorship: There is no individual whose preferences are automatically society's preferences independent of the preferences of all other individuals."

Now, I won't reproduce all the mechanics of Arrow's proof. It's readily available for those who want to examine it more closely. What Arrow proved (in the mathematical sense of "proof") was that no social choice function fulfilling these conditions could guarantee satisfactory results when there are more than two individuals in the society and more than two alternatives to choose from. We can see what this means if we look at a simple version of Condorcet's version of the "paradox."

Imagine three people (a, b, and c) trying to choose between three alternatives (A, B, and C). They've decided to use "Majority Rule" as the method for making the social choice. Majority rule is a social choice function which fits all of Arrow's conditions. We imagine that each of the three people forms an individual preference ranking which turns out to be as follows:

| a | b | c |
|---|---|---|
| A | B | C |
| B | C | A |
| C | A | B |

Now, what's the social choice? A majority prefers A to B; a majority prefers B to C; but, alas, a majority also prefers C to A. So no matter what ranking one tries to write down as the social preference ranking, it will be intransitive. A is preferred to C, *and* C is preferred to A—by a majority.

Of course, as striking as Condorcet's example is, Arrow has gone even farther. He showed that *any* social choice function (not just majority rule) which fulfills his conditions is subject to the possibility of paradoxical results. For our purposes it's important to note that a market based on ordinal preferences can be represented by such a social choice function. So the market's claim to be able to guarantee the most efficient result has to be rejected. In a market defined by ordinal preferences, Adam Smith's "invisible hand" can't be depended on not to slip.

Before the committed socialists get all excited about this, we'd better point out that if a socialist government tries to make decisions for a society as a whole, and if these decisions are to be based on the ordinal preferences of the citizens, and if a social choice function is adopted which fits Arrow's conditions; then they're in trouble too. They can't guarantee that they'll arrive at a satisfactory result.

**THE CONDITIONS ON SOCIAL CHOICE** Everyone who looks at Arrow's proof immediately thinks that there must be something wrong with the conditions placed on social choice functions. The temptation is to look back at the conditions, one by one, to see if they can be rejected or modified. We can do that ourselves.

First, how about the conditions of connexity and transitivity—both for individual and for social rankings? Well, we've already been through this. At the individual level these conditions are part of the rock-bottom definition of the rational economic man. So the market theorist has to hold on to them. And if we don't insist that the social ranking be rational in the same way, then we give up all claim to be able to guarantee a rational social decision.

Second, the condition of collective rationality is precisely the condition that the market theorist wants and needs. The social ordering (for example price) is to be a function of individual preferences and nothing more. That's the whole point of market theory.

Similarly, the market theorist cannot give up the Pareto condition or the condition of non-dictatorship without casting away the principle of consumer sovereignty.

That leaves us with the "independence of irrelevant alternatives" to examine. In fact, most of the people who have grappled with Arrow's proof have settled on this condition as the one to work on.

The condition is fulfilled by theories of revealed preference but not fulfilled by the other theories of utility, so the first way in which you might attack the condition is to argue for some ratio or quantitative theory of utility. I assume that by now you understand the nature of *that* task. We needn't go over it again. I think, though, that there are troubles with the "independence of irrelevant alternatives" which are worth looking at. These troubles are related to some questions we had about the theory of revealed preference, but we haven't examined them thoroughly before. The best way to start is with an example:

I'm going backpacking and want to select the things to take along: food, tools, sleeping bag, and so forth. I make a long list of possible things to take, knowing full well that I can't take everything on the list. My "budget constraints," so to speak, are given by the amount I can load on the pack board and by the weight that I can lug for the number of miles I intend to walk. At some point on the long list I'll have to draw the line.

Now, first we notice that I have to hope that the line is drawn so that it doesn't exclude anything necessary. I'd better list all the necessary things first, then the optional ones, and hope that I can carry all the necessities. Now suppose high on the list of necessities is an "Italian Army Knife," with all its component parts: knife, scissors, punch, picture of my mother, corkscrew, screwdriver, and more. Far down the list of optional items are: knife, scissors, corkscrew, and screwdriver. Imagine that the line is drawn *above* these items. Further suppose that when I finally come to pack for the trip I find that an Italian Army Knife is unavailable. If I insist on the independence of irrelevant alternatives, I'll be in real trouble. The line will move down one item (to include, say, a hairbrush), and I'll be left without a number of things necessary for the trip. Obviously, when I find out that I can't get an Italian Army Knife, I ought to move some items from the list of optionals to the list of necessities: that is, I'll reorder the items when one proves to be unavailable—explicitly violating the condition of the independence of irrelevant alternatives.

Now we need to know two things: Why in the world anyone would want to hold onto the independence of irrelevant alternatives in the face of examples like the one given? Can we, after all, find some way of saving the condition from such examples? The answers to these questions will show us a whole lot about the foundational assumptions of market theory.

Maybe if we didn't distinguish necessities from optional items the problem wouldn't arise. If everything were optional, then, when some item became unavailable, I would simply move the line down one item without changing the order. The trouble is that in the backpacking example it's just absurd not to distinguish necessities from optionals, and I've a suspicion that lots of real-world situations are of that sort. We need food in a way we don't need a TV set.

The real trouble in the example seems to be that in a fundamental way the items on the list are not themselves independent of one another. There are duplicates and substitutes. Everything appears on the list *as* something or other. It's no surprise that when I need a knife—and there are two on the list, when one becomes unavailable, I take the other *in its place.* Thus, if we want to retain the independence of irrelevant alternatives, we have to worry about the way we identify things on the list. In the backpacking example the reasonable thing to do seems to be to identify the items as something to cut with, something to sleep in, something to cook in, something to eat, and so forth—thus lumping all the duplicates and substitutes together. This could still leave us with a distinction between necessities and optionals, since low on the list we could put: something to watch birds through, something to make music around the campfire with, something to read in the tent when it rains, and so on. If I can't fit them in, there's no disaster if I leave them out—given my priorities.

An immediate consequence of this way of identifying things on the list is that secondary lists will now begin to appear within the categories selected. For example, within "things to cut with," I'm sure to have preferences between the possible alternatives. Furthermore, given weight and bulk constraints, the availability of items in one category could very well affect the ranking of items in other categories. The corkscrew in the Italian Army Knife may be worse than some others, but if

I select the Italian Army Knife as a "thing to cut with," I probably won't bother with another "thing to open the wine with."

As the Italian Army Knife shows us, lots of items won't stay put in one category. This causes trouble when we try to apply these categories in a market situation. When someone traded for something in a market, we wouldn't know what she was trading for. If we tried to see if there was a substitute for what was chosen, we wouldn't know how to do it. Life would be very simple if everything that could be bought and sold fit exactly into one of the categories we would need to preserve the independence of irrelevant alternatives. But as long as people have imaginations and a wide range of purposes, life isn't going to be that simple.

One of the main results of all this is that there is no reason to believe that, in general, market behavior consists in the simple pairwise choice between two bundles. Granted, there are bound to be *some* cases where this sort of comparison is all that's involved. A choice between breakfast cereals might be a pure preference of this sort. But generally a choice between two things is much more complicated. As we saw when we discussed $O$'s need for aspirin, there are many possible reasons for choosing one thing over another. Most of these reasons will lead into a consideration of what's available, what's likely to be available in the future, present and future purposes and needs, present and future budgetary constraints. In short, market choices will seldom be pure preferences. So, all the questions we had about the theory of revealed preference can be raised again here. The effect is to make us doubt that the "independence of irrelevant alternatives" is a condition that holds very often in the real world. However, it remains true that the condition must hold if we are to define commodities in such a way that we can construct indifference curves. They are constructed on the basis of pairwise comparisons.[11]

In summary: if the market's theoretical claim to efficiency is to be successful, then the market must be representable as a social choice function fulfilling all Arrow's conditions. But, paradoxically, Arrow proved that a social choice function of this kind can't guarantee efficiency. Furthermore, if the market must fulfill the condition of the independence of irrelevant alternatives, then a market hardly ever exists.

---

[11]The condition of the independence of irrelevant alternatives insures that individual ranking will be ordinal, not interval, rankings, since the gambles required to calibrate the interval rankings involve alternatives not present in the domain of alternatives. In addition, of course, it rules out interpersonal comparisons. (See footnote 10.)

## CHAPTER SEVEN

# Freedom
# and the Market

---

We can now turn to the claim that the market is the only economic system which can preserve our individual freedom. This claim isn't as easy to evaluate as some people would like to think it is. There's a serious problem in deciding just what sort of freedom we're talking about. Different people have different conceptions of freedom. What I'll do is lay out three representative ways of conceiving freedom, and we'll see how they fare when combined with a market economy. It may turn out that your own considered thoughts on freedom aren't explicitly discussed. In that case you have a do-it-yourself project on your hands: You have to match up your own conception of freedom with what you know about market economies. I hope that the material in this chapter will at least serve as a guide in your deliberations.[1]

---

[1]The three conceptions of freedom presented here are relatively standard, though not always discussed in these terms. A good general discussion of freedom can be found in Bowie and Simon, op. cit., along with further bibliography. The classic defense of the market on grounds of freedom is found in Milton Friedman, *Capitalism and Freedom,* (Chicago: University of Chicago Press, 1962) or F. A. Von Hayek, *The Constitution of Liberty* (Chicago: University of Chicago Press, 1960).

**FREEDOM AS
ANARCHY**
The first conception of freedom is "freedom as anarchy." Please don't be put off by the word "anarchy." Anarchists needn't be bomb–throwing maniacs. In fact, you'll see that you have anarchist sympathies yourself. Nearly all Americans do. It's part of our tradition.

"Anarchy," of course, refers to a situation where there is no mechanism for making authoritative central decisions. It normally ranks on a continuum with "monarchy," "oligarchy," and "polyarchy"; but while each of those terms points to the way in which central decisions are reached, "anarchy" points *away* from the making of central decisions. It's important to notice that the lack of central decisions doesn't necessarily mean the lack of order or rationality. An example often used to show this is the following: Two crowds of people face each other on opposite corners of a city street. Each crowd begins to move across the street. First there's a chaotic-looking mixture in the middle of the street; then people begin to arrive at the corner to which they were headed. Soon the street is clear, and all of them have arrived where they wanted to go. No central decisions were made. Every individual made little decisions about moving to the right or left, speeding up or slowing down. The fact that people almost always get where they are going under such circumstances proves that there is order and rationality to the process. So, if you think that anarchy necessarily involves disorder, you're probably confusing it with nihilism—which *is* the rejection of rationality and order.[2]

Anarchy is freedom precisely in the sense that if anarchy prevails, then people are free from the control of central decisions. The people walking across the street are free to walk as they please, guided only by their determination to get to the other side—and, if we're lucky, by their unwillingness to push, shove, and bowl over others. No one has set up rules or laws about how they have to walk. Individual judgment prevails.

Insofar as we want our own judgment to prevail—not subject to the control of other persons or institutions—we'll have anarchist sympathies. That doesn't mean that we want chaos to prevail. It just means that we think that good rational results can be obtained without having to resort to a centralized control system. I say that this is part of the American tradition because there has always been a strong undercurrent of distrust for centralized government here. It's as evident today as it ever was. The frontier spirit of independence is another manifestation of the tradition of anarchism. Our hero in this regard is Daniel Boone. Yet another source

[2]The example of the street-crossing to illustrate the decentralized decisions of the market comes from Charles E. Lindblom, *The Intelligence of Democracy* (New York: The Free Press, 1965).

of our attraction to anarchism is the Protestant tradition. In opposition to the authority of the priesthood in the Roman church, Protestantism tends toward the anarchic authority of individual consciences. In fact, you can rank the Protestant sects with respect to their degree of anarchy—with, I suppose, the Society of Friends very near the anarchic extreme.

It should come as no surprise that the market is the economic system which fits best with a conception of freedom as anarchy. In fact, the anarchy of the market is often put forward as its most attractive feature. In analogy to the freedom of the Protestant conscience, the market offers the freedom of the sovereign consumer. In place of centralized economic planning, it offers the anarchic rationality of the market. No one tells anyone else what to produce or what to consume. Production and consumption decisions are left to the free judgment of the market participants; prices are left to be the results of their free trading.

You might wonder how sympathy for the anarchic freedom of the market fits with the possible suspicion that the efficiency claim for the market may not be defensible. The relationship is pretty clear: If we're attracted to freedom as anarchy, and if we think that the market will turn out to be efficient, then there's no problem. On the other hand, if we think that the market can't be depended on to be efficient, then we're probably going to have to try to balance the defects in efficiency against the advantages of freedom as anarchy. If the market turns out badly for some people (for example, as an extinction game for them) then they're sure to want to try to rearrange things, perhaps under a centralized system of planning. A defender of the market would have to try to convince them that the benefits of freedom given up in the move to central control were more precious than any other benefits which could be gained. The attempt might succeed if the market defender could appeal to the Daniel Boone instincts of his opponents: independence, self-reliance, and a fierce pride in both. He could try to point out that the security of central control is not worth the price paid in loss of independence.

The opponent might reply that in Daniel Boone's time there was plenty of free land (if you could get rid of the Indians) and, in general, a lot fewer people competing for economic space. He might even concede that, at some times and in some places, this freedom from central economic control has surely been the best available alternative—although the Indians might not agree, but that times have changed. The competition for resources has tightened up under a system of private property; some people can accumulate enough resources to make life hard for others. Then the bitter side of freedom as anarchism appears. People who would like nothing better than independent, self-reliant success find it impossible to obtain. The economic opportunity space is all filled up by others who got there first.

It's interesting, with regard to the foregoing give-and-take, that one of the earliest modern defenders of private property and the market, John Locke, felt that the accumulation of property beyond the limits of your needs was justified only because the good God in heaven had provided enough to go around. Any rational man, thought Locke, was sure to fare well. This optimism of a bygone generation isn't as common today as it was then.

Before we leave freedom as anarchy, we have to look at some possible limits to that freedom. Let's start back at the street crossing. People managed to get across the street—despite all the foot traffic—without having to submit to central control. There's no reason in the world why they'd need central control to get across the street, *as long as* we can be sure that they'd have sense enough to get where they want to go, and *as long as* they're willing to respect the people who are crossing the street at the same time. Once barging into people and knocking them over became common, either some control would have to be exercised or crossing the street would no longer be a civilized activity.

Everyone recognizes, in some way, that civilized street crossing depends on an underlying acceptance of civility by the crossers. As long as this civility is maintained, no central control needs to be exercised. It's also important that we're talking about pedestrians. As soon as we begin to think of cars crossing through intersections, we begin to think about how vehicular traffic has to be regulated—centrally, by traffic lights, traffic signs, and traffic laws. These considerations seem to show that we're willing to accept the anarchist solution only insofar as behavior stays within certain bounds. The question for the market theorists is whether or not we can be sure that economic activity will stay within the bounds of the civilized. This is a touchier problem than it otherwise might be, because market theory insists on rational self-interest as the sole legitimate motivating factor. Will the rational economic man resort to fraud or pocket-picking, for example? This seems to depend on his calculation of the expected gains and losses and on the odds on getting caught. Adam Smith tells us not to depend on the benevolence of the butcher. Can we depend on him to keep his thumb off the scales?

Every known society has found it necessary to make laws regulating economic behavior: laws which hold freedom within bounds. We've discussed this a bit in the chapter on property. The apparent necessity for laws means two things: First, our anarchic freedom is bound to be limited; and second, once regulation of behavior is conceded to be necessary, then public dispute about *which* activities ought to be placed under central control is bound to arise. Why, for example, should the activities of bargaining and trading be precisely the ones left free? The answer to this question is usually given in terms of the efficiency claim—and that may not inspire our full confidence at this stage.

**FREEDOM AS**
**ELBOW-ROOM**

Freedom as anarchy is based on a conception of human beings as independent, self-reliant, and self-contained. The next theory of freedom is based on a very similar conception. We'll call the theory "freedom as elbow-room." The theory begins with the realization that my doing what I want to do may be inconsistent with your doing what you want to do. For instance, I want to sleep late Sunday morning; and you, in the apartment upstairs, want to practice on your bagpipes. One of us is bound to lose out. Or, again, I want to keep pigs in my back lot, and you want to have a patio and swimming pool in your yard next door, where you can entertain your friends in serene suburban elegance. Not only will my pigs reduce the elegance of your parties, but the noise of your parties is going to annoy me.

Many activities—in fact most activities—have what economists call "spill-over effects." That is, they have consequences for other people that those people don't bargain for. Of course, not all spill-over effects need be bad ones. If I'm a bagpipe freak, then the sounds seeping down from upstairs on Sunday morning might be serendipitous. They're pleasant, and I don't have to pay for them. The classic instances of spill-over effects are industrial wastes: smoke in the air, noxious chemicals in streams. Lately we've become very aware of these effects. A parallel example of a *good* spill-over might be found in the case of a nursery operation next door to where you live. The trees, shrubs, and flowers might be very pleasant, and you get to enjoy them for nothing.

There are two basic characteristics of spill-over effects. The first we've seen. They're something you don't bargain for; they're present whether you want them or not. The second is that they alter the desirability of things you want to do. If they're negative spill-overs, they make what you want to do less pleasant and/or more costly. If they're positive spill-overs, they make what you want to do more pleasant and/or less costly. It's easy to see how this works. Think of your pool and patio next to my pig farm. If you do nothing about my pigs, your poolside parties are very unpleasant. On the other hand, doing something about them (and in this case I'm not sure what you could do) might cost so much that you'd decide to forget about the pool and patio.

The constant presence of spill-overs leads directly to the conception of freedom as elbow-room. My pigs crowd out your enjoyment of your back yard. In some trivial sense you're still free to have a pool and patio, but you're clearly not free to enjoy them. I've made that impossible for you. Similarly, my freedom to take long walks in the woods and fields disappears when the woods and fields are filled with housing developments and shopping centers. My chosen activity is crowded out. Notice that people don't have to be evil or obnoxious to limit or destroy my freedom. The people who move into the housing development are simply trying to pursue a decent life as rational economic men, as fathers and mothers of families, and so forth. They aren't trying to crowd me out; they're just honestly trying to find a nice place to live. Nonetheless we spill over on each other. When people spilled over on Daniel Boone, he just picked up and moved to the frontier. This imposed a cost of moving and resettlement on him, but he judged that it was better to pay the cost rather than to give up his freedom to roam.

There are three ways to deal with spill-overs—if you count just gritting your teeth and trying to ignore them. The way a market theorist might handle them is by making them the subject of bargaining and trading. For instance, my neighbor who wants the pool might offer the use of it to me if I give up the idea of keeping pigs. He might be willing to let me hold some parties at his place if I'm willing to offer him the possibility of holding enjoyable parties of his own. Cases of industrial pollution are similar. If there's a lot of acrid smoke in the air, I'm not free to breathe enjoyably. If the generation of electric power has air pollution as a spill-over byproduct, then we all might bargain with the electric company. We could offer to pay more for electricity if they'd install pollution control devices and burn cleaner fuel. If the bargain is struck, then in paying out electric bills we'd be paying part of the money for electricity and part of the money for breathable air. As you know, in the industrialized parts of the world clean air is beginning to cost a lot.

If we're interested in how this market solution to the problem of spill-overs fits with freedom as elbow-room, then I suppose we have to go back to an examination of the efficiency and justice of the market result. We'd run into a lot of old familiar problems. For instance, if we had a satisfactory way of measuring utilities, then we could measure freedom as elbow-room. It would turn out to be just another commodity, identified in terms of the greater or lesser pleasure there would be in our various activities. But, on the other hand, if we have no satisfactory way to measure utilities, it's going to be impossible to know whether or not the market will achieve the maximum amount of freedom. Furthermore, we might want to know whether or not freedom as elbow-room is distributed justly. Offhand it seems as though people who are rich will be able to have a much wider opportunity for enjoyment than poor people. In addition, they'll have the means to cause a lot of spill-overs that poor people won't be able to afford to get rid of. The offhand judgment shouldn't satisfy us, but it at least tells us that it's a serious question whether or not the market really is the best means of obtaining a satisfactory level and distribution of freedom as elbow-room.

In our society, the most common way to deal with spill-overs is by submitting them to central control. We pass laws about them. The most common of these laws are land-use laws of which we have an enormous number. For instance, it really isn't up to me whether or not I keep pigs in my back yard. The zoning laws say I can't. I also can't turn my house into a store or a factory, build another house on my lot, store junk cars on my property, and a whole lot of other things, some of which I'm probably not even aware of. The potential spill-overs of these forbidden activities are controlled by prior public decision. They're not left to private bargaining. My freedom is restricted by these laws, as is the freedom of everyone else. In compensation, freedom is guaranteed in other ways. We're all sure of a little open space around us and we won't be bothered by factory noise or pollution, so our freedom to enjoy many activities is enhanced. Our society has judged that overall freedom as elbow-room is higher when certain restrictions are imposed in order to eliminate bad spill-overs.

Well, this last solution to the problem of spill-overs is certainly not a market solution. How is it to be justified? The key premise is that no single person should have to bear the entire cost of eliminating spill-overs. Furthermore, many spill-overs would be so costly to eliminate that no single person *could* bear the cost of eliminating them. As an extreme case, think of my pig farm again. Suppose I live in a large neighborhood in which everyone but me wants a pool and patio. I want to keep pigs. My pigs have effects that spill over on all these neighbors. If I'm stubborn and mean enough (and why not?), I can demand enormous sums from them as compensation for not keeping pigs. The situation begins to look a lot like blackmail, but if my neighbors try to accuse me of *that,* I simply point out to them that we're engaged in the operation of a free market and that the invisible hand must be allowed to lead us to the best result. (I have a feeling that the invisible hand would sneak over some night and slaughter my pigs.)

It's clear that as long as I can threaten to keep pigs I have an enormous bargaining advantage, one that my neighbors can overcome only at great cost. Our society—and most others—has decided that this sort of bargaining advantage is intolerable; hence the land use laws.

Lately, similar thinking has led us to pass "environmental protection" laws, including laws requiring industries to practice pollution control. Our freedom to breathe clean air and drink pure water has seemed important enough to us to warrant the restriction of the freedom of industries to pollute as they please; but a funny thing happens in these cases. When a company installs pollution control devices, it begins to charge more for its product, "passing along" the increased cost to the consumers. Again this raises the question of the just distribution of the costs for the removal of spill-overs. Consumers far out of the range of the spill-overs pay for their removal. The companies producing the spill-overs do not. Is this really the way we want to distribute the costs? We as a society are still ambivalent about this situation, but at least we're beginning to see the problem in the right light.[3]

**FREEDOM AS** The third conception of freedom goes beyond the
**SELF-FULFILLMENT** ideas of elbow-room and spill-overs to a more positive idea: the fulfillment of human potential. This is a very old idea; it can be found in the works of the ancient Greeks. It entered the Anglo-American political tradition as an important ideal in the nineteenth century. The basic idea is that persons are free when they have the opportunity and means to develop the potentials they are born with. We have to look at two aspects of this conception of freedom: the nature of the potentialities and then the providing of means and opportunities.

Everyone is born with innumerable potentialities: that is, with innumerable possible choices of things to be, to have, and to do. Among these possibilities there's some good news and some bad news. For instance, someone might have at the same time the potential to be a great concert pianist and the potential to be a contract killer for the local crime syndicate. To use old-fashioned language, we all seem to have the capacity to do evil as well as good. The proof of this is that we're good sometimes and bad sometimes, and there's no denying it. But no one who thinks of freedom as the fulfillment of potential nowadays would push for the development of the capacity to murder. This means that there must be a link between freedom as the fulfillment of potential and some theory of value—some theory of what's worth being, worth having, and worth doing.

Equally clearly, the theory of value connected to this conception of freedom must be public and shared. The reason for this is that if we don't get together about the potentialities we want to support, then we're not

[3]I once worked out a conception of freedom in terms of externalities: "Freedom, Consent, and the Costs of Interaction" in Eugene Rostow, ed., *Is Law Dead?* (New York: Simon and Schuster, 1971). The claim there is that if the measurement problem can be solved in general, the result can be used to measure freedom. Not what you might call a promising program. An important discussion of externalities is William Baumol, *Welfare Economics and the Theory of the State* (Cambridge: Harvard University Press 1952). The discussion of "freedom as elbow room" recalls John Stuart Mill's distinction between "self-regarding" acts. By the time we have reached chapter 3 of *On Liberty*, however, we have moved to a conception of freedom more closely related to "freedom as the fulfillment of potential." This has been pointed out by many commentators.

likely to be able to fulfill our own potentialities by ourselves. If someone has a potentiality that I don't respect—like the capacity to murder me— then I'm going to make it as hard as possible for him to realize his potential. The potentialities to be supported have to be ones that fit into a world where *everyone* can fulfill potentialities. Because of this, when we live according to the idea of freedom as the fulfillment of potential we're linked very closely to each other. We can contrast this with the situation in which we're only concerned with freedom as elbow-room. There, we needn't care at all about the other people around us, except insofar as they're crowding us, and we're crowding them. If we can make some sort of deal to hold the mutual crowding to a minimum, then we needn't concern ourselves any further.

When we ask for our freedom to fulfill our potential, we're really saying to other people: "Listen, I want to *be* thus and so, and *do* thus and so; to do this I'm going to *need* thus and so. I'm asking you to recognize, appreciate, and respect the things I am and the things I do. I'm going to need your support if I'm going to make it. Of course, I'm ready to help you in any way I can in your own development and fulfillment."

Because of the close ties of mutual appreciation and support required, people normally think of the context of the closely knit family when they think of the mutual fulfillment of potential. This makes a lot of sense— if you have the right sort of family in mind. Unfortunately, the model of the family that's been dominant in our society up until very recently may not be totally suited to the purpose. The man of the family gets to fulfill his potential just as long as that's consistent with bringing home the bacon. (That is, his chance to fulfill his potential is secondary to his economic success.) The children, while they're still children, are helped to develop their potential. Their education—important support in their early years—is well taken care of. Money for college might even be an important item in the family budget. Then there's the woman. She makes out fine if the potentialities she wants to fulfill are those of wife and mother. And, of course, as these roles are traditionally defined, they amount to supporting roles for the fulfillment of husband and children. I guess within this model of the family the woman is supposed to feel fulfilled at second-hand: through her husband's success, through the growth and development of her children. Well, this may be all right for some women (and some men, for that matter), but more and more women are unhappy to have their potential development limited in this way. They can't see why they have to have the supporting role all the time. Consequently, we're beginning to see a new-model family in which an attempt is made to care for the potential development of everyone in the family. Everyone grows and develops; everyone supports. (Notice that in our society "support" almost always means "supply money." I'm obviously thinking of a much broader range of things that we can do for each other.) So, if we have the appropriate picture of the family, then we can use it as a model for how people have to be related in order to embark on the mutual development of their potential.

But watch out. If we start out with the family as a model, we immediately begin to wonder if any group much larger than a family can contain people so tightly bound to one another, so mutually respectful and appreciative of one another. Remember, the people in the group have to think of their mutual ties as a positive contribution to their own freedom, not as an annoying limitation. If this conception appeals to you, then you'd do well to look carefully at the requirements for its success. We must have a mutual respect and concern for one another. Our values and aspirations must be compatible so that the fulfillment of one person doesn't prevent the fulfillment of another. (From an economic point of view this means that the means to our freedom can't be scarce.) We must think of our freedom as a common project rather than as an individual prerogative. We must approach each other openly and candidly, offering our help and asking for the help of others.

Are we capable of this, even if it appeals to us as an ideal? No one knows for sure, although everyone seems to have an opinion. For the most part the opinions are based on guesses, and I think we ought to be able to do better than that if we're going to make an intelligent decision.

**FREEDOM AND THE MARKET** Now that the three conceptions of freedom are in front of us, I think it's fairly clear how they fit with market theory and other possible economic theories. Freedom as anarchy is a willing mate for market theory. Freedom as fulfillment of potential violates some of the specifications of the rational economic man; hence it's almost certainly incompatible with market theory. In working out the conditions for freedom as elbow-room, the success of decentralized market decision-making seems to become doubtful. The management of spill-overs may require some central—cooperative—decisions. A look back at the Prisoners' Dilemma may help you see why.

Now, historically, the theory of freedom as the development of potential came into prominence at a time when market theory was highly regarded. Many theorists argued for both at the same time. But as time went on, the compatibility between the two began to be doubted. More and more people, especially outside the United States, began to think that if the capacities and aspirations of all people were going to have the chance to be fulfilled, then the first step was to reorganize the economy for that purpose. This meant centralizing the planning of production, attempting to make the distribution of goods more equal, and promoting the concept of economic life as the collective cooperative concern of the society rather than the private concern of isolated individuals. In short, freedom as the development of potential began to be associated with socialism.[4]

Unfortunately, over the last one hundred years the socialist systems haven't seemed to be any more successful in providing for self-fulfillment than the market systems. Now, you have to understand that this judgment is a matter of contention. Furthermore, even if it's correct, we're still left with the problem of deciding why it's correct. Many reasons are put forward, and, of course, the ardent defenders of each of the systems have their favored explanations. This leaves us with a major task on our hands if we want to come to our own considered judgment. Without a serious study of the historical issues in addition to the theoretical ones, we aren't able to make an intelligent decision. This would require us to press on well beyond the confines of this book.

**MARX AND FREEDOM**    While you're thinking about which conception of freedom is most important to you (possibly one not even mentioned here), and what sort of economic system would be most compatible with your sort of freedom, you might want a look at another aspect of Marx's theory.[5]

First, Marx is one of the thinkers who conceives freedom as the development of potential. Human history shows a highly intelligent, remarkably able species working to realize its vast potential. Being no humanitarian dreamer, Marx believes that this development can only take place if new classes of people periodically assert their demands for freedom against other classes of people who stand in the way of that freedom. The new classes can only realize their freedom by overturning the world of the old oppressing classes. In our world, Marx identifies the capitalist entrepreneurs as the oppressing class, and the working class as the new class which must assert its demand for freedom. All this is familiar Marxian lore. But now comes an interesting point. Marx thinks that socialism —the collective ownership of all property and the centralization of economic decisions—is the last and worst stage of oppression. While the

[4]For the claim that liberalism contains two incompatible conceptions of freedom, see C. B. MacPherson, *Democratic Theory: Essays in Retrieval* (Oxford: Oxford University Press, 1973) and Unger, op. cit.

[5]Marx's conception of freedom is well discussed in Carol Gould, *Marx's Social Ontology* (Cambridge: MIT Press, 1978). The book makes important references to the *Grundrisse,* op. cit. Marx expresses his views on state socialism most clearly in the 1844 manuscripts, Easton and Guddat, op. cit. p. 299 ff, near the beginning of his career; and, near the end of his career, in *Critique of the Gotha Program* (New York: International Publishers, 1938).

workers' revolution must pass through this stage, it will not be completed until the socialist state decays—"withers away"—in favor of the genuinely satisfactory stage which he calls "the higher form of communism."

Believers in freedom as anarchy will see, maybe with mixed emotions, that the higher form of communism is anarchic. In it the socialist state has withered away. A central decision-making body has become unnecessary and, in fact, inhibiting. Of course the anarchism of the higher form of communism isn't the anarchy of rational economic men, independent self-interested maximizers. It's the anarchy of unalienated persons as I described them in an earlier chapter: mutually appreciating, mutually respecting people as much concerned about the self-fulfillment of others as about their own self-fulfillment.

Two sobering comments have to be made here. First, the realization of the higher form of communism, no matter how attractive it might be to some, presupposes a radical change in the way that most of us think of ourselves and our lives. Some way would have to be found to create the mutual recognition and respect without which the higher form of communism would be impossible. Second, Marx thought that there were forces already present within capitalist society sufficient to drive the historical process through socialism all the way to the higher form of communism. So far, socialist societies have always gotten stuck in socialism with no apparent prospect of getting to the next stage. If, like Marx, you think that socialism is the worst of all possible worlds, you might well worry about the prospect of getting past it to something better. And if there's no way to get past socialism, then the higher form of communism with its attractive combination of freedom as anarchy and freedom as self-fulfillment will end up being nothing more than an idle dream.

**INVITATION**          There's no way to sum up this chapter, because only you know your own conception of freedom. Consequently, only you know which form of economic organization is likely to be congenial to your life as you like to lead it. But what I've said here ought to give you at least a starting point for some careful thinking about yourself. I can only hope that you're willing to exercise your freedom to think about yourself and maybe even to try to act on the basis of your thinking. Too often these days people approach these issues by resigning themselves to what they think they're stuck with and have to put up with. This attitude defeats you before you even start—and, incidentally, is inconsistent with each of the three conceptions of freedom mentioned in this chapter.

## CHAPTER EIGHT

# Economics: Science of Abstractions

So far we've worked through three potential criticisms of market theory. Two of them depend on decisions we all have to make. We have to compare our conceptions of value with those available to market theory and decide if market theory can do justice to our conception of value. Then we have to decide what freedom means to us and whether or not that freedom is promoted by the market. The third criticism is of a different sort. Market theorists claim to be able to say that the market is guaranteed to achieve the most efficient use of given initial "resources," and we've seen that there's no reason to believe that claim. If the market is treated in terms of game theory, then we find that efficiency can only be guaranteed if it can be guaranteed that no Prisoners' Dilemma situations will arise. I don't think that guarantee can be made. On the other hand, if the market is treated as a social choice function fulfilling Arrow's conditions (as it must in all orthodox formulations), then, again, it can't guarantee efficiency.

These arguments seem to be at a high theoretical level—although, if your sense of values and freedom has any practical importance for you, they really aren't. Staying at this theoretical level has its dangers. For one thing, no matter how good you are at following the theoretical discussion, it may still be hard to connect the theory to the everyday world. Furthermore, if that connection is difficult, it is correspondingly difficult to decide whether or not to accept the theoretical material. What, after all, makes a theory satisfactory, worth accepting?

In the following chapters I'll try to ease these difficulties. First we'll deal with the nature of economic theorizing and with the grounds on which theories can hope to be accepted. Then we'll try to confront market theory with something we may all be able to recognize as our own world.

**LAWS AND CONSTRAINTS: SUPPLY AND DEMAND**

Economics has long wanted to be a science—or at least, to be as scientific as possible. There are several reasons for this aspiration. As the natural sciences have developed, they've contributed enormously to our ability to deal with the natural world. Not only do the natural sciences underwrite technology (engineering and medicine, for example), but they provide us with an ever clearer sense of what is physically, chemically, or biologically possible. Couldn't an economics be developed which did the same sort of thing?[1]

Physics and chemistry give us a sense of the possible by formulating laws. Some chemicals will combine, others not; nothing violates the laws of thermodynamics; nothing and no one breaks the law of gravity. Physics and chemistry, at each stage of their development, give us our best estimate of the constraints within which we must act. They tell us what we can't do anything about; consequently they tell us what we have to do to achieve our purposes. For example, the physicist tells us that if we want to get to the moon, then we're simply going to have to build a rocket with enough thrust to overcome the gravitational pull of the earth. There's no way around it. We can't wish our way up there. If economics is a science like physics or chemistry, then we ought to expect it to tell us about similar constraints.

[1]The standard positivist account of economic laws is found in Milton Friedman, "The Methodology of Positive Economics," in *Essays in Positive Economics* (Chicago: University of Chicago Press, 1953); also Tjalling C. Koopmans, *Three Essays on the State of Economic Science* (New York: McGraw-Hill, 1957) especially the second essay. A slightly modified version of the analysis can be found in Alexander Rosenberg, *Microeconomic Laws: A Philosophical Analysis* (Pittsburgh: University of Pittsburgh Press, 1976). The canonical statement of the positivist account can be found in Carl Hempel, *Philosophy of Natural Science* (Englewood Cliffs, N.J.: Prentice-Hall, 1966). A recent account of explanation is Peter D. McClelland, *Causal Explanation and Model Building in History, Economics and the New Economic History* (Ithaca: N.Y.: Cornell University Press, 1975). My account differs from the positivist account. Among its roots are Adolph Lowe, *On Economic Knowledge* (New York: Harper & Row, 1965); and Martin Hollis and Edward Nell, *Rational Economic Man* (Cambridge: Cambridge University Press, 1975).

There are real problems in thinking of economics as an exact parallel to the physical sciences. In particular, the kinds of constraints spoken of by economic theory turn out, with a few exceptions, to be self-imposed constraints. This is certainly not something you could say about the law of gravity.

We can start with the most famous "law" in economics: the law of supply and demand. It's fundamental, we already have a familiarity with it, and it's hard not to feel that there's something right about it.

The attraction of the law of supply and demand has always been that it seemed to capture an inexorable truth about the world, an underlying truth to which human beings *must* conform. People have wanted to see the law of supply and demand not as a part of one among many economic systems but rather as a necessary feature of *any* economic system that *could* be set up. The parallel case may again be the law of gravity. While there are indefinitely many blueprints we could draw up for indefinitely many houses, any blueprint that will result in a real house must be consistent with the law of gravity. If you design a roof that weighs x pounds, then you have to include in your blueprint supporting members that will bear at least x pounds. No way around it. Many would like to think that the law of supply and demand embodies a similar necessity. So, let's see if we can build it from its foundations.

First, we notice that you can't make something out of nothing. Theologians have argued that this must have happened once, but even if so, it's not a trick *we* can perform. Since you can't make something out of nothing, everything available in an economy will either already exist or will be manufactured out of "raw materials" that already exist. Whether something already exists or is manufactured, it will require work to put it to use. We're at the point of being able to formulate a law: *The use of anything requires the expenditure of work.* Now, I think that we can get general agreement on this law, but only if we're careful about what we mean by "work." If "work" has the precise meaning the physicist gives to it, we have simply an idiosyncratic formulation of a law of thermodynamics. It's true of everything we know: macromolecules in a primordial soup as well as human beings, and everything in between. On the other hand, suppose we mean by "work" the expenditure of time and effort. This gets us closer to our basic picture of human activity, and I think we can still get general agreement on the resulting law: *The use of anything by human beings requires the expenditure (perhaps very small) of their time and effort.* This too seems to be a natural consequence of our inability to violate the laws of thermodynamics.

Second, we examine the division of labor. Adam Smith was fascinated with the division of labor and gave us a number of examples described with great gusto. He rightfully pointed out that the law of supply and demand is secondary to the division of labor. The law of supply and demand is meant to hold for trading situations. Trading arises because some people have some goods and other people have other goods, and this presupposes the division of labor.

The principle of the division of labor is this: The quantity of time and effort necessary in order to prepare some given set of things for use is minimized by dividing the suboperations of this preparation among several working units rather than assigning them all to one unit. (That's an awful mouthful; but, then, any attempt to formulate a law precisely ends up producing a mouthful.) A simpler formulation of a similar thought is the proverb "Many hands make light work"; and while we're mentioning proverbs, let's not forget that "Too many cooks spoil the broth." Taken together, these two proverbs tell us that there will be some division of any work process which will maximize the efficiency of the process in terms of time and effort. Economists and industrial designers spend lots of time figuring out this optimal division of work for different productive processes. What we ought to notice here is that the principle of the division of labor is about groups of people thought of as parts of a production machine. The principle says that when we design a production machine with people as the working units the most efficient design will be one with a division of labor. Efficiency here is the ratio between goods produced and time and effort expended to produce them.

By this time you ought to be beginning to detect a whiff of sulfur. Lurking in this concept of efficiency are many of the problems that bedeviled us in earlier chapters. On the one hand, the principle of the division of labor looks like an engineering principle—and, given the design of the human animal, a *sound* engineering principle. So far so good. Next, we have the measure of efficiency. As usual, efficiency is expressed as the ratio of output to input. The input is time and effort, easily measurable quantities. The output is another story. Here we have to depart from the normal thermodynamic definition of efficiency. It isn't just the output of work that we're interested in but the output of goods or commodities. We can only make the transition from sound thermodynamics to economics if we can get a measure of output that will satisfy us. Here we are right back to the earlier chapters on value. If we can't solve the problem of measurement of values, we can't express the principle of the division of labor as an economic law.

Come to think of it, we've been too kind to the input part of the efficiency ratio too. In order to think of time and effort as inputs, we have to think of them as something expended, a cost to be paid in the hope of gaining a return. In other words time and effort have to be thought of as exact analogs to the fuel expended to run machines. Furthermore, if the concept of efficiency is to have its normal meaning, we have to think of a smaller expenditure as better than a larger one. Time and effort are in the denominator of the efficiency ratio.

Now, we'll be content with this concept of efficiency, and, more important, we will seek to organize our lives in its terms, only so long as our own conception of our time and effort corresponds to the conception required. "Many hands make light work" makes good sense only insofar as we're trying to lighten the work. If I want to lose weight or get in shape, it doesn't make much sense for me to get a bunch of people to share the exercise. If I want the satisfactions of independence and self-sufficiency it's silly not to do as much as I can by myself. Finally, and most important, the time and effort I "spend" in those activities that I love and that give me great satisfaction aren't "costs" at all. That time and that effort doesn't belong in the denominator of an efficiency ratio: they belong in the numerator. For those activities, the model of thermodynamic efficiency just doesn't make much sense. Of course, we know more generally that efficiency isn't everything. If you need a graphic example, think of the gas chambers at Auschwitz. We need to make very sure that efficiency furthers our values.

All this seems to mean that we may well reject the division of labor as an organizer of our lives. We could do that, by the way, without denying that the principle of the division of labor is true, given an appropriate concept of efficiency. In fact, under certain circumstances it might be foolhardy not to take advantage of the thermodynamic benefits of the sharing out of responsibilities. Just as the economist says, whenever resources are scarce the division of labor must be considered seriously as a way of organizing our lives. But we have to remember that nothing is scarce by itself; it's always scarce in the light of wants, needs, and purposes. As long as we face scarcity in those things we need for the life we want to lead, then the efficiency of the division of labor is indeed a *choice* on our part. It may be a choice we can ill afford to reject.

By now I think we have a basic picture of the way in which the principle of the division of labor could underlie all our activity. At its core is the claim that we, as parts of the physical world, are subject to physical (thermodynamic) constraints. As long as our operative concept of efficiency remains tied to these thermodynamic constraints—for example, when we're scrabbling along at the subsistence level—the principle of the division of labor will be important, even crucial, to us. As the conception of "output" changes to accommodate our values and as these values diverge from biological necessities, then the principle of the division of labor shifts from something we *have to* conform to (if we want to survive), through something we *should* conform to (if we have any sense of our well-being), to something we might or might not conform to (depending on the overall purposes we have).

So, in short, the principle of efficiency of the division of labor can't be specified without the introduction of conceptions of value and consideration of the ways of life that go with them. This, you might notice, is a vindication of Von Mises, who insisted upon the foundation of any economic theory on an underlying theory of human nature, hence human values.

But suppose we do have a division of labor. Some additional steps are needed to get to the law of supply and demand. We need to build a market.

With many people in the market, we have to be sure we find a way to protect consumer sovereignty. We want each person in the market to be as free to trade as any other. We want each person's wants and needs to have the same effect on the market. The only way to ensure these conditions for a large market is to insist that all be related to the market marginally, that is, that each person only make a tiny difference in the market process. This will be true if there are always many competing buyers and sellers, none of whom has a much larger share of the market than any other.

In particular we want to make sure that no one has more than a fair share of control over prices. In the saga of $X$ and $O$ we saw that the setting of prices prior to trading was inconsistent with the operation of the free market. The same is true here, and we have to notice that if one of the traders in the market has a lot more influence on price than the others, then it will seem to these others as if a price has been set. The price at which they'll be able to trade will be different from the one which would be expected as the result of free rational bargaining. Both the efficiency claim of the market and its claim to promote freedom depend on the notion of price reached through free bargaining, so it's essential that we not lose sight of the fact that market participants must be marginally related to the market.

Now we have to see how prices emerge out of the bargaining activity of all these many marginally-related participants in the market. Our key concepts will be the ones we saw briefly in our discussion of Adam Smith.

In the course of their bargaining, $X$ and $O$ made offers to one another for bananas or apples at a certain price. These were legitimate offers in that $X$ and $O$ were genuinely willing to buy at the offered price, and they were capable of buying at that price. If we add up all the legitimate offers for a commodity at a given price, then we have the total demand for that commodity at that price. In addition, we can move on and find the demand for the commodity at all the other prices within a reasonable range. When we plot these on a graph we get a demand curve such as the one on Figure 18.

In just the same way, we can discover the amount of the commodity producers are willing to bring to the market at any given price and draw a supply curve. In each case price is measured horizontally, and quantity demanded or supply is measured vertically. The direction of the curves reflects the usual assumptions defining the rational economic man. The price may be in whatever units we please—from lambchops to dollars.

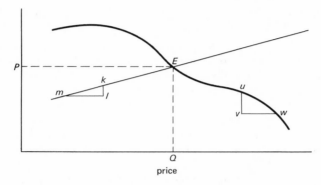

**Figure 18**

In any particular market, the supply and demand curves must be considered to be "givens." They are the basic data we start with. This is especially true of the demand curve. Here we have an exact parallel to the way we treated indifference curves. They were constructed on the basis of revealed preference, and these preferences were taken as basic data—not to be tampered with. Now we can think of a demand curve as the summation of a whole lot of indifference maps, and we can see two good reasons for considering demand curves as basic and given. First, to tamper with demand curves is to tamper with consumer sovereignty. If we seriously want consumers to be sovereign, then we must honor the preferences they reveal; the summation of these preferences is the demand. Furthermore, if we're interested in economics as a science, we must find the factual data upon which we can build our theories. Demand as expressed by the sovereign consumers is an important part of that basic data. Again here we notice that it's not the business of the economist as scientist to ask *why* the demand is as it is; it just *is*.

When we look at the supply and demand curves given in Figure 18, we see that there is a point *E* where they cross. At this point the price is *P* and the quantity supplied and demanded is *Q*. At the price *P* and the quantity *Q* the entire supply of the commodity will be bought up. The market will be cleared of the commodity.

Point $E$ is thought of as an equilibrium point, where supply and demand are in balance. If the suppliers bring more than $Q$ to market, they'll have some left over. If they want to sell this remainder, they'll have to reduce the price at which they're willing to sell. If the buyers can see this situation in the offing, then none of them will be willing to pay more than the price at which the supplier will have to sell his last remaining quantity. To pay a higher price would be irrational. In consequence, it would be irrational for the producer to continue to oversupply a commodity. He can do best by supplying exactly $Q$. The buyer sees that it would be irrational to pay more than necessary; the seller sees that it would be irrational to supply more than he can sell at a profitable price. These are the market pressures which steer prices to equilibrium at points like $E$. Once again the rationality of the rational economic man appears as the invisible hand.

Point $E$ on Figure 18 is exactly analogous to our old point $T$ in the saga of $X$ and $O$ (Figure 15). That is, $E$ is a point at which neither the suppliers nor the demanders can do better without the other doing worse. If there are no serious bargaining disadvantages on either side, then point $E$ is the point which rational economic men will reach if they are left to bargain freely. An argument to show that $E$ was the best just result under the circumstances would be exactly parallel to the argument intended to show that $T$ was the best just result in the bargaining between $X$ and $O$. In fact, you might try to ask some of the same questions about point $E$ that we asked about point $T$.

Notice how far we are from a sense of the laws of supply and demand as inexorable conditions of our existence. In particular, in setting out the laws we've had to suppose that the suppliers and the demanders are, and are acting as, rational economic men. What sorts of creatures are these rational economic men? How are they related to us, to the people we find in the world around us? In order to answer this question we have to examine the role of abstraction in economic theory.

**ABSTRACTION AND ITS CONSEQUENCES** Economic theory seems to be talking about us, products, money, and the institutions such as banks and corporations which engage in economic activity. Similarly, chemistry talks about atoms, molecules, compounds, and reactions. Now the basic objects of chemistry seem to exist by themselves. We discover things about them, find ways of taking them apart and putting them together, and so on, but we firmly believe that they were there to be discovered and played with long before we arrived on the scene. On the other hand, economic institutions are things we created ourselves—not that any one person came along and made them up single-handedly, but over a long period of history they've evolved as a result of human ingenuity in response to need. Consequently, while atoms and molecules can apparently be understood without reference to human purposes and needs, banks and stock exchanges cannot. They embody human purposes, reflect ways in which people conceive and organize their lives, and, in short, make no sense at all except against this background of human purposes and, of course, human values. So economic objects are secondary objects, dependent, in the last analysis, on the human values that give them meaning and, in fact, give them their existence in the first place.

What about some of the other objects of economics: money, for instance? There are many very sophisticated theories of money. Basically they fall into one of two categories: First, money can be thought of as a quantity of some precious, durable good such as gold; and second, it can be thought of as a stand-in for any economic asset—a convenience adopted for the purpose of smooth and easy economic transactions. In the first case money is obviously secondary to human values and beliefs. Only human values and beliefs can *make* a durable substance "precious." There are lots of durable substances in the world, some of them rare, that are worthless. And if people stopped wanting gold, it wouldn't be worth anything either. On the other hand, if money is simply a stand-in for any set of assets involved in economic exchange, then its existence surely depends on people's values and beliefs. We can think of how it depends on our beliefs if we think of what happens when we lose confidence in a currency. We say that it becomes worthless, which is to say that it's not money any more. Furthermore, even when it's worth something, its meaning has to be given in terms of the "something" that it's worth. In other words, if money is a stand-in for products, then its existence is secondary—dependent on the prior existence of the products for which it "stands in."

This brings us to the next object of economics: the product. We've already seen how the existence of anything *as a product* depends on underlying human values. For anything to be a product it must be demanded, and behind demand are the reasons people have for demanding. Here we have to add one more thought. Anything that's treated in economics *as a product* is treated as an abstraction. In the first place, as we've seen, economics abstracts from the reasons for demand in order to take demand as given and basic. To put it in the old terms, economics ignores use value in order to be able to deal with products as exchange values. So, for all the things we might say about the items that enter into exchange (items that we think of in many ways), the economist only considers one abstract aspect of them: their exchange value. Of course even this is a second-level abstraction, for even to talk of something's use value—

its place in the life and purposes of some person—is to abstract from all the other aspects of the thing. We can accept this abstraction best when we realize that most objects that enter into exchange are human artifacts. They wouldn't exist if no one had made them, so they wouldn't exist if they didn't fit with human purposes in some way or other. An interesting example of this is the steer that ends up in pieces on your dinner table. Not many steers would exist in nature, without the intervention of human activity. In fact, if Darwin's theory of natural selection is right, not many *could* exist in nature.

So all these objects of economics are abstractions. Of all the ways we could think of them, the economist makes an abstraction and thinks of them in one way: as objects of exchange. We've seen clearly how this is so in the case of commodities. Something is a commodity just insofar as it occurs on someone's indifference map; that is, just as soon as a rate of exchange can be established for it. What that thing might be and might mean in any other context is no part of the defined task of the economist.

Isn't there any object of economics that isn't an abstraction? Well, there's us. Economics is about us, and we're certainly more than just abstractions. I'm afraid we're in for a disappointment. Economics talks about us as abstractions too. We've seen over and over again that we appear in market theory as rational economic men—much as someone might appear in a soccer game as a goalie, or in a chorus as a soprano. For the purposes of the market we are "buyer," "seller," "producer," or "consumer." These simply specify the activities of the rational economic man within the market system. Any further understanding of us as people is barred by the theoretical constraints on how the market must be described. As we've seen, we can't even infer the reasons and values of market participants from their market behavior.

Each of the objects of economic theory—especially market theory—is an abstraction. The reasonable reply to this is "So what?" After all, *all* of the social sciences deal with abstractions: the voter, the father, the leader, the follower, and so forth. Isn't this the only way we can get any *general* understanding of people and societies? If we dealt with each person in his or her full particularity, how could we extend our understanding from case to case? Furthermore, even the physical sciences deal in abstractions: point particles, frictionless planes, weightless string, Carnot engines, and so forth. These abstractions are crucial in the development of physical theories.

The use of abstractions in the social and natural sciences is undeniable. It raises a lot of interesting questions, some of which are as deep as "What is it to think?" We'll concentrate on two consequences of importance. The first can be stated briefly; the second will occupy us in the next section.

One of the conspicuous features of the market is that there are many participants, all of whom enter the market anonymously. In the market, the important facts are the offers and counter-offers, not the identity of those who make the offers. All who enter the market enter as equals, and they aren't discriminated against. Any discrimination between market participants willing, say, to make offers for a product is thought to be an imperfection in the market. Think of what would happen to the theory of price if suppliers charged each of their customers a different price, depending on who the customer was. Often when anonymity is violated by suppliers who discriminate between potential customers, we get upset. We think that some people aren't being granted the opportunity that others enjoy. Our sense of justice rebels against this. We insist that everyone be treated equally, hence anonymously and as an abstraction: "potential buyer."

In general, market theorists believe that justice in the market is underwritten by the rationality of the rational economic man. If a producer discriminates against potential buyers, the producer is irrationally turning down potential profits. Thus market theorists are always exasperated with racial discrimination. If a restaurant owner selects customers by race, the owner is obviously restricting the opportunity for profits. When this is pointed out, the owner has a choice: Continue to discriminate, thus acting irrationally from an economic point of view, or stop discriminating, thus becoming a rational economic man. It seems obvious to the market theorist that given the choice, rationality will eventually win out over racism. On the other hand, if a consumer discriminates against potential suppliers, then he interferes with competition and runs the serious risk of having to pay higher prices for what he wants. For these reasons, I think, market theorists since Adam Smith have thought that justice ought to take care of itself in a market system, and if it doesn't, then some people are being irrational. If we're willing to abstract away all our particular characteristics and act as rational economic men, justice will be promoted.

In the light of your thinking about freedom in the last chapter, you might notice that the market theorist's line of thought never takes spillovers into account, nor does it deal with their consequences for freedom. Before we can decide if the anonymity of the market is satisfactory, we have to decide whether or not the abstraction on which it's based is itself satisfactory. We have all the apparatus on hand to do so. We have to decide if the market really does promote our well-being as rational economic men (the efficiency claim); we have to decide if the well-being the market offers to rational economic men fits with the well-being we want for ourselves as whole people; we have to decide if the concept of rationality embodied in the rational economic man is, of all the ways of being rational, the one we want; and we have to decide if our conception of freedom is the freedom of economic abstractions, or is compatible with such abstractions. For instance, I can't imagine how a mutual recognition and concern for self-fulfillment could fit well with the facelessness of the rational economic man. But at any rate, these judgments are ones that you eventually have to make for yourself. A full discussion would distract us from our present concerns.[2]


**ABSTRACTION AND**         In order to move on to the second consequence of
**VERIFICATION**            abstraction, we have to ask how economic theory
stacks up as scientific theory. Any scientific theory has to be tested to see if it works or not. In the natural sciences we assume this as obvious, any theory is subject to experimental testing. Until the testing has taken place we (generally) hold back from accepting the theory. But it's often pointed out that the kinds of experimenting done in the natural sciences are either impossible or unethical in the social sciences. Think of what it would be like to perform a real experiment in economics. You'd have to set up a variety of different economic systems and play around with them to see what happens. In the course of doing this you'd be making some people rich and some people poor, you'd be risking depressions and inflation, and, in general, you'd make an enormous impact on people's lives. Of course, on a smaller scale you might be able to make local experiments within the limits of an ongoing basic economic structure. But would you be right in calling these attempts "experiments?" Experiments are useful in the natural sciences just because they can be set up very carefully. When a natural scientist sets out to investigate the effect of one factor on another he has to make sure that the factor he's testing is the only one that could be having an effect. For instance, if a biologist were trying to determine the effect of vitamin C on health, he would have to try to create a situation in which all the other nutritional factors were held constant, and in which all other factors affecting health were kept under control. If all manner of nutritional factors and environmental circumstances were allowed to vary willy-nilly, he could never be sure that the results he got were the effects of vitamin C. In addition, for an experiment to be convincing, it ought to be repeatable. It ought to work the same way each time it's tried. This is one of the main ways to be sure that all the extraneous factors are really under control. No one as yet knows how to control all the economic factors that might affect results. So we should doubt if economic theories will ever be testable by experiment. It all

---

[2]The immediate source of my discussion of economic abstractions is an interpretation of Marx's methodology contained in Pier Aldo Rovatti, *Critica e Scientificità in Marx* (Milano: Feltrinelli, 1973). For the difference between idealizations in economics and those in the natural sciences, see Hollis and Nell, op. cit. Appendix to Chapter 1.

depends on the theory to be tested, its scope, what factors are likely to have an effect, and so forth.

Experiments are not the only way that theories are tested, though. Every bridge that's built and every machine that's made is a test of the theories that lie behind it. If a bridge is built out of sound materials, if the design is just as the theory says it should be, and if there are no errors in construction, then if it falls down we can be sure that the theory was wrong. So in general, technological success can lead us to have confidence in some theories—namely the ones that work. Of course this is true only so long as we can readily identify technological success, not much of a problem with bridges.

But when we move over to economics, we have a bit more trouble identifying technological success. If we start with Adam Smith, the task looks easy enough. A theory has met the test if the system built on it has maximized the wealth of the nation. We know, though, that this simplicity is deceptive. First of all, we can't know if one system has maximized wealth unless we know what the level of wealth might have been under some other system, and this is virtually impossible to find out. More important, all our difficulties in measuring wealth and utility get in our way here. In fact, the usual ways of measuring wealth lead us to some strange results. For instance, let's go back to the old two-person trading situation in which value is measured by revealed preference. We'll be testing the theory of free trade in a free market. What will be the mark of success? Well, I guess this has to be stated in terms of the efficiency of the bargaining process. If it leads to a satisfactory result, then the theory of free trading has proved to be a good one. But now a lot of familiar problems start to arise. On the one hand we might try to compare the results of free bargaining with some other result arrived at in some other way. But, as we've seen, the theory of revealed preference gives us no way to make such a comparison. On the other hand we might define the result of free bargaining—whatever it turns out to be—as the best result. Now this is the strange alternative. It tells us that free trading can't fail to be a success no matter what result it brings about. It's as if we designed a new kind of automobile engine and defined success as anything the engine happened to do—not run, run with no power, run with a lot of power, use a lot of gas or a little. To select one of these results over the others as the satisfactory result requires a criterion of success independent of the actual performance of the engine. Without this independent criterion of success, the only concept of success available is a silly one. "Did you test your engine?" "Yep." "Did it pass the test?" "Yep." "Did it run?" "Nope."

Thus, testing a theory of trading based on revealed preference by using a concept of efficiency defined in terms of revealed preference just doesn't make any sense. If we want to know whether or not the theory of free bargaining is a technological success, we're just going to have to find a theory of value other than that of revealed preference. So far we haven't seen a theory of value that looks capable of doing the job.

Have I accurately described the situation that economists are faced with in the real world? Yes, I think so, but at a level of generality that makes the real world hard to recognize. For instance, when government economists adopt measures to stimulate or slow down the economy, and the economy either speeds up or slows down in response to the measures taken, it certainly looks as if technological success bears out the validity of the theories they're working with. But let's look at what this judgment depends on. First, they must have already decided what's valuable and what isn't. Typically they measure the Gross National Product, which is calculated on the basis of a collection of goods and services produced over the course of a year. This means that they've found a way of telling goods from trash and services from disservices. Do they make these value decisions on the basis of a theory of revealed preference? Not really. Of course some economists like to think that all goods and services are ultimately identified in terms of revealed preference, but the accounting procedures used to measure the Gross National Product don't trace the process back that far. Economic practice is to depend on the fact that at any given time there's a fairly common sense understanding of what's a good and what isn't; what's a service and what isn't. This is reinforced by the fact that at any given time some things can be sold, and some things can't. This guarantees some link between what's accounted a good and what's in demand. The link isn't very tight. For instance, many things are produced in anticipation of future demand, and then the demand may not materialize. But in general it's assumed that the link is tight enough to give us a reasonable accounting procedure. At any rate, once this common sense identification of goods and services is established, we can go on about the task of deciding how to stimulate or slow down the production of goods and services; if efforts are successful, this seems to argue for the success of the theories used. The ability to make things happen in the way we want them to happen thus seems, in economics as in engineering, to be a way of testing theories. But there are still deeper problems to be dealt with. Again, they are problems stemming from the fact that economics deals with abstractions. In fact, in the last analysis, I don't think that it makes sense to talk of testing economic theories at all.

**ABSTRACT IDEALS**     As we well know, the pure theory of the market defines its participants as rational economic men. It then defines the relationships between participants in terms of free bargaining in a perfectly competitive market. Finally, it predicts that such participants, in such relationships, will make the most efficient use of any given set of initial resources. On the surface, this looks to be exactly analogous to the sorts of things that a chemist might tell us. For example, a chemist might say that if oxygen molecules and hydrogen molecules were brought together under certain conditions of temperature and pressure, then a certain amount of water would be formed, proportional to the amount of oxygen and hydrogen initially present. The chemist's claim could be tested easily. We'd measure the initial amounts of hydrogen and oxygen; then we'd measure the amount of water that resulted from their combination. Now, suppose we had the means to make analogous measurements of initial resources and final results in the market process. (I know this is a shaky assumption, but if we don't make it, the analogy with chemistry can't even get off the ground.) Would the analogy between economics and chemistry then be a good one? I don't think so. We can see why by looking at the role of abstraction and idealization in each.

When putting the oxygen and hydrogen together, the chemist knows that the predicted amount of water to be formed is an idealized estimate of amount. In any real-world trials the amount of water actually produced might well differ from the exact amount predicted. But over the course of a large number of trials, the difference between the amount produced and the amount predicted will always be very small. So the ideal relationship on the basis of which the predictions are calculated is useful and satisfactory—even though the ideal is seldom if ever met with perfect exactness. Furthermore, by working back to an understanding of the chemical reaction at the molecular level, the chemist is able to see *why* the exact amount of water predicted isn't always produced. Some stray molecules of hydrogen and oxygen manage to float around without making contact in the necessary way. In fact, you know that this situation really does occur, because there's a certain amount of hydrogen in the atmosphere and a considerable amount of oxygen. If they *always* got together in the right proportion, there wouldn't be any free hydrogen in the atmosphere. Well, having hydrogen molecules floating around among oxygen molecules without the two combining isn't a very tidy situation. It means that the real-world results obtained by the chemist are always a little different from the calculated results. But the chemist learns to live with this. It doesn't grieve her too deeply. In particular, the chemist does not start to yell at oxygen molecules as if it's their fault that the calculations don't work out perfectly neatly. She knows that they couldn't care less about calculations and would combine if they happened to come in contact with hydrogen in the right proportion at the right temperature. Oxygen atoms aren't perverse, naughty, sulky, or distracted; and they don't make mistakes. They only know one tune to march to, the tune is always playing, and they march whenever they get the chance.

But when *we* don't behave the way market theory says we should, the market theorists yell at us for being irrational. They *know* we're being irrational, because if we were rational, things would work out the way the theory says they should. They know we're being perverse, naughty, sulky, or distracted; or we've been making mistakes. Rational economic men would never act like that. Aren't we ashamed of ourselves?

Of course we might not be ashamed at all. We know lots of tunes we might march to, and the tune the rational economic man marches to might not be the one we choose. For example, his tune might not fit our conception of freedom or the values we have. We well recognize that if we don't march to the market theorists' tune, we'll get results far from the ones they predict on the assumption that we *are* rational economic men. But that may not worry us very much.

The rational economic man is an abstraction chosen from all the possible things that a human being might be. The market defines a way of life abstracted from all the possible ways of life a human being might choose. Consequently, when market theorists go to the real world to test the predictions they make on the assumption that we're rational economic men, they're not testing their theories. They're testing us. An analogy will help us see this more clearly.

As soon as automobiles became common, we had to work up a set of traffic laws: Drive on the right, stop at stop signs, don't cross a solid line in your lane, don't exceed the speed limit, and so forth. These laws tell the driver how she's expected to drive. There's no attempt to think of traffic laws in the same way we think of the laws of physics. We can't fall up, only down; but we can pass in no-passing zones. This is just to remind you of a point of grammar drilled into you by your grade school teacher: Don't say "can" when you mean "may," "can't" when you mean "shouldn't."

There are many ways to phrase such laws as traffic laws. Most often they're phrased in terms of "must" and "must not"—in order to give them the sound of necessity. "Drivers should stay to the right of the highway except to pass" just doesn't have a tough enough sound to it. The prohibition against driving on the left has to sound more urgent. But here again, we have to be careful not to think of the "must" of the traffic laws as the "must" in: "In a closed system, the total amount of matter and energy must remain constant."

But, whatever the words in terms of which we want to express traffic laws, it turns out that there's a way to avoid all the "shoulds," "musts," "cans," and "mays" in spelling them out. At least, there's a way to avoid the *words*. You simply describe the safe driver. The safe driver always keeps to the right, passes only in passing zones, keeps within the speed limit, in short, obeys all the traffic laws. In addition, of course, the safe driver develops driving habits that aren't specified by the law. How attentive the driver is and how defensively she drives would be hard things to legislate. Nonetheless, many of the things that constitute the safe driver can be summed up as "obedience to the traffic laws." Then, when the safe driver has been fully described, the content of the traffic laws has been built into her.

This way of illuminating laws or moral principles is very old. If you look into the Bible, you'll find that Job is described in the following way: "There was a man in the land of Uz, whose name was Job; and that man was perfect and upright, and one that feared God, and eschewed evil." Job is obviously being held up to us as an exemplar. His story would have no impact if this weren't so. His perfection, uprightness, and eschewal of evil have to be filled in with specifics, but it's quite clear that they could be summarized in terms of his obedience to God's laws. He's put forth as the kind of person God meant us all to be, the kind of person we ought to be—according to the tradition within which we find his story. God's laws constitute Job in his perfection and uprightness. They make him what he is. Similarly (if more mundanely) the traffic laws largely constitute the safe driver.

Both Job and the safe driver are idealizations and maybe *mere* idealizations, although it's not inconceivable that Job could have existed or that we could locate a safe driver somewhere. A main difference between Job and the safe driver—at least on the surface—is that there can be as many ideals of the safe driver as there are sets of traffic laws to define alternative ideals. The presumption is that there's only one ideal of the perfect man, one set of God's laws to define him. But in both cases, the match-up between the ideals and the laws is clear. Furthermore, once we know what the laws are, we can describe what the ideal *is* and *does* (or would be and would do) instead of what those of us who fall short of the ideal *ought* to be and do. So we say "The safe driver stops at all stop signs," as if this were a fact about this strange beast, the safe driver. But it's not hard to see the "shoulds" and "shouldn'ts" lurking in the back seat. For, when we teach people to drive, we try to instill habits in them which result in their approaching the ideal "safe driver" as closely as possible. In addition, we give them good reasons for wanting to develop the necessary habits: "If you don't drive safely, you're bound to waffle your car—or maybe even get killed." And, if those reasons aren't enough we also provide penalties for failure to obey.

Once a particular set of traffic laws is established, and once we're sure that people could avoid accidents and expedite traffic flow if they were safe drivers, then we can go to the real world to see what's actually happening. If we find that there are lots of accidents, then we know that drivers are falling short of the ideal safe driver. Again, this may mean that they're badly trained, or that they're stupid or irresponsible, or that they have other concerns which override their commitment to the benefits of safe driving. In no way, however, are the traffic laws being tested. There are two reasons for this: First, it would be very odd to think that traffic laws were hypotheses about human behavior in the way that Newton's laws are hypotheses about the behavior of, say, falling bodies. Second, and more important, the only way that traffic laws could be "tested' would be to find out if they worked to prevent accidents and to smooth traffic flow. That is, testing them wouldn't determine their truth or falsity; it would determine their efficiency. Furthermore, if we wanted to test even the efficiency of traffic laws *as such* and the ideal of the safe driver that goes with them, then we'd have to be sure that all real-world drivers were living up to the ideal. Otherwise we could always attribute apparent failures of the laws to the failures of people to obey them; thus leaving the question of the efficiency of the laws undecided. Because of this indeterminacy, debate over the success or failure of traffic laws is perpetually open-ended—if the debate proceeds in terms of what would happen in the ideal case. On the other hand, if the question is whether or not the laws are acceptable enough to the average driver for him to obey them, hence avoid accidents, by and large, then we have another matter on our hands. We could, in fact, find out if the laws were more or less acceptable. Then, I would guess, we'd find that innumerable, different sets of traffic laws were acceptable at roughly the same level.

Now, with these analogies in mind, what can we conclude about market theory and the ideal of the rational economic man? First, we can see that "safe driver," and "rational economic man" are idealizations of the same sort. They abstract a particular capacity or possible way of behaving from the sum of capacities and possible ways of being that we find among people. They tell us what ought to happen if we behave ideally in terms of the abstraction: In one case we ought to be able to drive from place to place without wiping each other out; in the second case we ought to be able to maximize utilities given an initial set of resources.

In each case there are alternative ways we could behave. In each case we can ask "Do people really behave in accordance with the ideal?" In each case the answer is "Sometimes yes, sometimes no." As an actual description of what we do, none of the ideals fits us very exactly. But whether or not we actually do behave according to the ideal really isn't the important point. The main question is whether or not we *ought* to aspire to the ideal.

The reasons for teaching people to be safe drivers are pretty compelling. But it's important to see that there's a big difference between reasons for teaching people to be good drivers on the basis of *some traffic laws or other* and reasons for teaching them to be safe drivers on the basis of a *particular* set of traffic laws. Within limits, it might not matter which set of traffic laws we used, so long as everyone used the same ones. So, in two different parts of the world, we train safe drivers, but the safe drivers in one part of the world could fulfill an ideal different from the one that defined safe drivers in the other part. So long as the twain didn't meet they'd be all right.

"Testing" is relevant in this case: (A) to find out how well drivers have been trained; and, more generally, (B) to find out how closely they approach the ideal of the safe driver. Furthermore, as we saw, we could find out if we had a good set of traffic laws—but only on the condition that people lived up to the ideal of the safe driver. And last, there's one other possible test we could conduct. It might happen that we had formulated a good set of traffic laws that would work if everyone lived up to the ideal of the safe driver, but that people just couldn't or wouldn't measure up to the ideal. An example of traffic laws that people *couldn't* live up to might involve a system of traffic lights that required a reaction time far too short for normal human reflexes. An example of traffic laws that people *wouldn't* live up to might involve a 55 mile an hour speed limit. In either case, the fit between the laws and the people expected to obey them would be a bad one; if people really couldn't or wouldn't obey the laws, there'd be no choice but to change the laws. Over a period of time we could become convinced that we were stuck with such a misfit, and in some sense we could count this as a testing of the laws.

Now we come to market theory. What are the reasons for teaching people to be rational economic men? Well, *if* we think that the efficiency claim is sound, and *if* we think that the market fits our conception of freedom, and *if* we can see how to solve the measurement problem to our satisfaction, then there might well be reasons to teach ourselves and others to be rational economic men. Otherwise not. This brings us back to our old stamping grounds, and suggests why our investigation of the efficiency claim was worth the time. We've seen some reasons to doubt the efficiency claim already. We can now ask whether the claim could be tested in the real world. There are a couple of interesting possibilities.

In analogy with the "testing" of traffic laws, we can see that a really conclusive test of market theory would require that the participants in the economic system tested conform to the abstract ideal. In other words, we'd have to convince them (or force them) to be rational economic men before we'd have a real-world test that would show if it's a good thing to be a rational economic man. This is why the theoretical arguments for efficiency are so important. Only if Adam Smith's dream is theoretically compelling will we be justified in getting into a situation where a "test" of market theory is possible. So the market has to be painted for us in glowing terms. And if it doesn't seem to be working, our enthusiasm can be sustained on the grounds that the reasons it isn't working are our failure to measure up as rational economic men and, in general, our failure to create the conditions under which the market can work. By the way, we find the same line of argument on the opposite side of the fence. Many socialists, when faced with the apparent difficulties in socialist systems, are inclined to argue that no "real" socialist system has ever been achieved—thus appealing to an ideal of their own.

Now, you might notice that if market theory really were like the theories of chemistry and physics, all this urging, encouraging, and scolding wouldn't make much sense. Oxygen molecules don't need to be persuaded to combine with hydrogen. That's the way they are. And if market theory were about the way *we* are, we wouldn't need to be persuaded either. But market theory isn't about the way we are; it's about the way we *would* be *if* we conformed to a particular abstract ideal. Market theory hides the "shoulds" and the "oughts" by expressing itself in terms of the rational economic man. The rational economic man maximizes gains just as surely as Job eschews evil. Both are what they ought to be, given the laws that constitute them in their perfection. The "oughts" only disappear because they've been swallowed up in the definition of the ideal. But since they're still there, we have a right to suspect that the laws of economics are more like traffic laws than they are like the laws of physics. The question is not whether we *do* conform to the laws, but whether we *should*. Furthermore, conclusive evidence about what would happen if we were to conform to the laws is impossible to get until we conform. So whether we *should* conform or not has to be decided on the basis of the sorts of considerations we have examined in the previous chapters, not on the basis of experiment and testing.

## COULD WE BE RATIONAL ECONOMIC MEN?

We have to look a bit more closely at whether or not people could or would fulfill the ideal of the rational economic man. If we couldn't or wouldn't conform to the ideal, then it would be silly to waste our time spinning out the tale of what would happen if we did.

Reasons why we wouldn't conform to the ideal are easily found in our discussions of value, justice, and freedom. If we decide that our values, sense of justice, and conception of freedom didn't fit with the ideal of the rational economic man, then we wouldn't conform. As I've said, the decisions involved are ultimately up to each of us, so I'll leave them to your best judgment. This leaves us with the question whether or not we *could* conform to the ideal. How would we ever determine this? We're really asking: "Is a world of perfect, rational economic men organizing their lives in terms of a perfect market possible? Is human nature capable of reaching such an ideal?"

Questions of this sort are notoriously difficult. On the one hand, we could know for sure that it was a possibility if it ever happened. But it never has happened. On the other hand, it's virtually impossible to say that it *isn't* a possibility. The fact that it hasn't happened is far from conclusive. Lots of things that are possible haven't happened yet. Judgments about what can or cannot happen, when not based on what *has* happened, have to be based on solidly grounded theories. For instance, physicists tell us with great confidence that a perpetual motion machine is impossible. No one ever built one. They base this judgment on the laws of thermodynamics, laws which are well confirmed by experiment and technology. Of course, their proof that a perpetual motion machine is impossible doesn't seem to deter enterprising inventors from trying to make one. It's no surprise that the inventors haven't come up with one yet, and you can safely bet that they won't. The U. S. Patent office is so confident of this that when someone sends them a candidate, they immediately set out to decide which law of thermodynamics it violates. In fact, they classify "perpetual motion machines" in terms of which law of thermodynamics is violated.

Unfortunately, there are no "laws of human nature" analogous to the laws of thermodynamics, laws grounded on experiment and technological success. So when we're called on to assess a possibility or impossibility concerning people, we're stuck with the educated guesses we formulate on the basis of common sense. The guesses aren't going to give us any definitive answers. The question as to whether or not we could be rational economic men is forever open.

Of course there's the possibility that someone could try to *make* us act like rational economic men, just as they could try to make us be safe drivers. But the market theorist couldn't be very happy about that. What would have happened to the claim that the market gives us freedom from central control?

**SECOND BEST**      Given any doubts at all about the real-world possibility of a perfect market, shouldn't we start to think about approximations to it? Maybe the problem of testing market theory lies in the tightness of the abstraction, and if we loosen it a bit we'll have an easier time. But here the market theorists are their own worst enemies. Suppose, for example, that we looked back in history to periods during which a reasonable approximation to free markets and rational economic men seem to have been present. And suppose we thought that in such periods things hadn't gone so well as they should have: Maybe there was poverty, the ups and downs of prosperity and depression, etc. Would this be evidence that the market system wasn't satisfactory? The market theorist would say no and leap right in to try to convince us that the bad economic results were due to imperfections in the market, violations of market condition, irrationality. So, the theorist would say, we can't conclude that market theory is at all unsatisfactory. We've seen this sort of situation before—in the context of traffic laws. The ideal is testable only under ideal conditions. The consequence is that the market theorist is locked tight to an ideal and is cut off from the examination of approximations.

There's a further difficulty in evaluating approximations to an ideal. You'd think that if an ideal were unattainable, then the next best thing to it would be sure to be the closest approximation to it that you could get. Unfortunately you can't reason that way. Again we can make use of a couple of analogies. There's an old maxim in the game of bridge: Seek the best result possible, not the best possible result. This is called the "half-a-loaf" maxim, since it resembles the ancient adage "Half a loaf is better than none." The idea here is that when you start to play a hand at bridge you can see the ideal result—which will be possible *if* all the cards are perfectly placed. But it may be stupid to play the hand on this basis. Either you have information that tells you that the cards aren't perfectly placed, or, more commonly, you know the probability that the cards are perfectly placed is so small that the odds on your achieving the ideal result are prohibitively against you. So you ought to play the hand so as to achieve the best result possible *under the circumstances.* In doing so you may well give up all chance of achieving the ideal result. But so what? It would be foolhardy to pursue the ideal—marching steadfastly into the jaws of defeat. Of course while this may be good advice, you know that some people clutch very hard at ideals. Kibbitzing at a bridge game can be like standing on a cliff watching the lemmings plop down into the sea.

Next we can think of taking a sea voyage. Suppose that for the particular voyage we're going to take we know exactly what the perfect ship would be. And suppose we found one, but, alas, it was a bit old, rotten and likely to spring leaks. It would be ideal if it were perfect, but it has a few defects. Are we sure that we ought to take it anyway, as the closest approximation to the ideal? Not really. There might be some other ship, very unlike the ideal, which would be more likely to bring about the best result possible *under the circumstances.* Once the ideal is known to be unattainable, we might well have to rethink the choice of a ship from start to finish. Knowing what the ideal would be doesn't automatically tell us what the next best alternative would be.

Now back to the main track: Suppose we were confident that the best possible economic system would be one in which there was pure private

property, perfectly rational economic men, perfect information, perfectly competitive markets, and perfectly free access to markets. And suppose that we knew that one or more of these perfect conditions was unlikely to be attainable—given the world as we find it. Would we know that the next best economic system would be one in which the perfect conditions were approximated as closely as possible under the circumstances? No, not at all. The second best economic system might be very different from the ideal. There's no way to be sure that an inch-by-inch retreat from the ideal is the sensible way to proceed. It may very well be foolhardy. The imperfections in the ideal might be just the ones which would have disastrous results for some or all participants in the system. Extinction games might emerge; gross inequalities might develop; bad spill-overs might be maximized; imperfections might chronically increase rather than decrease. A wholesale rethinking of what we want out of an economic system might be necessary. But, as we know, ideals die hard. Sometimes, watching economists and politicians deal with a real-world problem is like standing on a cliff watching the lemmings plop down into the sea.

Before we leave this we have to make sure that socialists don't get to feeling too cocky. What's been said about approximations to the perfect market can be said equally tellingly against any central planning system which sets up ideal conditions for success. If the central plan will only produce its intended results if certain ideal conditions (of manpower, production, etc.) are met, and if these ideal conditions prove to be unattainable, then we can't be sure that the next best alternative would result from minor modifications of the original plan. It could be that the best result possible under the circumstances would require scrapping the plan altogether. But remember, the half-a-loaf maxim doesn't tell us what will be the second best alternative once the ideal is unattainable. It only tells us that it's probably wise to rethink the whole problem.

Traditionally there's a lot of resistance to the half-a-loaf maxim. "Strive for perfection!" we're told, even when we know we can't reach it. The Judeo-Christian tradition has it that because of the sins of Adam we have fallen to a position somewhere below the angels. Yet unlikely as it is that we'll ever achieve the state of grace, we ought to try. Of course, the world will need some strongly enforced laws to keep us sinners from doing harm to each other. Not being ideal, we deserve the restriction of these laws.

I really don't know what to make of that line of thought, but somehow, somewhere along the way, market theory was identified as part of the godly straight and narrow. So abandonment of the market looks to some like Adam's fall into sin. I don't know what to make of that either.

# In Search of Economic Reality

It's time to take that step closer to the real world that I promised earlier. The way we'll do it is by asking if we can expect people to act as rational economic men and what consequences we can expect if they do.

Now, as we work through answers to these questions we'll have to remember to be somewhat modest. It will be possible in this chapter to send out probes. These probes can bring us back samples which we can hope are accurate samples of the terrain we're probing. But as often as they satisfy our curiosity, the probes will raise new questions which would have to be pursued beyond the confines of what's presented here.

Let's not forget, though, that we're really in no position to despair of getting to the definitive last word on the issues we'll probe. Economic life goes on, indifferent to the current state of our knowledge or ignorance. Economic decisions are made and have to be made—now. If we're the ones making those decisions, then they'll have to be made on the basis of the understanding we have—now. While we'll always be aware of large areas of ignorance, we have every right to try to bring the results of our philosophical thinking to bear on the decisions we make.

So, can we expect people to act as rational economic men, and what will happen if they do?[1]

**PROBE 1: AVOIDING THE BONDS OF THE MARKET**
We've seen a standard account of supply and demand. We've seen that the theory of a consumer sovereignty requires that demand be taken as given. Producers are to take their instructions from the market and rationally adjust supply to demand. This puts limitations on the knowledge that producers are supposed to use. It would be interesting to see if the rational economic man—as producer—would, or ought to, accept these limitations. Let's set up the situation clearly again:

Participants in the market must base their economic activity only on the information they obtain in the marketplace. In particular, if they are buyers, they can know what price suppliers are asking and what price competing buyers are offering. If they are sellers, they know what prices are being offered, and they know what prices their competing suppliers are asking. It's assumed that the real control over prices is in the hands of those who form the demand. The theory of consumer sovereignty now takes on a causal sense. When we trace back the reasons why a price is what it is, the final link in the chain is on the side of demand. Producers "take their instructions from the market" with respect to *what* they produce and *how much* they produce.

Furthermore, if the market is to function right, the instructions of the market have to be understood in a certain way. A rise in price must be a signal for producers to supply more, and it must be a signal for consumers to buy less. If the signals are read in any other way, then there's no guarantee that the market will reach an equilibrium price.

Now, put yourself in the place of the producer. It may be annoying for you to be under the control of consumers: "to be taking instructions from the market." Maybe you'd like the market to be taking instructions from you, for a change. First off, there may be something you *like* to produce. This isn't a motivation that has a legitimate place in the market, but it's perfectly understandable, and it's hard to see what's wrong with having it. Second, you may be stuck with a set of production facilities that aren't very flexible; they're only good for producing one thing, and if that one thing isn't in demand, you're in trouble. Third, even if your production facilities are flexible, it probably takes time to convert them to new uses,

[1]A useful book to read in conjunction with this chapter is John Kenneth Galbraith, *The New Industrial State* (Boston: Houghton Mifflin 1967). Another is Herbert Marcuse, *One Dimensional Man,* op. cit.

and it's a bit risky to be stuck with a guess about what people will be demanding at the end of your conversion period. If you guess wrong, you're in trouble again. It will be no consolation that you'll be looked upon as one of the tragic heroes martyred to consumer sovereignty. Here's where courage and a sense of adventure come in as important motivations—even though they have no theoretical place in the definition of the rational economic man. If you have a sense of adventure, you might be willing (even eager) to risk your productive facilities in a guess about what future demand will be like. On the other hand, if you want to secure your resources against the chanciness of the market, you might want to look around to see if you can do better than take your chances. You might want to exercise control over your future.

Now turn around and put yourself in the place of the consumer. Suppose there's something really important for the kind of life you want to lead, but which you can't produce for yourself. Suppose further that virtually nobody else wants or needs this thing. The demand is extremely low, so the item is probably not going to be worth producing except at a very high price, maybe even a prohibitive price. It might be well worth your while to try to get other people to want what you want. After all, it's only because the wants of many people conform to each other that enough demand is created in the market to stimulate supply. If you don't try to get others to want what you do, then when you go to the market you'll find that you're stuck with a choice between all the things that everyone else wants. Of course the alternative is to learn to like what everyone else likes: Live as everyone else lives. Keep reminding yourself that you're a sovereign consumer.

Now, again from the point of view of the consumer, look at this situation: You go to the market and you find that the price of one of your favorite things has gone up. Suppose you think that this is a sign that the price of the thing is going to keep going up, so you better buy it now; it will never be cheaper. If a lot of people think as you do, demand will increase, and, lo and behold, the price will continue to go up. "But hold it," says the market theorist, "This inflationary psychology is irrational. If the consumers would interpret the change in price the way they should, then prices would retreat back to an equilibrium." But it's far from clear that inflationary behavior is irrational, even from the point of view of the rational economic man. He may live in a world where the prices of things continually *do* go up. This is the world he has to interpret and deal with rationally. Is it obvious that in such a world he would be irrational to buy as quickly as he could? Remember the Prisoners' Dilemma.

Now return to the plight of producers who want to be able to predict what will sell several years in the future. They want to eliminate guesswork and be free from the uncertainty of the whims of the sovereign consumers. In general, there are two ways to do this: They can get tastes to conform to what they want to produce; or they can try to make people buy their products because there are no other choices. We'll first look at the manipulation of tastes. It's clear that the manipulation of tastes is not a market activity. It's an activity that operates behind the level of indifference maps. In trying to ensure that people will buy a certain product, a producer is trying to ensure that (A) some demand curve will have at least a certain height and a certain slope; hence (B) that a certain number of individual indifference maps will have the product on one of the axes, and the indifference curves on that map will reflect a willingness to trade for the product at the price the producer wants to charge. In attempting to influence people so that they have the appropriate preferences, the producer is certainly not taking demand as given but is trying to modify or even create demand. This obviously puts the concept of consumer sovereignty into question.

But if you don't look at the way your values develop and how the world around you is trying to influence them, you're not making the best use of your right to choose. In particular, for our present purposes, you have to realize that many of your co-participants in the economic system have a strong interest in modifying and creating your sense of values so that you'll serve their purposes, so that you'll contribute to the demand for their products. Consumer sovereignty isn't the simple concept you might have thought it was.

Incidentally, the market theorist interprets a piece of advertising as a notice that a certain product is available. With that notice the consumer decides if he or she wants the product. Now, there may have been a time when this interpretation had to be taken seriously. But not now. I'm sorry, but some things are too far beyond belief to bother with. To say that a piece of present-day advertising is a notice that a product is available is like saying that a missionary's sermon is a notice that there's a god.

**ELASTICITY**     For the next step in the discussion of the manipulation of demand we have to go back to something we first talked about in the first chapter, the distinction between wants and needs. This time we can put the distinction together with what we know about supply and demand. We want to look at wants and needs again because it's pretty obvious that the possibility of manipulating demand varies depending on whether the demand is for something needed or just for something wanted.

The term for the rate of change of supply or demand as price changes is "elasticity." For instance, the demand curve on Figure 18 looks "normal"; it tells us that as a price goes up, the amount that people will be willing to buy goes down. Since the elasticity of demand can be measured within any small length of the curve, I put a little triangle down in a corner to illustrate. The elasticity of demand is measured by the ratio of line $VW$ to line $UV$. If $VW$ equals $UV$, then $UV/VW = 1$; the elasticity is unitary. If $UV/VW$ is greater than 1, then demand is said to be elastic; if $UV/VW$ is less than 1, the demand is said to be inelastic. If a demand curve is wavy like that of Figure 18, then there will be short lengths on it where demand is elastic and other short lengths where it's inelastic. Down where $UVW$ is located demand is quite elastic. The same sort of ratio expresses the elasticity of supply. The ratio of change in supply to change in price is measured by $KL/ML$.

Obviously, when you're talking about elasticity of demand, you're measuring the rate at which people want a commodity relative to its price. If the amount demanded varies greatly as the price goes up or down, this means that people can pretty much take the commodity or leave it— depending on whether or not its price is favorable. On the other hand, when the demand for a commodity is inelastic, this means that people must have a certain quantity of the commodity no matter what its cost (within reason). Thus, the most obvious use of the concept of elasticity is to distinguish between necessities and luxuries, or, in the language we used several chapters ago, needs and wants. If the demand for a commodity is inelastic, this means that people have to have it (or at least think they do). By looking at the demand curve as given, economists can distinguish between necessities and luxuries on a factual basis. They simply watch the shape taken on by the demand curve. If they like they can even construct a continuum of relative necessities and relative luxuries.

We understand why economists will take the elasticity or inelasticity of demand curves as given and will think that it's not their task to question them. But for us, this is just another instance where "one more question" might lead us to something interesting. So we'll ask why demand curves tend to be shaped the way they are. In particular, why are the demands for some commodities elastic and the demands for other commodities inelastic?

The short answer is that demand curves give us a portrait of the value system of a society, insofar as this value system is expressed in the market. Some commodities (such as salt) tend to have an inelastic demand in virtually all societies. This reflects the importance of salt in everyone's diet and, ultimately, reflects the need of all animals for sodium. The demand for salt is so dependably inelastic that innumerable societies have made salt a state monopoly. This serves two functions: It prevents individuals from gaining a monopoly in salt, and it insures the state a dependable source of revenue.

Consider another example. We've evolved a society where an automobile is virtually a necessity. Almost everyone claims to be unable to get along without one. At the present time we're wrestling with the elasticity of demand for gasoline. There are lots of reasons why it would be good to reduce the demand for gas: For example, petroleum resources could be converted from use to make gasoline to, say, heating oil; we could reduce the quantity of petroleum we import, thus making our trade deficit decrease. But, within a very broad price range, it seems that our demand for gas is inelastic: it's such a necessity that we're willing to buy it at almost any price—complaining as we wait in line but buying nonetheless. The consequence is that any attempt to regulate demand for gasoline by regulating price seems doomed to failure. Television sets are another item for which the demand is becoming less and less elastic. In these cases we find certain commodities sliding toward the "necessities" end of the necessity-luxury continuum. When we remember that many people in the world get along perfectly well without a car or a TV set, we begin to get a feeling for the degree to which we are locking ourselves into a way of life which defines necessities for us. For this reason, it might be wise to remember that any necessity is a necessity *for* something. If we say that something is a need rather than just a want, then we have to be ready to explain what it's a need *for.* When we ask what we need a car for, we find that we have to describe a life lived over a considerable area, where home and work are at some distance, and where we've developed the expectation to be able to cover a lot of ground for purposes of recreation. When we look at our need for a car in the light of public transportation as an alternative, then we begin to see how we've come to expect to be able to be where we want in our own sweet time and on our own terms. Others looking at us say, "What luxury!" We say that for us it's not a luxury but a necessity.

Questions about elasticity and inelasticity of demand aren't confined to the mundane. For example, many religions require their adherents to observe a holy day each week, a day when worldly activity stops and spiritual activity takes place. At some times, and in some places the demand for such a day of rest has been so inelastic that people have been willing to pay for it with their lives. Once upon a time the observance of the sabbath was so important to the people of some of the United States that they felt justified in passing laws prohibiting economic activity on Sunday: the "Blue Laws." In doing this, people exhibited some of the roots of their value system. In our own time, as you know, we tend to find the cost of this day of rest too high, so more and more stores are open on Sunday, most real estate is sold on Sunday, etc. We'd still rather not work on Sunday though. What this all means is that the demand for a sabbath is becoming more elastic, especially relative to our opportunity to be consumers. This exhibits the roots of our values just as the demand for a sabbath did for our ancestors.

At any rate, the elasticity or inelasticity of demand for various things is a key indicator of the shape of our value system. And if we pursue the underlying reasons for the shape of our demand curves, we find out some very interesting things about ourselves. This is especially important if we ask the kinds of questions about ourselves that we asked in the chapters on rationality and value. Behind every demand curve in an economy is a vast set of individual indifference maps which account for the demand curve. Behind every individual indifference map is a set of reasons why things are preferred or indifferent. And, if you have any awareness of your life as a whole, behind the reasons for any given preference is a sense of where these reasons fit in the overall pattern of your life. An economist may be able to get away with taking demand curves as given. As reflective human beings, we can't get away with it. As soon as we begin to think of alternatives to the habitual patterns of our lives, we're forced back through the chain of reasons to a basic examination of ourselves.[2]

**PROBE 2: MONOPOLY**    With an understanding of elasticity, we can move on to another strategy for influencing demand, the development of monopoly. Market theory tends to think of monopoly as irrational—that is, impossible among rational economic men. The idea is that if someone were to obtain a monopoly of something, then rational consumers would search around for substitutes. It would be worth their time to find suitable substitutes, and when they'd gotten them the monopolistic supplier would be stuck with the original commodity. So it wouldn't have done him any good to have become the sole supplier. At best, he would have to sell his commodity at the price the market would have established if there had been competition for consumer trade with other suppliers.

In this century, defenders of the market have conceded that monopolies might develop (since they seem to be profitable) and that one of the services of the government might be to watch out for monopolies to prevent them from being established. Our major anti-trust laws were passed by defenders of the market system.

In any case, monopoly is inconsistent with the working of the market. The market requires perfect competition, which means that no individual participant in the market may have the power to set prices single-handedly. On the other hand, monopoly is a great way to ensure the stability

[2]On the measurement of the Gross National Product and its relevance to our well-being, see Oskar Morgenstern, *On the Accuracy of Economic Observations* (Princeton: Princeton University Press, 1963); Tibor Scitovsky, *The Joyless Economy*, op. cit.; and Arthur Okun, *Equality and Efficiency* (Washington: Brookings Institute, 1975). The classic work is John Maynard Keynes, *The General Theory of Employment Interest, and Money* (New York: Harcourt, Brace, and World, 1964). It is a great help to read, along with Keynes, Lavin H. Hansen, *A Guide to Keynes*, (New York: McGraw-Hill, 1953); and Robert Lekachman, *The Age of Keynes* (New York: McGraw-Hill, 1966).

of your enterprise. If you're the only one who can supply something people want or need, they're going to have to come to you to get it. Even if you could only charge the normal market price for your product, you'd still be in great shape, since that price would always be paid to you. Of course, if you had a monopoly of a product for which the demand was inelastic, then you'd *really* have it made. As I said before, this is the basis for governmental salt monopolies.

You have to remember, though, that you can only have a monopoly as long as there are no substitutes for your product. If people can shift their demand to some equivalent product, monopoly is impossible. So you're constantly going to have to be on the lookout for potential substitutes for your product. How are you going to tell one when you see one?

Here we are right back at the problem of identity. We've seen similar problems before, in connection with Arrow's Paradox. Let's begin with some ABC's. Lots of companies in the world make cars, but only GM makes Chevrolets. Lots of companies now make plastic disks for scaling, but only Whammo makes Frisbees. Lots of books are published, but only Prentice-Hall publishes this one. If companies weren't so concerned to distinguish their products and make them seem unique, they wouldn't be so worried about brand names. Only 3M Company makes Scotch Brand Cellophane Tape, but everyone calls the stuff Scotch tape whether it's made by 3M or not. This makes 3M unhappy. The same thing is true of Kleenex. Who wants to call it facial tissue when you need a piece to sneeze into? In some cases, *all* that differentiates two products is the brand name, but this doesn't always prevent some people from having strong preferences for one over the other. So the problem of identifying a commodity is a strange one.

Having a monopoly means having all the (      ), so that anyone who wants any has to come to you to get it. What can fit in the blank? "Chevrolets" *cannot* fit into the blank, despite the fact that GM *trivially* has a monopoly of them (they own the brand name). On the other hand, "automobiles" would fit in the blank if everyone but GM went out of the automobile business. What's the difference? Well, first, under present circumstances there are lots of substitutes for Chevrolets. True enough, some people might have great loyalty to Chevrolets, but it really doesn't take much (a better trade-in at the Ford dealer's) to shift them over to another car. You really have to get down to the fine points to find where cars differ from one another. On the other hand, if only GM made cars, then *in our world as we're used to living in it* GM would have a monopoly. There are, in fact, substitutes for automobiles: mass transit, private aircraft, bicycles, horses and wagons, walking, etc. But as our society has developed, these substitutes seem unacceptable. Their extensive adoption in place of automobiles would cause a radical change in our lives (for good or ill). Think of the craziness of someone hopping into the car and driving a mile to the drugstore, driving back, getting out of the car, and then jogging off three miles in the other direction for the exercise. Unbelievable.

So, in the case of automobiles, the possibility of monopoly is the consequence of the adoption of a way of life that makes potential substitutes unacceptable. Once we start to talk of the uses and purposes things have, and once we've spelled out the requirements for a way of life as people have gotten used to living it, then identifying commodities becomes a manageable job. Without the background of purposes and ways of life, the job is impossible. Sure enough, at the level of biological necessity we can think of, say, someone having monopoly of food. But to picture the situation sensibly we'd have to think of something like a desert island where there is nothing to eat but coconuts. Outside the desert island, there's just too much stuff around that's edible. Biologists and anthropologists tell us plainly that the human being is the most adaptable of animals. We can successfully exploit more various environments than can most other animals. Our digestive systems can handle an enormous range of vegetable and animal nutritional sources. But once we start to develop eating habits, rejecting a lot of potential food sources as "unpalatable" or "unappetizing," then we put ourselves in the position of being subject to monopoly. We've narrowed the ways in which we're willing to satisfy our biological needs. We accept no substitutes for the old familiar food.

Now we have to be a bit more careful in talking about substitutes. If we think back to the indifference maps, we might remember that anything at all can be placed on an axis of the map. Then, when two commodities are placed on the two axes, we can start to discuss the rate at which a person is willing to trade or substitute one for the other. Any willingness to trade is a willingness to substitute. It follows that virtually everything is a substitute for everything else in some circumstances or other. Anything seems to be able to replace anything else at some rate in someone's budget. If the monopolist has to worry about substitutes in this sense, he's in trouble before he starts.

We might get closer to a useful sense of "substitute" if we look at demand in an economy as a whole. Suppose that there were two commodities related in such a way that when the demand for one went up, the demand for the other went down—and vice versa. Would that not show that they were substitutes? No, not in any important sense. Over any period during which we followed the ups and downs of demand there could be a number of different reasons why the demand for some always went up when the demand for others went down. This would be especially true under conditions of affluence, where people were changing their minds about how to use the money they had left over after the necessities were taken care of—just for the sake of variety. Still, in some general way we might be able to get some sensible information about substitution in these cases if we were (A) willing to talk about purposes; and (B) willing to identify the commodities in terms of these purposes when we considered them as substitutes. For instance, we might find that the demand for sailboats went up and the demand for golf clubs went down. As instruments for leisure time activities they could be understood as substitutes. Once the purposes involved in hobby and recreation are established then both a sailboat and a set of golf clubs are, in the appropriate sense, "the same thing," hence substitutes. They are "recreational gear." This doesn't make them substitutes in any more general sense, though. I defy you to cross a lake on a nine iron, or putt with a boom.

We can find non-recreational examples too. I'm staring out the window at a roll of number-ten wire mesh, manufactured to be used to reinforce concrete floors. But the particular wire I'm looking at is a substitute for (and improvement on) wooden tomato stakes. With respect to *that* purpose they're roughly the same, but when I pour the floor of my shop I'm not going to lay down wood lathe as reinforcement.

It seems then that the identification of purposes is basic to the identification of substitutes. This is yet another way in which values—this time expressed in terms of use or purpose—must be understood if we're to understand economic behavior. Specifically, if we're going to know whether we've gotten a monopoly or not, we've got to know why people are demanding our product.


**WILL THERE BE**          Each person's indifference curves reflect her will-
**MARKETS?**               ingness to substitute one commodity for another in
her bundle, and the rate at which she's willing to make such substitutions. Thus it's in the potential monopolist's interests to try to influence this rate of substitution. This gets us right back to the persuasive devises we talked about two sections back. To take a bizarre example: if GM could convince lots of people that (A) they simply had to have a car and (B) that there is no real substitute for a Chevrolet, then, despite what I said before, Chevrolets could become monopoly commodities. It's only because we and GM see the futility of this that we don't take a possible Chevrolet monopoly seriously.

But what about part (A) of GM's task? It's hard to get into the automobile-making business, especially in this day and age. The number of manufacturers will be small. Suppose that GM (and the other companies) could really convince us that we had to have a car—and maybe more than one. Suppose they could even convince us that we had to get a new car every couple of years. Then, on our indifference maps, automobiles would have virtually no substitutes, the rate of substitution of automobiles for other commodities would be very high, and the resulting demand curve for automobiles would become less and less elastic.

Now you ask, "What good does this do GM? It doesn't have a monopoly of automobiles." There are only a few automobile manufacturers, though. If they each could be sure of a given percentage of the market, then they could stabilize and secure their future success. The percentage might vary a little, but the limits of variation might be tolerably small, consistent with secure planning, and sure enough to eliminate major risks. Furthermore, it might be to the advantage of all the automobile companies to settle for this fixed percentage of automobile sales. They might even pursue a pricing policy designed to stabilize the percentage. They wouldn't need to get together to agree on price. They could just watch each other closely, take instructions from each other rather than from the market, and recognize when they were well off.

No *one* of the automobile companies would have a monopoly, but together they would have control over all the automobiles in the market. This situation is called oligopoly. The competition between members of an oligopoly is known to be very different from that between individual participants in a market.

Clearly, if the automobile manufacturers each have to settle for a more or less fixed share of the automobile market, it will be to their mutual benefit to make the market as large as possible. It will even be worthwhile to cooperate in the effort to enlarge the market. Thus, some people have said that automobile advertising on TV is only secondarily concerned with selling a particular brand of automobile. Its primary function, they say, is to promote demand for cars in general, for example, by making us feel embarrassed about having a five-year-old car, no matter which new car we'll eventually buy. This speculation about car advertising makes sense in light of the speculation that the automobile industry is oligopic.

The general message in these considerations about the manipulation of demand is that the more flexible we are in our needs and the more different we are from one another in our values, the less likely it is that monopolies or oligopolies will develop. The opposite side of the same coin is that the larger business enterprises become, the less flexible they become in their ability to shift production. The more they become concerned with stabilizing future demand, then the more they need the buying public to be inflexible in its needs and uniform in its values. The total effect of this situation is that the conditions for a freely operating market become more and more rarely found. Price is not established by free bargaining but by a few people who calculate the best way to exploit their opportunities over a period of time. Management decisions are no longer based simply on "instructions from the market" but are sophisticated decisions based on many different factors—including estimates of their ability to manipulate demand in the future.

Market theorists should be up in arms about this, and, in fact, a few of them are. But many of them try to continue to have us believe that the free market is still working, even when the participants in the market are a handful of industrial giants. A good part of the reason for this is that the concept of the free market and the concept of capitalism have become confused in the public mind. As we saw, capitalism can be defined as a system of production in which those owning the producing enterprises hire employees to work for them and then divide the profit of the enterprise with employees in terms of a wage bargain. The concept of the free market has as its core the establishment of price as a consequence of a free bargaining process between many parties, none of whom has the power to set the price by himself. I said before that it's possible to think of a free market economy without capitalism. Now it appears that it's possible to think of a capitalist economy without a free market to go along with it. In fact, that may be the system we're living under, to a large extent. A free market might become an annoying inconvenience to a capitalist economy.

As long as demand is taken as given, the situation I've just described would be impossible. But in this day and age, no intelligent large enterprise can sit still and not try to manipulate demand. Furthermore, times are exactly right for the successful manipulation of demand. First, there has recently been a tremendous increase in the ability of producers to influence potential consumers: The electronic media account for that. Second, the sheer size of major corporations makes their role in the economy of the nation as a whole something that everyone has to worry about. People have come to realize, at least in a vague way, that their day to day prosperity is linked to the success of the economy as a whole, and that the success of the economy depends on the success of the giant corporations which dominate it. Not everyone agrees that what's good for General Motors is good for the country, but everyone seems to concede that what's bad for General Motors is, sooner or later, bad for them. Consequently, falling in line with the way of life promoted by the major powers in the economy becomes a kind of public service, a patriotic duty.

This sense of patriotic duty rebounds to the benefit of major corporations. We've become used to hearing about the efforts of the Federal Reserve System (through regulation of interest rate and money supply) and the Federal Government (though tax increases and decreases and spending programs) to keep the economy going at the best possible rate.

In general, these days, "best rate" seems to be indicated by the lowest possible rates of both unemployment and inflation. This reflects the society's commitment to general well-being that we talked about earlier. The effort to meet this commitment has two major effects. First, it tends to promote the stable conditions that large corporations need in order to secure their success. This is so even when attempts to regulate the economy don't seem successful to the average person. Second, it gives consumers the feeling that their consumption is an integral part of the national effort to stimulate and stabilize the economy. It's no surprise that all this is accomplished by public relations efforts (pep talks and warnings) on the part of those who are trying to manage the economy. Demand isn't taken as given these days. Far from it, it's the subject of constant manipulation.

Well, if all this makes the operation of a capitalist system possible and the operation of a market system impossible, why are we still treated to the rhetoric of the free market? The main reason is that, more often than not, our allegiance to capitalism is based on our allegiance to the free market. The main institution being protected is private ownership of the large industrial corporations. The main threat to this ownership is that, as people see the importance of these giants to the overall well-being of the society, it occurs to them that the giants ought to be under public control. In most countries this public control has come about. Naturally, the private owners in the industrial system want to avoid this happening here. So they appeal to our tradition of supporting private initiative and freedom of economic activity. Unfortunately, most of the good arguments in favor of private ownership and against public ownership depend upon the existence of free markets. For instance, the argument that free bargaining will result in the most efficient price depends upon the existence of free markets and perfect competition. The large corporations themselves destroy these conditions. In addition, one of the main attractions of private ownership is the freedom implied in consumer sovereignty. Large corporations must regulate demand in order to succeed. It's only rational of them to do so. So we seem to have evolved into a system where capitalism is maintained, largely by creating and maintaining the illusion that free markets and consumer sovereignty still exist.

Finally, it might be thought that any system of private property must operate through free markets. Therefore, since we have a system of private property, we must have a system of free markets. But this isn't very convincing. It could only be true of a system of *pure* private property, and the world has never seen such a system in action. You might also ask yourself if such a system is consistent with the existence of the enormous, highly developed economies we have today. I don't think it is.

**PROBE 3:**                      The equilbrium of supply and demand is supposed
**OVERPRODUCTION**      to produce the best rational results within an economy. One facet of this claim is that an excess supply of a commodity will
not continue to be present in the market-place for very long. Taking their
instructions from the consumers, producers will refrain from overpro-
ducing things they can't sell. Of course, the instructions from consumers
are embodied in the demand curves.

Now, to say that producers will adjust supply to meet demand is to say
that supply is elastic enough to come to equilibrium with demand at a
level satisfactory to both producers and consumers. For supply to be
inelastic there would have to be some reason for there to be a chronic
overproduction of some commodity. This reason could not be found
within the market itself. Within the market the only reason for production
is the maximization of utility, and this has to be calculated on the basis
of demand. So if inelasticities of supply occur and if overproduction
results from them, it must be because reasons outside the market are
affecting supply in some way. Do such reasons operate? If they do, then
they will interfere with the ability of the market to produce good results.

Imagine the following combination of circumstances: A nation has
assumed a commitment to the well-being of its citizens. In particular, it's
committed to keeping them employed, ensuring decent medical care, and
ensuring a decent standard of living. As we often hear nowadays from our
U. S. Senators, a job, medical care, and a decent standard of living can
be considered to be rights which all citizens have. Imagine further that
there is an industry, such as our steel industry, which is a key to the overall
health of the economy. For example, at a given time it employs an enormous number of people, and many more people are employed in industries which use steel as raw material for the commodity they produce. If
the steel industry were to close down, unemployment would increase
beyond the point that the nation would tolerate. The chain reaction of
unemployment and lack of business would make the nation's commitment to employment and well-being impossible to honor. The nation
could not afford an unhealthy steel industry.

Under these conditions the steel industry might be forced to over-
produce. For example, if, for some reason, demand for steel fell, the
industry might have to continue to operate at near capacity in order to
prevent the recessionary shockwaves of unemployment from spreading
throughout the economy. In other words, the total requirements of the
economy might make it disastrous for the steel industry to respond to
market pressures in the way it's supposed to according to market theory.
We're faced with an inelastic supply curve, given the requirements of the
economy as a whole.

Are there any other ways in which overproduction could come about? I think there might be. Remember that market theory assumes that a producer makes decisions about how much to supply and what price to charge on the basis of the "instructions received from the market." This information is given in the demand curves. The consumer is sovereign only if demand functions this way in the producer's thinking.

But suppose the producer thinks in the following way: "I'm going to manufacture commodity C. In fact, that's the business I'm in and doing something else would mean starting all over again. This would be disastrous for me. Now, to stay in business I'll have to sell a certain amount of C at a certain price. The amount and price will have to be determined by what it costs me to make C: the cost of raw materials, the salaries of my workers, rent and other overhead costs, plus the profit I need to make in order to keep myself going. I know that if I sell $x$ number of C's, I'll have to charge price $p$ for them. For any number of units sold there's a corresponding price that will have to be charged if the total return is going to cover costs and the necessary bit of profit. But people won't pay more than $p$ for C's. Therefore I'll have to manage to sell $x$ of them." This kind of thinking can lead to chronic overproduction for the following reason: Each producer of C is under the same pressure to sell $x$ number of them. There's a sharp difference between selling $x$ of them and selling less, the difference between success and failure. Now, since all the producers of C's are competitors, hence uncertain whose C's will finally be bought by consumers, they'll have to make a decision based on a guess about the probability of their being able to sell all their C's. Suppose there are ten producers. And suppose that at the price $p$, at which each has to sell $x$ C's, $x$ turns out to be a bit more than a tenth of all the C's that will be sold. It might still be rational for each of them to produce more than 1/10 of the total to be sold. The reasoning would be exactly parallel to that which might lead you to buy a lottery ticket. That is, the expected gain might be high enough for them to take the risk of failing. If this is so, C's will be overproduced.

The line of reasoning we've just seen offers us a look at an aspect of the theory of price we haven't seen before. In it, the price of C is not set solely by the market but also by the cost of making C's plus profit. Once a producer starts to think in these terms, people who want this commodity are just going to have to "pay the price" for it; that is, they'll have to be willing to pay the unit cost of production plus profit. If they are not willing to pay the price, then the commodity simply won't be available.

Theories of price based on production costs can become very elaborate, depending on how costs are computed. They can also be related to market determinations of price: The cost of production sets limits within which the market price must fluctuate. The exact relationship between production determinations of price and market determinations of price is still debated within economics. For instance, it isn't absolutely clear how real-world producers set prices for their products. But for our purposes here the important point is that it's in no way irrational for the producers in the situation I've described to reason the way they did. However, if they do reason in this way we can't be sure that there'll be a nice equilibrium between supply and demand. There may be overproduction.

**POTENTIAL CURES FOR OVERPRODUCTION**    Chronic overproduction has nothing to recommend it. It's not a healthy situation. Let's look at the example of the overproduction of steel. Can anything be done about it? Various economists give various answers. The committed market theorist says, of course, that we ought to have the steel industry behave rationally and respond to market pressures. The industry ought to cut back steel production to meet the level of demand. Then it should think of other commodities it might bring to market instead of steel. Investors in the steel industry ought to think of shifting their investment into other areas where demand is sufficient to make investment profitable. The market theorist goes on to point out that the bad situation was created in the first place by the inflexible commitment to employment and well-being. This prevents the market from doing its job. In the long run, according to the theory, the only way to maximize employment and well-being is through the mechanism of the market.

At this point the critic of the market says that the consequences of letting market pressures work in this case are intolerable. Unemployment and depression are likely to occur, especially while the steel industry is searching around for alternative commodities to produce. In this case, the critic says, we can't afford to wait around and let the market do its work. *Even if* in the long run the economy would come to a new equilibrium, the long run might take a long time. In the medium and short run millions of people would suffer. This is where the attempt to isolate economics from the rest of life can hurt the most. The world of industrial nations that's been built over the last few centuries has been developing a commitment to a stable, prosperous life for all people. No nation dares to trust the market to work out "in the long run." The *economist* can wait out the long run (especially if he has tenure); the politician can't. Furthermore, this is assuming that the market system will work out for the best in the long run, which is far from certain.

Let's be really clear about how long the "long run" of the market theorist could be. I'll use our old lottery example as an analogy—though we could as well use the example of coin tossing.

The definition of rationality we came up with while analyzing the lottery, and which led us to the conception of the rational economic man, depended on a notion of the long run. We had to calculate rational expectations, in the long run. Now, suppose that over a very long run (and it could be as long as you pleased), you never won. Could you conclude that the theory of rationality was wrong? No. Could you conclude that the lottery was rigged? No. It's perfectly consistent with the conception of rationality and with the fairness of the lottery that you lose every time for a long time or that you win every time for a long time. All that's claimed is that in the "long run" things ought to even out. If you've lost every time, that simply means that the theoretical long run isn't over yet. Maybe you've got something to look forward to in your old age; maybe not.

The notion of the long run involved in market equilibrium is analogous to the one involved in the lottery. *Even if* we are convinced that market equilibrium is bound to be reached, it might take forever to reach it. That's perfectly consistent with the theory. Generations could be born and die, and the equilibrium not be reached. The "long run" is a theoretical ideal. Life is short.

Faith in equilibrium in the long run is exactly analogous to faith that the lottery is a fair one. If some one person always won the lottery, you'd begin to lose faith in its fairness. The theory tells you it *could* still be fair, but you'd have your doubts. You'd want some assurance that the lottery is fair. Maybe you'd want to watch them put the tickets in the barrel and pull out the winning ones.

Now, it's interesting that in the case of the market we know we can't get the assurance we need that equilibrium is bound to occur. The efficiency guarantee can't be made. So, when people become impatient with claims about what will happen in the market in the long run, we're in a position to sympathize. This makes it worth looking at alternative solutions to the problem of overproduction.

Well, if the market solution to the overproduction of steel is rejected, what are the other alternatives? First, there's a solution that will be familiar to you from the saga of X and O. We can set a price for steel which will increase the amount that will be sold, until it reaches the amount we want to produce. But if we do this, we'll have to subsidize the steel industry so that it will remain possible for them to produce steel profitably—meet their costs, pay their workers, etc. Presumably this subsidy would have to be paid out of tax funds; so, in effect, we would be spreading the cost of steel through the entire taxpaying population. If the production of steel in great quantities is as important to the overall health of the economy as we imagine it to be, it might be worth it to the society as a whole to pay the price in taxation. After all, in the long run everybody benefits from healthy economic conditions.

Against this, the market theorist might appeal to our suspicion that this solution is just robbing Peter to pay Paul. If the high price of maintaining the steel industry at a high level of production can be paid by taxation and subsidization, then that must mean that the resources are available in the economy to pay the higher price directly in the market. So it ought to be possible to stimulate enough demand for steel to make use of the supply we want to provide. That is, there must be some way to change the shape of the demand curve, and then let the market do its work.

If someone were trying to decide whether this was so, he would have to look at the demand curve in a new way. Instead of being looked at as *given,* it would have to be looked at as potentially changeable. The demand curve for steel is composed of the indifference curves of a number of people and enterprises having a use for steel. Given those indifference maps as they are, the demand for steel is not sufficient to use up the supply. So it looks as though we have to change the indifference maps if we're going to get the demand for steel up to the right level. Either more people are going to have to contribute to the demand for steel, or new people and enterprises will have to be persuaded to use it. It looks as if a job of salesmanship is needed. Otherwise there's no choice but to subsidize the steel industry, under the conditions we've set up.

Rather than speculate about how all this would actually work, we better resolve to take a good hard look at the contemporary economic situation. But there's a theoretical point to be made here. If economists were to accept the commitment to employment and well-being in the short and medium run, and if they wanted to avoid the taxation-subsidization scheme, then they would have to find some way to change the pattern and level of demand. They could not do this intelligently without examining the pattern of preferences behind the demand curves. Furthermore, if they're going to modify those preferences intelligently, then they need to examine the reasons behind the preferences. Then they have to cook up new reasons to convince people to change their preferences. The upshot of all this is that once goals such as employment are set for an economy, economists must venture out of their chosen confines. They can't take demand as given. They must get behind it to try to change it.

**KEYNES**  The last method for dealing with the problems of overproduction and with similar problems must be set off by itself. The thinking behind it is important enough to have been called a "conceptual revolution"—the Keynesian revolution. We're going to have to try to see the fundamentals of this approach on the basis of what we've learned so far, and in terms of the simple example of the overproduction of steel. A full understanding of the sort that economists seek would require an understanding of capital, money, the relationship of investment, saving, and consumption, and other matters we haven't touched on very seriously. Nonetheless, we're in a position to see the basic issues. We just can't think that when we're finished we'll be ready to try to run the Federal Reserve System.

The problem once again is that there are compelling reasons to run the steel industry at a rate where the supply of steel is greater than the demand. Now, if the society really does have this productive capacity, it seems a shame to let it go to waste—especially when we think of the importance of a healthy steel industry to the well-being of virtually everyone in the society. So maybe the problem shouldn't be looked at as a problem of overproduction, but rather as a problem of under-utilization, not a problem of too much supply but of too little demand.

Here we have to make a distinction within the concept of demand. Many people might be "willing" to pay the price for something they want or need, but they can't afford these things. Obviously, their willingness to pay the price is irrelevant to the *effective demand* for those things in the real-world economy. But if their willingness to pay the price could be made effective by making them able to pay the price, then their demand would become part of the total demand in the market. Furthermore, it might be possible somehow for an economic system to afford to make this *latent demand* effective.

Now we have to pause to let the market theorist get his word in. It's his view that if the economy can afford a greater demand for, say, steel, yet doesn't translate this into an effective demand for steel; then this really means that the resources we propose to use to increase the demand for steel would be better spent on something else. In other words, an economy left to itself is bound to develop a pattern of consumption (and saving and investment) which will allocate the resources of the economy most efficiently. If the effective demand for steel is thus-and-so, then that's how much steel ought to be produced. In terms of market theory, the distinction between latent and effective demand makes no sense at all. This was emphasized even by Adam Smith, who insisted that we be concerned only with what he called "effectual demand."

On the other hand, the Keynesian approach is based on the assumption that there are reasons why a gap will develop between latent and effective demand, even when there are enough productive capacities in the economy to make the demand effective were we to choose to do so. The gap must be closed. In most modern societies, the gap is closed by public spending. At any rate, public spending has to be a normal part of a national economy as long as the government has to provide public works, roads, harbors, defense, and is a major purchaser of materials and services. Consequently, by expanding the range of services it provides, the government can contribute substantially to demand. (And don't forget the contribution it can make to the demand for labor.)

We're all familiar with the size of the U. S. defense budget these days. It's easy to see how the demand for steel can be increased if tanks, ships, and other military hardware are produced at a great rate. So it's equally clear how public spending could effect patterns of demand throughout the economy. The complicated part of the story is how the government gets the money to pay for the goods and services it buys. I'm afraid we're going to have to leave that issue aside, except to say that most of the major battles between defenders of the market economy on one side and Keynesians on the other are fought over the competing conceptions of the national economy which underlie government spending. When we think of the pervasiveness and importance of these issues for our own lives, we might well decide to go beyond the confines of this book to learn the economics it would take to understand the competing positions, and decide between them.

For our purposes, however, we can again see how the day-to-day operation of our economic system can lead us right back to a consideration of our basic values. If we grant that a government can enter a spending program designed to influence the pattern of demand in the economy, then we're again forced to think of demand, not as given, but as a subject of investigation and control. When government spending itself is a major component of demand, we have to ask what the government is spending for and why. After all, it's our government. Its spending is in some sense our spending. We have to know what values are reflected in the government's economic activity.

We first notice that if the government is simply trying to increase effective demand—for steel, in our little example—then it doesn't matter what the steel is used for. It's often said that if we just want to stimulate demand, we might as well build mile-high pyramids in the desert. But it seems silly to use the government's enormous spending capacity for something as useless as a steel pyramid. If there are other wants and needs to be served, then it seems reasonable for governmental spending to be directed to serving them. So, instead of building mile-high pyramids we build nuclear aircraft carriers. This reflects the importance that military strength—national security—has for us, relative to other things for which the government could be spending its money. Even people who are otherwise ardent defenders of the free market are willing to have the government enter the economy as the major (and sometimes the only) purchaser of the products of the "defense industry." Support for programs expressing other values (welfare, the arts, ecology, for example) ebbs and flows in our Congress. Support for military spending remains firm and steady.

If all goes well, then the pattern of government spending will reflect the values of those who are governed. If it does, then the sovereignty we might have enjoyed as consumers will have been converted into the sovereignty of voters in a democracy. Presumably, in a democracy the government is responsive to the wishes of the governed.

It should be obvious that the Keynesian alternative—even in the scaled-down version presented here—requires us to draw the boundaries of economics differently from the way that the market theorist wants to draw them. For the Keynesian, the government has important management decisions to make and management functions to perform within the economy. It can't be thought of simply as an agency hired to perform these management services. For one thing, once we decide that employment, welfare, and other goals ought to be pursued by governmental contribution to demand, then the nature of our economic sovereignty has changed. Instead of being individual sovereign consumers pursuing our own values in the market, we become individual voters trying to make our values felt in public decisions about spending, saving, and investing. To protect this sovereignty, it looks as though we'd better look at the government as a part of the economy over which we have control, rather than as an agency hired to do a job.

We can't forget that even to begin to talk about the necessity for management decisions with respect to the economy as a whole is to reject the claim that the market by itself can be depended upon to reach a totally satisfactory result. Our discussion of the efficiency claim ought to be some help toward a judgment about the necessity for Keynesian measures. But in addition, since the nature of our sovereignty changes when we begin to have the government make management decisions, we ought to be sure that the freedom promised to us by the market isn't given away as we move away from a pure market system.

**MONETARY AND FISCAL POLICY**     A closer look at the ways in which Keynesian thinking is put into practice will give us a chance to apply what we learned in the last chapter. We've seen reasons why we might want to stimulate demand or slow it down. Insufficient demand might be depressing the economy and causing unemployment; excess demand might be exerting inflationary pressure. Monetarists and fiscalists are concerned with the methods of stimulating or slowing down the economy. The monetarists believe that the only effective way to influence demand is by regulating the amount of money available in the economy.

The fiscalists believe that the level of demand can be raised or lowered by a policy of increased or decreased taxation, or increased or decreased government spending. The issue is important enough and touchy enough so that we ought to see it stated clearly.

Professor Galbraith sets out the two theories in the following way:

> Monetary policy seeks to control the economy by regulating the amount of borrowing from the banks, and the spending and respending of the money so created. It expands aggregate demand for goods and services, if that is indicated, by having more spending from borrowed money. If the need is to restrain spending because of the danger of inflation, then the central bank can cut back on spending from borrowed funds.

> Fiscal measures . . . work through the management of the government budget. If there is unemployment, you cut taxes; that leaves people with more private income to spend, and the resulting demand means more jobs. Or you increase public expenditures without increasing taxes, and so the government adds to demand with the same effect. Furthermore, the people the government employs spend and add more to demand—what economists call the multiplier effect. If inflation is the problem, you put the policy into reverse. You raise taxes, and this cuts down on private spending. You cut back on public expenditures, and that means the government contributes less to the demand for goods and services, reduces aggregate demand.[3]

The effectiveness of these policy alternatives and their relative merit have been the subject of constant controversy among economists for a long time, and the battle rages on. My opinion on this, as a sophisticated theoretical issue in economics, isn't worth a dime. But since I'm someone who lives in a country where economic decisions are made according to prevailing opinion on the issue, I have to try to come to some sort of judgment. I have to think hard about some of the issues we've examined over the course of this book and try to apply them here. The answers I come up with are two:

First, I don't know which of the two theories is right, and the events of the last thirty years make it extremely difficult for anyone to know for sure. Varying combinations of the two theories have been used in the national economy. Monetarist theory in particular insists that long-run results are what count, but in the long run so many different policies have been layered atop one another that it gets harder rather than easier to say which measures and which factors have caused a given economic change. This is one of the reasons why it's so hard to choose between competing theories. The times when you find anything like a decisive test of monetarism or fiscalism are very few. In addition, in politically sensitive times, when unemployment and inflation are major political issues,

[3]Galbraith and Salinger, *Almost Everyone's Guide,* op. cit. p. 91.

no one seems to dare to pursue a strictly monetarist or strictly fiscalist policy long enough to produce a fair scientific test of it.

The second answer I come up with is a methodological one: If we all wanted the monetarists to be right, we could get together and *make* their theory the right one; and we could do the same for the fiscalists if we were so inclined. This might seem a bit strange, but we've already seen how it could be so. Both monetarist and fiscalist theories are, in large part, theories about how people will act under particular circumstances. They're theories which embody assumptions about how we're motivated. They're theories about what information is going to be available to us (for example, what our take-home pay is going to be, whether or not credit will be available to us, what interest we'll have to pay on a mortgage), how we will interpret this information, and how we'll behave on the basis of the information so interpreted. If one of the theories is right about us, then the predictions made on the basis of the theory will come true. This is because we make them come true.

Now, it would be silly to think that it's a simple matter to make an economic theory come true. For one thing, it would take a concerted effort on the part of most of the people in the world. In addition, some people—political leaders, the owners and managers of large industries and businesses—would have a lot more to do with making the theory come true than ordinary people would. The effect of *their* policy decisions on the economy as a whole is enormous; my economic policy decisions don't cause the slightest ripple outside my family.

Second, the stakes involved in making an economic theory come true might be enormous. This would surely be so if we wanted to make market theory or Marx's theory come true. Everyone knows that Marx's theory is a revolutionary theory. That is, for Marx's goals to be realized a revolution must take place. On the other hand it's often assumed that the ideals of market theory are within our grasp—if we just change a few things here and there to eliminate "imperfections." But it may be time to take a look at all the participants in our economy who have a vested interest in the violation of the conditions for the market. In fact all the giant corporations in our economy, including those in the automobile, oil, and metals industries for example, make policy and price in ways that are inconsistent with a competitive free market. A move to a fully competitive market system would require a revolution too.

In addition, there are other ways of having a stake in the violation of the market. Marx, in the context of a discussion of consumption, spoke of "parasites and gluttonous drones," he was talking about the flock of civil servants and bureaucrats who pushed paper around for the governments of his time. The importance of these people is that the government (and eventually the taxpayers) support their consumption. Well, it looks as if the welfare states which have grown up since Marx's time have managed to make parasites and gluttonous drones of us all. You immediately think of welfare recipients and the defense industry, but in fact we're *all* supported by the government in some way or other. Consider agricultural subsidies, which help support farmers but which also hold food prices artificially low; petroleum subsidies, which let us pay about a dollar twenty-five for a gallon of gas while our friends in Europe were paying about three dollars, still insuring the oil companies a good profit; government housing; and mortgage subsidies. Everyone is a beneficiary of some item on this list and of other items which could be added. The consequence is that a return to the market would mean a vast upheaval in the lives of all of us.

The stakes may still be high even when we're talking about changes in overall plan that aren't so extreme. Some theories are more advantagous to particular economic interest groups than others. To make the advantageous theories come true would be to favor some over others. Furthermore, any economic theory provides everyone with a way of predicting the consequences of his own activity. We can imagine what would happen if people who were acting rationally according to one theory were suddenly confronted with a system conforming to another—different— theory. It could be like starting out to play chess, and finding, after a few moves, that you were suddenly in a game of checkers. The good chess moves you had made might have landed you in a disastrous position for the checkers game.

We saw how it might be rational, profitable, and tempting for producers to violate the conditions of the market. Suppose they'd been doing this for some time and, in fact, had come to gear their policy to the assumption that they could continue to manipulate demand, control prices, and suppress competition. It would then come as a rude shock to them if someone forced them to conform to the market. The whole structure of their planning would have to change. They might strenuously resist such attempts to make them behave as they should from the point of view of market theory.

**REVERSE PSYCHOLOGY AND SELF-FULFILLING PROPHECY**     People might actively try to subvert a particular theory because they judge that they can gain an advantage in doing so. An interesting statement of this possibility is contained in the following open letter from a state governor to the President. The governor is questioning fiscal theory. His first point is that conditions have changed a lot since fiscalist theory was formulated. In particular, the public sector of the economy has grown very large. As a consequence, he argues, fiscal theory might have become obsolete, might not have the consequences it used to have. He then goes on to say:

> But the element that, I think, has changed the most is the reaction of the citizens whom the theory calls on to "invest" in increased plant when they "see" the stimulus producing increased mass consumption. The investors are no longer buying the Keynesian doctrine.
>
> For quite some time now, capital investments have lagged far behind both need and expectation. In fact, corporate capital investments have run regularly only a little more than half of the levels planned by boards of directors. Managers are not even investing what they are authorized to invest.
>
> On a grander scale, both the number of investors and the share of the national wealth that they are willing to invest have been dropping dramatically for close to 20 years. I submit that any modern "game theory" contains an essential postulate that the game must change when all the players understand the rules.
>
> Investors are becoming concerned when they see "stimulus" because they know that it is external, not inherent in market dynamics or demand and temporary.
>
> Therefore, it would appear imprudent to invest in increased capacity if you doubt that the demand will last long enough to pay off the investment and justify capacity increase. Since by definition governmental action to apply stimulus occurs only when natural demand has "wound down," investors view stimulus-occasioned demands on capacity as being phony and temporary. Accordingly, for many there is a great temptation to hold back from investing.[4]

In other words, people, especially investors, aren't behaving as they're supposed to behave if fiscal theory is going to work. They could; but they seem to have decided that it's against their interests to do so.

The same point could be made about monetarist theory, but in a more complicated way. The monetarist points out that the major determinant of how much money we spend, save, or invest is the amount of money we have. How much we have depends, ultimately, on how much there is. Our spending, saving, and investment decisions, says the monetarist, will be based on judgments we make as rational economic men in a free market, given the constraints of the money supply. At this point there are two ways to question monetarist theory. Can we beat the market game? (Many people seem to be very successful doing this.) And, second, our old question: Should we behave as rational economic men? By now I've said enough about that question.

You might have noticed that the points raised in the previous paragraphs are related to a pair of familiar quirks in our behavior. You've undoubtedly heard of "self-fulfilling prophesies" and "reverse psychology." You come up with a self-fulfilling prophesy when you make

---

[4]An excerpt from Vermont Governor Richard A. Snelling's letter to President Carter, *The New York Times*, March 5, 1978, III, 14:3.

a prediction, and the prediction itself is instrumental in making the prediction come true. For instance, you get up in the morning and predict that you're going to have a miserable day. Then the prediction and the sense of doom that goes with it result in your having a miserable day. In "reverse psychology," on the other hand, a prediction is instrumental in the prediction's turning out false. For instance, you tell children that if they keep playing beside the water they will get their feet wet; so, just to show you up, they're very careful and don't get their feet wet.

As the governor suggests, economic models can fall prey to behavior very much like the self-fulfillment of prophesy and the operation of reverse psychology. The model itself serves as a source of information and motivation for the people whose actions are supposed to be explained and predicted by the mode. So, as the governor says, when investors see the government acting to stimulate demand, instead of taking this as a sign that things will be better, they take it as a sign that things must be pretty bad, so they better hold off on their investments. When they hold off, things do get pretty bad—as a result. The governor might have reinforced his point by describing the way in which the stock market reacts to various sorts of information. If you have a theory about how people will behave in the stock market, and if it's a theory about what rational behavior would be, and if you act rationally according to the theory just as everyone else does; then you have a theory about your own behavior. By acting according to the theory, you help it to come true.[5]

"Self-fulfilling prophesies" and "reverse psychology" are just symptoms of the general point I made in the last chapter. Economic laws (even as imbedded in the theories of the fiscalists and the monetarists) are more like traffic laws than the laws of physics. Electrons don't turn around and move the other way in their orbitals to spite the physicist or to outwit his system. Nor are the physicist's predictions instrumental in the behavior of the electrons.

**SUMMARY**     These probes ask, at a certain level of theoretical pretension, what most ordinary people ask at the level of their pay check and tax return. It's been my contention all along that the minute you start asking such questions seriously and pursuing them systematically, you're led to ask some very fundamental questions about yourself, your values, and the rational course of your life. Intelligent pursuit of these matters isn't beyond anybody's capacity. We all can do it—given some time and a little help. I can only hope that I've provided a little help.

[5]The most famous discussion of self-fulfilling prophecies in this context is in Ernest Nagel, *The Structure of Science* (New York: Harcourt, Brace, Jovanovich, 1961), p. 469 ff.

It's also my view that the answers to most of the important questions posed in this book require decisions on everyone's part, rather than the discovery of definitive or eternal truths. So, as I said at the beginning, you're continually left with questions to answer for yourself rather than authoritative advice or solace. Furthermore, there's no point in pretending to provide an ending—happy or otherwise—to these investigations and explorations. Any endings would have to be found in life, not on the printed page.

# FOR FURTHER READING

## CHAPTER 1

ARISTOTLE, "Nichomachaean Ethics" in Richard McKeon, ed., *Introduction to Aristotle* (New York: Modern Library, 1947).

AUSTIN, J. L., *Philosophical Papers* (Oxford: Oxford University Press, 1961).

BACHRACH, PETER and BARATZ, MORTON, *The Theory of Democratic Elitism: a Critique* (Boston: Little Brown, 1967).

DAHL, ROBERT, *Who Governs?* (New Haven: Yale University Press, 1961).

DAVIS, LAWRENCE H. *Theory of Action* (Englewood Cliffs, N.J.: Prentice-Hall, 1979).

GALBRAITH, J. K., and SALINGER, NICOLE, *Almost Everyone's Guide to Economics* (Boston: Houghton Mifflin, 1978).

HABERMAS, JÜRGEN, *Theory and Practice* (Boston: Beacon Press, 1973).

LOUCH, A. R., *Explanation and Human Action* (Berkeley: University of California, 1966).

LUCE, ROBERT D. and RAIFFA, H., *Games and Decisions* (New York: Wiley, 1957).

MARCUSE, HERBERT, *One Dimensional Man* (Boston: Beacon Press, 1964).

MYRDAL, GUNNAR, *Beyond the Welfare State* (New Haven: Yale University Press, 1960).

RUNCIMAN, WALTER G., *Relative Deprivation and Social Justice* (Berkeley: University of California Press, 1966).

WEBER, MAX, *The Theory of Social and Economic Organization* (New York: The Free Press, 1947).
WILSON, BRYAN R. ed., *Rationality* (Oxford: Basil Blackwell, 1970).
WINCH, PETER, *The Idea of a Social Science* (London, New York: Humanities Press, 1958).

## CHAPTER 2

BENTHAM, JEREMY, *An Introduction to the Principles of Morals and Legislation* (New York: Hafner, 1948).
MYRDAL, GUNNAR, *Objectivity in Social Research* (New York: Random House, 1969).
RICARDO, DAVID, *Principles of Political Economy and Taxation* (New York: Dutton, 1933).
SCITOVSKY, TIBOR, *The Joyless Economy* (New York: Oxford University Press, 1976).
SMITH, ADAM, *The Wealth of Nations*, Bruce Mazlish, ed., (Indianapolis: Bobbs-Merrill, 1961).
UNGER, ROBERTO, *Knowledge and Politics* (New York: The Free Press, 1975).
WITTGENSTEIN, LUDWIG, *Philosophical Investigations* (New York: Macmillan, 1953).

## CHAPTER 3

BOWIE, NORMAN E. and SIMON, R. L., *The Individual and the Social Order* (Englewood Cliffs, N.J.: Prentice-Hall, 1977).
DE GRAAFF, JOHANNES, *Theoretical Welfare Economics* (Cambridge: Cambridge University Press, 1957).
FEINBERG, JOEL, *Social Philosophy* (Englewood Cliffs, N.J.: Prentice-Hall, 1973).
GOLDING, MARTIN, *Philosophy of Law* (Englewood Cliffs, N.J.: Prentice-Hall, 1973).
LITTLE, I. M. D., *A Critique of Welfare Economics* (Oxford: Oxford University Press, 1950).
MILL, J. S., *On Liberty* (Indianapolis: Hackett, 1978).
MURAKAMI, Y., *Logic and Social Choice* (New York: Routledge & Kegan Paul, 1968).
RAPOPORT, ANATOL, *N-Person Game Theory* (Ann Arbor: University of Michigan Press, 1970).
RAPOPORT, ANATOL, *Two-Person Game Theory* (Ann Arbor: University of Michigan Press, 1966).
SAMUELSON, PAUL, *Foundations of Economic Analysis* (New York: Atheneum, 1965).
SEN, AMARTYA K., *Collective Choice and Social Welfare* (San Francisco: Holden-Day, 1970).

## CHAPTER 4

EASTON, LLOYD and GUDDAT, KURT, eds., *Writings of the Young Marx on Philosophy and Society* (New York: Doubleday, 1967).
MARX, KARL, *Capital* (New York: The Modern Library, 1936).
MARX, KARL, *Grundrisse*, Martin Nicolaus, tr. (New York: Vintage, 1974).
ROBINSON, JOAN, *Economic Philosophy* (Chicago: Aldine, 1962).

ROBINSON, JOAN, *An Essay on Marxian Economics,* 2nd edition (New York: St. Martin's, 1967).

VON MISES, LUDWIG, *Human Action* (New York: Yale University Press, 1949).

## CHAPTER 5

GODWIN, WILLIAM, *Enquiry Concerning Political Justice,* K. Codell Carter, ed. (Oxford: Oxford University Press, 1971).

HELD, VIRGINIA, ed., *Property, Profits, and Economic Justice* (Belmont, Ca.: Wadsworth, 1980).

LOCKE, JOHN, *Two Treatises of Government,* Peter Laslett, ed. (Cambridge: Cambridge University Press, 1960).

NICHOLAS, BARRY, *An Introduction to Roman Law* (Oxford: Oxford University Press, 1962).

## CHAPTER 6

ARROW, KENNETH, *Social Choice and Individual Values* (New York: Wiley, 1951).

BOULDING, KENNETH, *Conflict and Defense* (New York: Harper & Row, 1962).

BUCHANAN, JAMES M., and TULLOCK, GORDON, *The Calculus of Consent* (Ann Arbor: University of Michigan Press, 1962).

LERNER, ABBA, *Flation* (Baltimore: Penguin Books, 1973).

NOZICK, ROBERT, *Anarchy, State, and Utopia* (New York: Basic Books, 1974).

RAWLS, JOHN, *A Theory of Justice* (Cambridge: Harvard University Press, 1971).

## CHAPTER 7

FRIEDMAN, MILTON, *Capitalism and Freedom* (Chicago: University of Chicago Press, 1962).

GOULD, CAROL, *Marx's Social Ontology* (Cambridge: MIT Press, 1978).

HAYEK, FRIEDRICH A., *The Constitution of Liberty* (Chicago: University of Chicago Press, 1960).

MARX, KARL, *The Critique of the Gotha Program* (New York: International Publishers, 1938).

MACPHERSON, C. B., *Democratic Theory: Essays in Retrieval* (Oxford: Oxford University Press, 1973).

## CHAPTER 8

BERNSTEIN, RICHARD, *The Restructuring of Social and Political Theory* (New York: Harcourt, Brace & Jovanovich, 1976).

FAY, BRIAN, *Social Theory and Political Practice* (Winchester, MA: Allen Unwin, 1975).

HAHN, FRANK, and HOLLIS, MARTIN, eds., *Philosophy and Economic Theory* (Oxford: Oxford University Press, 1979).

HOLLIS, MARTIN, and NELL, EDWARD, *Rational Economic Man* (Cambridge: Cambridge University Press, 1975).

KOOPMANS, TJALLING C., *Three Essays on the State of Economic Science* (New York: McGraw-Hill, 1957).

LOWE, ADOLPH, *On Economic Knowledge* (New York: Harper & Row, 1965).

POLANYI, KARL, *The Great Transformation* (Boston: Beacon Press, 1957).

ROSENBERG, ALEXANDER, *Microeconomic Laws: A Philosophical Analysis,* (Pittsburgh: University of Pittsburgh Press, 1976).

## CHAPTER 9

GALBRAITH, J. K., *The New Industrial State* (Boston: Houghton Mifflin, 1967).

HANSEN, ALVIN H., *A Guide to Keynes* (New York: McGraw-Hill, 1953).

KEYNES, JOHN MAYNARD, *The General Theory of Employment, Interest, and Money.* (New York: Harcourt, Brace, Jovanovich, 1965).

LEKACHMAN, ROBERT, *The Age of Keynes* (New York: McGraw-Hill, 1966).

OKUN, ARTHUR, *Equality and Efficiency* (Washington: Brookings Institute, 1975).

# INDEX